THE FILMS OF THE SEVENTIES

•

a social history

by

William J. Palmer

The Scarecrow Press, Inc.
Metuchen, N.J., & London
1987

Permission has been granted for the publication of revised versions of the following previously published material:

"Blow-Up: The Game With No Balls," was first published in Literature/Film Quarterly, Vol. 7, Number 4 (1979), pp. 314-321.

"The Vietnam War Films," was first published in Film Library Quarterly, Vol. 13, Number 4 (1980), pp. 4-15.

Special thanks to Donald Seybold, Shaun Hughes, Tobey Herzog, Tom Wiener, William Epstein, Alan McKenzie, Jerome Christiansen, Ann Moore and Joseph Duffy.

Library of Congress Cataloging-in-Publication Data

Palmer, William J., 1943–
    The films of the seventies.

    Includes index.
    1. Moving-pictures--Social aspects--United States.
I. Title.
PN1995.9.S6P34   1987   791.43'09'09355   86-21051
ISBN 0-8108-1955-4

This book is dedicated to Christy.

From <u>Blow-Up</u>, mechanical sex in an impotent world.
Courtesy of MOMA/Film Stills Archives.

THE MARQUEE

This is a book about the movies of the seventies.
The movies are the stars.
Not the decade or the actors or the critic.
This book offers critical readings of a large cast of American and Foreign films. Some films, however, because of their wide influence, light up the marquee more often than others. These key films--

> Antonioni's Blow-Up
> Coppola's The Godfather, I and II
> Coppola's The Conversation
> Polanski's Chinatown
> Lumet's Network
> Cimino's The Deer Hunter
> Post's Go Tell The Spartans
> Coppola's Apocalypse Now
> DePalma's Blow Out
> Weir's Gallipoli

--best define the major themes of the decade. They are the decade's most socio-historically symbolic motion pictures.

Though the title of this book is "The Films of the Seventies," the "seventies" in terms of this film history begin with Blow-Up in 1966. And, many of the trends, the themes and images that define "The Films of the Seventies" are still strong influences more than halfway into the eighties. Films from the late sixties are included because they either heavily influence or mark the point de depart of the most prominent thematic trends in the films of the seventies. A few eighties films, such as The

Stunt Man, are mentioned because they serve as clear bridges between the decades.

This book is based upon one straightforward premise: that movies both reflect and comment upon the society in which they are made; in other words, that films become metaphors for the dominant themes of social history.

This book focuses upon four major themes which dominate the films of the seventies:

1) corporate conspiracy;

2) man's inability to control and understand reality;

3) the failure of the Existential impulse of the forties, fifties and sixties;

4) and, the futility of contemporary war.

There were other isolated seventies film trends which ran counter to this approach, such as the Nostalgia craze (witness the well deserved popularity of American Graffiti) and the Revival frenzy (Heaven Can Wait or The Postman Always Rings Twice), but the major impetus in film in the seventies was to draw upon the social history of the time for metaphorical inspiration. Perhaps the hottest movie genre of the early seventies, the Disaster film, is one of the best indicators of the metaphorical ways in which motion pictures tend to tailor themselves to the temper of the times. Before dying out in the late seventies, this genre, from The Poseidon Adventure and Earthquake in 1972 to The Towering Inferno (1975) to Two-Minute Warning (1976) and Black Sunday (1977), presented a series of images of seemingly safe, solid structures being torn down. Similar, seemingly unassailable structures, like the Pentagon and the Presidency, were simultaneously falling in American society.

One telling exception to this approach is the series of blockbuster commercial films (all endlessly sequeled) of the late seventies and early eighties, particularly Raiders of the Lost Ark, the Rocky films, the Superman

films, and the noveau horror movies (the Halloween
series, the Friday the 13th series, et al). These films seem
to glory both in their technical virtuosity and in their
avoidance of any relation to history or contemporary
society. In the cases of the Superman and the Rocky
films, their sentimental optimism runs directly against the
grain of seventies life. In these films, the characters are
all stereotypes and the messages wouldn't qualify for
Fourth Class mail. Of all of these astoundingly popular
films which have cloned sequels, only the original Jaws,
which attains an interesting depth through
characterization, the thematic examination of the
corporate power in society and the ecological
relationship between man and nature, and the Star Wars
films, which place the individual in both mythic and
comic confrontation with corporate technology, make any
attempt to align themselves with the concerns of
seventies society.

The focus of this book, then, is upon some key
films and a few key socio-historical themes of the
decade of the seventies, but this book also analyzes in
some depth hundreds of other, less distinguished films
from The President's Analyst (shrinks and spies) to Nasty
Habits (nuns and buggers) to The Wild Bunch (cowboys
and Mexicans) which often make the same use of and
reach the same conclusions about the social history of
the decade as those major, critically acclaimed films. In
fact, this is as much a book about the influence of
films upon other films as it is a book about the
influence of society upon films and films upon society.

In the early days of film criticism, except for clear
exceptions like James Agee or Andre Bazin, critics read
films like books or critiqued films as if they were stage
plays. For these critics, meaning was carried by the
verbal statements in the film, messages were transmitted
via polemic speeches. The visual, non-verbal aspects of
films, the images which appeared on the edges of the
frame or in the background rather than in the very
center drew little critical attention. Citizen Kane changed
that oversight forever. Then, in the sixties, critical

attention shifted drastically to the opposite pole. The
movies became a Director's medium. What this book
hopes to present is a body of criticism which not only
recreates and analyzes the visual impact of these films'
striking and original images but also links those images
to the information and the ideas which surface in
dialogue or narration. This book is intent upon showing
the close relationship, especially in the best motion
pictures such as Chinatown and Apocalypse Now, between
the visual and the verbal modes of expression.

Finally, this book is about those films of a
particular time which not only attempt to capture reality
in their images and words but also try to analyze the
very nature of reality itself. The titles of the films of
the seventies blaze and blink up on the marquee. Those
films' value is found in the relationship between those
titles pulsing in the marquee lights and the audience
lined up in the street below to buy their tickets.

From Network, the corporate Sermon on the Mount.
Courtesy of MOMA/Film Stills Archives.

PREVIEWS OF COMING ATTRACTIONS

THE FILMS OF THE SEVENTIES

From <u>Chinatown</u>, lost innocence meets flawed sight --
"Forget it, Jake." Courtesy of MOMA/ Film Stills
Archives.

1. THE FILMS OF THE SEVENTIES: AN INTRODUCTION

Society and the Movies.

The Movies and Society.

Most often, the relationship between social history and the youngest art form has been a tenuous one which both social critics and film critics have felt rather uncomfortable in defining and analyzing. This "discomfiture of definition" probably originates in that ambiguous conception of a mythical "Hollywood" as the dream factory where the wizards of escapism dispense distortions of reality to anyone who buys a ticket into their technicolor land of Oz. Quite often, the result of this "discomfiture of definition" is the quick dismissal of any possibility of the existence of a viable relationship between contemporary social history and the subjects of contemporary motion pictures.

In the throes of this "discomfiture of definition," the generic term "Hollywood" becomes a derogatory presupposition which precludes any sort of serious consideration, analysis or even belief in its products. There are a number of familiar variations on this theme. "You can't take that seriously, it's the Hollywood version of life" is one. "They've taken history and Hollywoodized it" is another. "They've given reality a Hollywood ending" is perhaps heard more often than any of the others. These variations tend to harden into critical formulae which appear in film reviews and critical essays as a means of denying the necessity of pursuing and establishing any connection between the particular movie under discussion and real life in society. Yet, in many different ways, some literal, some metaphorical, movies _are_ related to the goings-on in society.

That is not to say, however, that in some genres, some periods of film history, the charge of "Hollywoodizing" is not well-deserved. Perhaps there is no better example than the John Wayne war movies, such as the early The Sands of Iwo Jima (1949) or the much later The Green Berets (1968), in which the "Hollywood version," purporting to present and interpret real events of social history, takes social history and exaggerates, heroizes, romanticizes, and distorts it to the point of unrecognizability. Perhaps the best example of all of this kind of Hollywood exaggeration is the film To Hell And Back (1955), the story of the exploits of World War II Congressional Medal of Honor winner Audie Murphy acted by the man himself. In that campy shoot-em-up, actor Murphy plays soldier Murphy as an angelic munchkin capable of cutting a wider swath through the Wehrmacht than Patton's whole 3rd Army. A more subtle example of "Hollywoodizing" can be found in the political bias toward the American presence in Vietnam represented in the Jane Fonda-dominated film project Coming Home (1978).

There have also been trends and periods in film history when the relationship between the movies and society has been painfully commercial, hostile and overtly exploitative. Witness the blaxploitation films of the late sixties and early seventies such as the Superfly (1972) series and the Shaft (1971) series. How about the exploitation of vulnerable young women in the "slice-n-dice" horror films of the late seventies or the exploitation of adolescent sexuality in the "puberty exploding" films of the early eighties which were simply more explicit renderings of the "beach blanket bingo" movies of the fifties?

In other periods of film history, the movie industry has consciously chosen to ignore social history because

that contemporary social history was simply too troubling
or too controversial to portray with any hope of
financial profit. This was certainly the case with the
movie industry's almost total avoidance of any aspect of
the Vietnam War in the period 1966-1976. Certainly, there
have been times and films which have underscored the
"discomfiture of definition" of the relationship between
the movies and society, but "the times they are a
changin'."

Pulitzer Prize-winning historian Arthur M. Schlesinger
Jr. in his lecture "Film and History: An Equivocal
Relationship" posits that

> Movies must have something to tell us
> not just about the surfaces but about the
> inner mysteries of American life. They must
> cast light on the way people seek meaning in
> daily existence, how they understand
> themselves, their society and their destiny.[1]

The whole intention of this book is to present a
revisionist view of the social involvement of the movie
industry in the portrayal of the crucial events and social
attitudes of our time. This revisionist view concentrates
upon denying the premise that "Hollywood" is
insensitive to and unrealistic about its portrayal of life
in the contemporary world. This analysis of the films of
the seventies advances the contrary premise that, in fact,
the movie industry recently has consciously reacted to,
commented upon and dramatized the social events,
trends and consciousnesses of its time. In other words,
despite the tension between the perceived unreality of
"Hollywood" (used as the generic term that it has
become because presently "Hollywood" exists all over the
world) and social history, that in recent years, as was the

---

[1]The 1984 Patricia Wise Lecture, sponsored by the
American Film Institute, AFI Theater, Washington, D.C.

case with the intense social consciousness films of the
thirties like I Am A Fugitive From A Chain Gang (1932)
and The Grapes of Wrath (1939), motion pictures have
frequently turned for dramatic and exciting subject
matter to the factual events of contemporary social
history and have portrayed those events in both realistic
and symbolic terms with perception, involvement and
impact. Though the "Hollywood" version of
contemporary social history has been the frequent target
of derisive criticism, much of that criticism is
undeserved. The films of the seventies do portray and
analyze the major events of contemporary social history.
They do not always do so mimetically with strict
adherence to the "mirror in the roadway" approach of
Flaubert, but they do it nonetheless, often metaphorically
rather than mimetically.

Therefore, the purpose of this book in combining
social history and film criticism is to go against the
grain of the accepted popular conception of the
relationship of the film industry to the social history of
the time. Instead of accepting that generic conception of
"Hollywood" with all of its negative connotations, a
positive look at all the ways in which recent films have
examined, grappled with, sensitively revealed and even
polemically analyzed the crucial events and trends of
contemporary social history is worth taking. Despite the
accepted stereotype of a film industry which is escapist,
exploitative and unrealistic in terms of established
literary conceptions of social realism, the contemporary
film industry is really quite conscious of, receptive to
and reactive toward contemporary social history and
contemporary societal trends.

"If God could do the tricks that we can do, he'd be
a happy man." That's what Eli Cross (Peter O'Toole), the
charismatic John Huston-like film director in Richard
Rush's The Stunt Man (1980), proclaims about the ability
of the art of the movies to imitate life. The Stunt Man
is one of the finest films of the early eighties because
it is a film which bridges the seventies and the eighties
perfectly. The Stunt Man recognizes itself as a document

to a time in social history when all is illusory, when nothing can be accepted at face value, where, in fact, art may be more comprehensible than reality ever could be. As Cameron (Steve Railsback), the young Vietnam veteran turned title character of The Stunt Man, says: "Reality can be pretty outrageous."

The Stunt Man is a movie consciously dramatizing the relationship between this young and tricky art form, the movies, and the "outrageous" post-Vietnam, post-Watergate reality of society in a specific time and place. Eli Cross's bias in favor of art as more real than reality is directly the opposite of the opinion of the young hooker (Nancy Allen) in Brian DePalma's late seventies film Blow-Out (1979) who says: "Movies are great but, like, this is like real life, on the streets." Art and life, movies and society, perhaps at no other time in film history was the young art form more responsive to what was going on around it than in the seventies. For the first time in a long time, the movies seemed inclined, actually went out of their way, not only to deal with the contemporary issues, events and people in their society but to actually examine their own function as an art form in relation to that society. It was a decade of art and reality meeting on the soundstage of contemporary social history.

A brief exchange between the two central characters in The Stunt Man sums up this particularly seventies movie consciousness (maybe "self-consciousness" is a better term) pretty well:

CROSS: Done any stunt work?
CAMERON: Got outa Nam in one piece.
          That's a hell of a stunt.

The fledgeling stunt man clearly thinks that making movies and making history are things not so far removed from each other. Julian Smith in his work on the movies and social history, Looking Away: Hollywood and Vietnam (Scribner's, 1975), written before any of the major Vietnam War films came out, certainly agrees with the young stunt man when he writes:

> Vietnam was like a movie that had gotten
> out of hand: gigantic cost overruns, a
> shooting schedule run amuck, squabbles on
> the set, and back in the studio, the first
> auteur dying with most of the script in his
> head, the second quitting in disgust, and the
> last swearing it was finally in the can, but
> sneaking back to shoot some extra scenes.
> (103)

More recently, other critics and social historians have similarly emphasized the cogency of the relationship between the movies and society in the seventies. Hollis Alpert, writing an introduction to a collection of retrospective essays entitled "Summing Up The Seventies" (American Film, December 1979) asks: "Was it the public that fostered change, or was it film and television that changed the public?" Social historian Morris Dickstein, in his contribution to that same series of articles, answers Alpert's question: "The films of the sixties, unlike the writing of that period, reflected very little of what was then going on . . . . we can say with some justice that the films of the sixties are finally being made in the seventies." Another, lighter view of this whole interplay between art and society was expressed by John Cassavetes as he looked back on an earlier decade: "Maybe there never was an America in the thirties. Maybe it was all Frank Capra."[2]

Since the late sixties, movies have also been getting more and more socially conscious. This recent social consciousness, however, doesn't resemble the heavy-handed parables and morality plays of the social consciousness films of the thirties such as Mervyn Leroy's and Paul

---

[2]Quoted by Jeanine Basinger in "America's Love Affair With Frank Capra," American Film, March 1982, p. 81.

Muni's I Am A Fugitive From A Chain Gang (1932) and
Fritz Lang's and Henry Fonda's You Only Live Once
(1937). Rather, the social consciousness films of the
seventies tend more to the political, the historical and
especially the self-referentially symbolic. The films of the
seventies are concerned not only with imitating life in
contemporary society but also with actually considering
their own relationship to the society with which they
deal.

WHAT IS THE RELATIONSHIP OF ART TO
SOCIETY?

That major question underlies any critical discussion
of artistic creation and its artifacts: paintings, statues,
poems, symphonies, novels, films. But it is simply too
big a question. Because it is too big a question, its
answers often are unsatisfying. They come out too vague
or expansive, too exclusive or incomplete. Art may be
"interpretive" of society or "critical" of society or
"propagandistic" toward society or "influenced by"
society or "instructive" to society or "informative" or
"subversive" or "contemptuous" of society. Yet, and most
people feel that this is art's greatest strength, it can be
all of these things simultaneously. The relationship of
art to society can be both the forest and the trees, the
dancer and the dance.

A workable relationship between art and society is
almost impossible to define unless justifiable limits are
placed on the question, unless, in other words, that
oversized question is cut down to size. Cutting the
question of the relationship between art and society
down to size has traditionally been done by critics, art
historians, social historians, whomever, by means of the
judicious wielding of the saws and axes of time and
space and species.

For example, rarely is all of art considered.
Commonly, a single art form is chosen for discussion be
it music, painting, the plastic arts or literature. Most
often, the art form is chosen because it is an influential
art form within the context of a particular time and
space: quattrocento painting in Renaissance Italy; heroic

couplet poetry in Augustan England; jazz in the
American Twenties. Because societies change, the
ascendent art forms of those societies also change.
Because in the past societies were insular, different art
forms tended to rise to ascendence with a geographical
exclusivity. But in the twentieth century, with the onset
of Marshall McLuhan's "global village" electronic definition of society, the spatial component in the art-society
relationship has become much less restrictive and insular.
Thus, when a book approaches this question of the
relationship between art and society, the only way to
avoid the inherent "discomfiture of definition" is to cut
the question down to size immediately by concentrating
on a particular art form such as film in a particular
time such as the seventies. Yet, even with this kind of
pruning of the overgrown question of the relationship of
art to society, another large question still lurks in the
underbrush.

   HOW DO FILMS FUNCTION IN THEIR
RELATIONSHIP TO SOCIETY?

   They expose. They place either past or ongoing
issues, events or information into a national or
worldwide spotlight. More importantly, films often bring
events or issues which have occurred or been raised in
the past but which have lain dormant, been ignored or
have been systematically suppressed, back into the
spotlight of national or world consciousness. The German
film, The Lost Honor of Katharina Blum (1975) about
the social harassment of innocent witnesses to crimes,
and the spate of late seventies films on the Vietnam
War discussed at length later in this book are salient
examples of the ability of films to expose issues in
social history.

   They raise future issues. Films like The Quiet
American (1958), The Ugly American (1963) and The
Sand Pebbles (1966), for example, all prefigured and
commented upon the futility of American involvement in
the Far East. Even more graphically, The China
Syndrome (1979) directly predicted two weeks before it
happened an actual socio-historical event, the Three Mile

Island nuclear accident.

They define social trends. When social history is examined over any arbitrary period of time, certain events may stand out as pivotal or highly influential. Perhaps the most obvious recent example of this formation of a trend around a single crucial event would be the Watergate burglary and its impact upon the ensuing social history of the seventies. But more often, when studied over a specific period of time, social history tends to form itself into themes or trends of concern or change in society. A number of similar events may occur which show a trend toward a certain type of behavior or attitude in society. Art forms, like the movies, tend to closely examine these themes or trends in the social history of the time period in which they appear.

They analyze social events and issues. They have the power to educate their audience in the workings of society, to instruct their audience in the meanings of the events which occur in society. By giving the events and themes of contemporary social history embodiment, movies make those events and themes more available to the audience, easier for people to understand, to deal with, to make decisions about. A film like The Formula (1980), for example, portrays the labyrinthine workings of "Big Oil" corporations.

Finally, and from an aesthetic point of view perhaps the most important, films can take the events and issues of social history and turn them into representative metaphors of national and global life. Films like Blow-Up and Chinatown which metaphorically comment upon social history demonstrate the ability of art to successfully monitor and mirror the movement of human consciousness in the life of the world.

By dealing with these two major questions-- qualifying the first and codifying the second -- the critic can profitably examine that relationship between art and society without experiencing or succumbing to the "discomfiture of definition." That is exactly what this book hopes to do: Examine the relationship of a particular art form, the movies, to the social history of a particular time, a period extending from approximately the late sixties to the early eighties, more precisely 1966 to the end of 1982, mainly the decade of the seventies.

In many ways, the structure of this book is almost mathematical. That structure is formulated on a kind of critical set theory which organizes the films of the decade (the prime set) into each of the individual sets (or prominent trends) to which they belong. The major events and trends of social history in the seventies formed mind sets which influenced the making of whole bodies of films dealing with single events or similar subject matter.

The major events of the decade are easy to remember, hard to understand and have all been dealt with in the films of the seventies with a diversity and complexity of attempted mimetic portrayal and metaphorical representation. The seventies was a complex and confusing decade. The films of the seventies mirror that complexity in their images and metaphors and consistently portray that confusion in the plights of their characters.

The seventies was the decade of the Vietnam War as the sixties had been. But the Vietnam War in the seventies was different. All through the sixties, the war ignited emotions, blazed incountry at its highest intensity of violence and betrayal, fragged society. But in the first three years of the seventies, Vietnam weighed heavily upon America: already lost, a lingering reminder of past sins, not understood at all, just there, hanging on, everyone from the politicians to the protestors to the grunts in I Corps trying to disengage from it, survive it. It hung on . . . on TV. It hung on as an embarrassment to the nation, to the Nixon administration, to the military establishment, to the anti-war movement on the campuses and in the streets. Never had America known such a long war. It seemed like it would never end.

Nixon was trapped in the maze of his own words, all that "Peace With Honor" rhetoric. The anti-war movement couldn't understand why they had been unable to march and chant the war to death. The military were frustrated because not only couldn't they wage and win the war but they couldn't even pull out of it gracefully because the news media were constantly peering over their shoulders. For everyone, no matter what their political persuasion or occupation or social class, the Vietnam War intruded and hung on.

Finally, in 1973, the American adventure in Vietnam ended. Yet the Vietnam War hung on. Its effects clung fiercely to the second half of the seventies. The war festered in the memories of Americans, changed the temper of the times, rearranged national and personal priorities, continued to confuse, to torture the millions of veterans and their families, to puzzle everyone who thought about it enough to realize that they probably never would understand it. That is when the movies took the event and made it into metaphor.

The Vietnam War films of the late seventies rekindled the American consciousness of the war which Washington had attempted to file away and forget. What the movies realized was that when a reality is so complex that no one can understand it, it is time to turn that reality into art because art has the ability to make connections metaphorically which life can never make realistically. Perhaps the best example of the metaphoric approach to the complex question of meaning in the Vietnam War is the striking Russian Roulette metaphor upon which Michael Cimino's The Deer Hunter (1978) bases its whole perception of the war's effect upon the individual. That Russian Roulette metaphor, inspired by the most famous newsphoto taken during the war-- the Saigon Chief of Police executing a suspected Viet Cong in the center of a busy Saigon street --had no basis in fact (no evidence has surfaced that American prisoners were forced to play Russian Roulette by their Vietnamese captors; Russian Roulette parlors did not exist in the city of Saigon and it was not a betting sport like cockfighting or kickboxing) yet in a single repeated movie image captured all of the loneliness, despair, frustration, risk and existential rebellion against the threat of death that soldiers playing the game of Vietnam experienced daily.

The seventies were also the decade of Watergate. Since that fateful day in March 1972 when a "second-rate burglary" managed to bungle its way into metaphor, myth and the national consciousness, Watergate seemed always to be with us, entangling and wrapping the seventies in its own web of words and images which hardly anyone could understand and some of which were erased before anyone ever got the chance to try to understand them.

Like the Vietnam War, Watergate, though seeming to be a simple thing, became more and more complex, escalated, got so far out of hand that it changed the whole temper of American life, changed America's whole conception of itself. Like Vietnam, Watergate also hung on, attached itself like a parasite to the national and global consciousness. It came to represent all that had gone wrong with America, with Democracy. Watergate became a guilt complex that made a whole nation neurotic. Watergate became a further motive for alienation, suspicion, paranoia, distrust and fear, all of which had been planted in the sixties to bear full fruit in the seventies.

Like the Vietnam War, TV made Watergate. Where TV had presented Vietnam as the ultimate in global village news reporting, the networks put Watergate on as a squalid afternoon soap opera with a complete cast of characters filling all the stereotyped roles and a plot so thick that it made As The World Turns and General Hospital look like uncomplicated nursery rhymes. Television photographed the reality and it seemed like fiction, but then the movies took the event and made it into metaphor.

Watergate fostered a whole cinema of paranoia, a series of movies like Three Days of the Condor (1975) or Capricorn One (1978) or Blow-Out (1981) in which reality is supposedly captured, taped, photographed or investigated, yet still can't be fully understood. Thus, once again, when reality as reality resists being grasped,

the metaphorical representation of reality as art becomes
the only remaining alternative.

The seventies were also the decade of the emergence
of international oil cartels, of artificial oil shortages, of
big business, international corporate conspiracy flexing its
muscles openly enough so that people around the world
finally became aware of its existence. Americans, for the
first time in the seventies, realized that because of their
own consumptive frenzy they had lost control of their
destiny. Multinational corporations became real entities
when they imprisoned individual Americans in gas lines,
doubled the price of a gallon of gas in a matter of
mere months and actually restricted the mobility, took
away a part of the freedom, of the American
population. The masses as individuals, for the first time,
became aware of the existence of international corporate
powers, felt the effects of international corporate conspiracy, but that was as far as it went.

Even TV couldn't present this particular aspect of
seventies life clearly. Even TV couldn't develop a format
to make international corporate maneuvering intelligible.
Once again, it was left to the movies to take the
shadowy realities of international finance and turn them
into metaphor. In a film set in the late seventies, The
Formula (1980), Marlon Brando in one of his memorable
seventies soliloquies (it seemed like each major film in
which Brando appeared-- The Missouri Breaks (1976),
Apocalypse Now (1979), The Formula --was built upon
the premise that Brando's reason for being there was to
deliver long philosophical Shakespearean soliloquies)
offers as clear a metaphor as can be imagined for
America's consumptive dependence. "Oil," Adam Stiefel,
international tycoon, matter-of-factly states, "is the great
American tit."

It was also the decade of Three Mile Island and
Love Canal and revelations about the results of past
atomic bomb tests. Americans were being asked to
believe that things they couldn't even see, much less
understand, were tangible threats to their lives and their
children's lives. As was the case with Vietnam and

Watergate, the public utilities and the corporate polluters and the government testers expended their mightiest efforts to cover-up and confuse and minimize and distort the reality of these threats to the environment. Again, TV found itself inadequate for presenting the reality of the situation. TV had nothing to photograph. The various threats of this particular type-- the radioactivity, the poisonous microbes --were invisible. It was left to the movies to take those events and turn them into metaphor.

It was the decade of disengagement and self-absorption, the "ME" decade. Existentialism, which had fueled the quests and movements and anguishes of self-expression in the sixties, faded into the pallid pragmatism of the seventies. Self-definition sank to the level of self-fulfillment. Students didn't care so much who they were anymore; what they cared about was getting a good job and making big bucks. Students lost interest in making the world better (thanks mostly to the frustrations of Vietnam and Watergate) and concentrated on making their resumes fatter. Long hair and faded jeans gave way to preppy alligators and Calvin Kliens. American Graffiti (1973) followed by Grease (1978) and television's Happy Days and Laverne and Shirley triggered a frenzy of regressive nostalgia for the more playful, more optimistic, safer fifties. Rock and Roll momentarily took a back seat to the pallid prancings of Disco. The temper of the times had changed most noticeably among the young. Where a blind idealism had driven the flower children of the sixties into the streets, an entrenched and fully justified cynicism drove the children of the seventies into tunnels of vocational education, caves of conservatism and unimaginative, circumscribed self-interest.

The students of the seventies learned a depressing lesson from their predecessors. Young people in the sixties had tried to understand reality, control it, and all of their efforts had been futile. Young people in the seventies didn't want to waste their time trying to understand. In reaction against the frustrations of the sixties, they threw themselves into work where they could achieve immediate, tangible results. It was the movies, starting with The Graduate (1967), that took the lostness and apathy and emptiness of imagination of the "ME" generation and turned it into metaphor.

These were the major social, historical facts, the events that made the seventies the seventies. Their effects spread throughout the society in obvious and less than obvious (even submerged) ways. The decade tried to deal with these events. The unblinking eye of the decade, Television, tried to capture and record and interpret these events and, in most instances, failed. Most of the time, the television news could only photograph the surface of reality, discuss the facts of reality. It couldn't get to the meanings that lurked beneath the surface. When the facts had all been found and set out in the limited images of the TV camera eye, they never fit totally together, nothing was ever what it seemed to be.

Even with armies of news commentators in voice-over analyzing the TV images, TV had trouble capturing the full meanings of the events because TV is limited to reality and there is nothing more unreal than the attempt to capture, explain, understand reality. The most frequent cause of TV's failure on the news or in public hearings or in special event coverage was TV's inability to structure reality, to organize and present it unfragmented. The movies can do what television cannot. They can take an event and structure it into metaphor.

That ability to structure reality into metaphor is why the movies have, throughout this century, been one of the most reliable of indicators, observers, interpreters of the social and historical attitudes of the society. Robert Sklar in his seminal work Movie-Made America: A Cultural History of American Movies (Random House, 1975) has stated that fact most clearly: "movies have historically been and still remain vital components in the network of cultural communication, and the nature of their content and control helps to shape the character and direction of American culture as a whole (vi)."

But the relationship of art and social history functions not only in time but also in space even though in the electronic age of McLuhan that space has been greatly widened. The movie art of turning the realities of social history into intelligible film metaphors was not just an American phenomenon of the seventies. For example, it is striking how similar the metaphors of the films of two places so separate from one another as America and Australia can be. The films of the late seventies in both America and Australia were obsessed with war. Of course, the war which obsessed them both, whether presented literally in <u>Apocalypse</u> <u>Now</u> or <u>The</u> <u>Odd</u> <u>Angry</u> <u>Shot</u> (1979) or metaphorically in <u>Breaker</u> <u>Morant</u> (1980), was the Vietnam War. American film themes, such as the sinister power of the corporate world, were acknowledged and expanded by major European filmmakers like Fassbinder and Wenders. European films, especially films like Antonioni's <u>Blow-Up</u> (1966) or Truffaut's "metamovies," his movies about moviemaking, became major influences on the dominant themes and metaphors of American films of the seventies. America, Western Europe, Australia: they were the places where film in the seventies was making the most, both literally and metaphorically, out of the events and trends of seventies social history.

Cutting the question of the nature of the relationship between art and society down to size and listing the different ways in which movies function in their relationship to society are two steps on the road to overcoming the "discomfiture of definition." But other critical and theoretical issues remain.

The purpose, the underlying premise and the justification for a book's existence are issues which ought to be examined early in any book of history or criticism. They are three different ways of answering the single straightforward question which challenges any book of history or criticism: "Why is this book necessary in this time and this place?"

The purpose and the major premise of this book

complement each other. The purpose of writing social history is to analyze the "society," the "time" and the "place" in which we live (or lived) in order to answer three essential questions. First, what were the most important events, trends, social attitudes which occurred within the specified time and place? Second, how did those events, trends, social attitudes change the society in which they occurred? Third, how did those events, trends, social attitudes influence the evolution of the society into its present-day state? In other words:

1. What happened?
2. What changes occurred?
3. How did that past make our present?

The purpose of writing a social history of film evolves from the same considerations. Film, like any valid art form, mirrors the life of the society which creates it. As Robert Sklar writes, the film historian/critic must "try to understand motion pictures in their largest sense, as a mass medium of cultural communication (v)." In the case of film in the seventies, the movies and the society were as inextricably connected as they had been in earlier decades. Witness the social consciousness films and escapist musicals of the thirties or the patriotic morality plays of the forties. In the seventies, the reciprocity of interest and concern and political motive between the movie industry and society which hadn't existed in either the safe fifties or the radical sixties was re-established. For instance, the movies as a social art form had been supplanted by the music industry of the sixties. In the seventies, the movies reasserted themselves as the most viable mass art form. They reestablished their mimetic/interpretive function, their social relationship with their audience, something they had studiously avoided doing during the turbulent and confusing sixties. Art comments upon society while simultaneously drawing art from that society. Art structures and dramatizes the facts and emotions of society in order to make those facts and emotions available and intelligible to the masses who make up that society.

The premise underlying this book is tailored to those three major purposes for the writing of social history. The events which created the major social issues of the seventies (the Vietnam War, Watergate, etc.) also planted submerged social attitudes within national societies (both in America and abroad) as well as within the film industry itself. These submerged attitudes-- guilt for Vietnam, embarrassment over Watergate, helplessness in the face of corporate power, confusion as to the very nature of reality --in turn inspired, shaped, even dictated the subject matter of the films being made in Hollywood, Frankfurt, Paris and Sydney. In other words, this book's intention is to show how individual movies, genres and sub-genres, Directors and even whole national film industries assimilated the social history of their particular "time" and "place," turned that history into mimetic metaphor, and, in doing so, interpreted that history through popular art thus making it intelligible to a mass audience.

The case of The China Syndrome (1979) is the most immediate example of this principle in action. No film of the seventies was better timed for the purpose of interpreting social history. On the evening news, the Three Mile Island nuclear accident was no more than an aerial long shot of three gray concrete domes. On the Eyewitness News, the radioactive threat was merely a few hisses of steam dissipating over a leaden Pennsylvania industrial river. The movie, however, appearing a scant two weeks before the real event, defined the concept "nuclear accident" in terms that people could understand. A metaphor from nuclear physics gave the film its title. Images of greed, corporate conspiracy and fear dramatized the concept in human terms.

Thus, purpose and premise complement one another but the justification for this book's existence is perhaps the simplest of all the theoretical issues to confront. Why a social history of film in the seventies?

BECAUSE it needs to be done. BECAUSE Robert Sklar's brilliant book <u>Movie-Made America: A Cultural History of American Movies</u> stops at 1970. Sklar's book is the model for a book of this sort which attempts to make the proper connections between society and the popular art which mimetically defines that society. BECAUSE as Ian Jarvie in his <u>Movies and Society</u> (Basic Books, 1970) so bluntly put it: "there is also a monumental ignorance about the nature of the cinema as a social institution-- among the most significant in the world . . . . This medium that is apparently so hard to understand was at one point the third largest of America's industries. Since the First World War it has been one of her principal exports. It is a major vehicle for the dissemination of her national culture (4)." Jarvie sets forth one major purpose for this approach to films, to examine "the interplay between the cinema and society-- the social conditions --it serves/portrays/attacks (7)." In fact, Jarvie rather militantly asserts that it "is time for a further confrontation with the widespread, commonsense theory that films do influence their audience, whether that influence is mediated or not, and do so quite radically (121) . . . . Film experience also provides: information; social, moral and political argument; distraction; and catharsis . . . . Every one of us learns an immense amount of facts about other countries whenever we see a foreign film. We not only learn what the place looks like; we learn things about the sensibility of that nation (123-4)." And finally, BECAUSE the film histories written in the last fifteen years tend to neglect the seventies and rarely attempt to make the connection between social history and film art.

Recent film history tends to sharply focus in, to emphasize the close-up rather than the long establishing shot. Recent film history tends to restrict itself to individual movements or Directors or genres or national cinemas or single film-related social events of earlier decades like the McCarthy hearings and the Blacklist rather than upon attempts to generalize about and specifically illustrate the relationship between the medium and the society as a whole (as demonstrated by the medium's participation in and portrayal of the temper of the times).

Recently published major film histories simply can't afford the space to examine in depth the relationship between movies and society in the seventies. Most of these recent major film histories consider that relationship in their discussions of earlier decades but when it comes to the seventies the focus inevitably moves to discussion of the dominant genres or the most prominent Directors.

David A. Cook's brilliant and definitive A History of Narrative Film (W.W. Norton and Co., 1980) is a good case in point. A fine film history especially strong in its definitions of the foriegn national cinemas in the fifties and sixties, when it comes to its two chapters on the seventies it is painfully obvious that some editor told Cook to cut and those chapters are where the major amputations took place. Gerald Mast's A Short History of the Movies (Bobbs-Merrill, 1981) first appeared in 1971 and went into an updated third edition in 1981. It also suffers from an acute lack of space when it comes to the seventies. Mast subscribes to Andrew Sarris's "Auteur" theory in his chapter on the seventies. He makes brief comments on the careers of the decade's most prominent Directors. Frank E. Beaver's On Film: A History of the Motion Picture (McGraw-Hill Inc., 1983) reserves more room for the films of the seventies and, at one point, in his discussion of the Vietnam War films, approaches the relationship of film art to society. At the beginning of his chapter entitled "The Strains of American Cinema" Beaver signals the direction his discussion is going to take when he writes: "American cinema after 1965 reveals a fascinating interplay among societal conditions, industrial struggle, and personal endeavor" (464). Beaver's 47 pages on the films of the seventies briefly cover the territory with insight. [3] There are understandable reasons for the dilution of these recent film histories at the contemporary end. Because they are written for classroom audiences and film history classes typically run out of

time and do little with the films of the seventies at
semester's end, that decade is the logical one to cut.
Also, because the films are so recent and there has been
so little time for study and judgement of their "lasting"
qualities, the safe route is to "wait and see" rather than
invest book space and class time in risky properties.

Two other books, both focused only on the films of
the seventies, Les Keyser's Hollywood In The Seventies
(A.S. Barnes and Co. Inc., 1981) and James Monaco's
American Film Now: The People*The Power*The
Money*The Movies (New American Library, 1979), don't
take the social history approach. Keyser's is a
coffee-table picture book structured in terms of short
discussions of the seventies work of Actors and
Directors. He is a member of the Variety school of film
criticism which posits that the best movies are the ones
which make the most money.

James Monaco's American Film Now: The People*
The Power*The Money*The Movies also focuses exclusively on the films of the seventies. It is a fascinating
book because it has a clearly defined approach for
examining American film within the context of the
seventies decade. That approach posits that film should
be studied as a business rather than an art form.
Monaco's book is authoritative and thoroughly
documented often from primary interview sources; if
Monaco isn't a Hollywood insider, he gives an excellent
and knowledgeable impression of one. Also, Monaco's
book is imaginatively written, entertaining, innovative in
its structure and its rhetorical excursions (for example:

---

[3]Flashback: A Brief History of Film by Louis
Giannetti and Scott Eyman (Prentice-Hall, 1986) appeared
while this book was in press and devotes 37 pages to
"American Cinema Since 1970." The authors write at the
beginning of this section: "History is not so tidy as
historians would wish it. the period under consideration
actually comprises two distinct eras, with the dividing
(Footnote continued)

the book opens with a fictional biography of a young
aspiring seventies filmmaker).

Yet, Monaco in <u>American</u> <u>Film</u> <u>Now</u> clearly states his
"discomfiture of definition" when approaching the
relationship between the movies ("Hollywood") and
American society. He denies the existence of that
relationship. "Are contemporary movies talking to us?"
he asks. "On the whole, I think not . . . . American
film in the seventies has a better reputation than it deserves" (preface). He underlines his denial when he
states: "It is only occasionally that a movie comes along
that presents the kinds of characters and situations that
we know from everyday life" (preface). The book which
you are now reading takes the opposing view that the
main sources of subject material for the best films of
the seventies (Vietnam, Watergate, the violation of reality
in their everyday lives) were the very events that the
people of America and the world were most interested in
seeing dramatized, were trying hardest to understand.

Monaco brilliantly defines filmmaking in the
seventies as a power struggle between art and the
corporate villainy of "Hollywood." For him, the
corporate villain in the seventies succeeded in strangling
any pretensions to art that the movies may have had.
Conversely, it can be argued that a great many of the
films of the seventies in the self-reflexivity of their
images, characters and themes demonstrate that creative
filmmakers have their own resources for fighting back
against the flabby devils who squat in the corporate
boardrooms plotting to make art bow down in worship

----

[3](continued)
line falling shortly after mid-decade. The earlier 1970s--
dominated by the unending war in Vietnam and the
Watergate scandals --represent a continuation of the
sensibility of the late 1960s. Most film historians point
to <u>Star</u> <u>Wars</u> (1977) as the beginning of a new epoch in
American filmmaking, characterized by a nostalgic
(Footnote continued)

to the gods of the bottom line. The history of film in
the seventies is a map of a guerrilla war against the
incorporation of the film industry. This war is being
fought up there on the screen with the film artist's most
powerful weapons-- his images, his themes, his visual and
verbal metaphors.

In a sense, James Monaco in American Film Now is
an archaeologist of the seventies film industry rather than
a historian or critic. American Film Now is an
authoritative, behind-the-scenes excavation which digs up
and puts on display the artifacts that get thrown away
or aren't recorded or documented on the screen when a
movie is made: the deals, the unwritten laws, the meet-
ings, the discarded doodles. His interest is in defining
why a film is made, how and why it becomes a hit,
rather than in what a film says about American society
in the seventies. At one point Monaco writes: "The main
thing new about American movies in the seventies is
what's old. The seventies have no culture of their own,
no style, unless it is nostalgia" (60). In the first couple
of years of the decade with the American Graffiti break
out, perhaps he was right. But, quickly the seventies
developed a distinct culture of insecurity, retrenchment,
paranoia and distrust of reality, all directly influenced
by Vietnam, Watergate and the pressures of a distinctive
1970s world. Monaco's American Film Now is the best
book yet to appear on the American film industry in
the seventies but it shows little interest in the study of
the relationship between the movies and society and
doesn't give the movies of the seventies enough credit as
a serious art form.

The images and the socio-historical subject matter of
the films of the seventies express their rebellion against

------

[3](continued)
longing for the simplicities of bygone days." Giannetti
and Eyman devote three pages to "The Vietnam-Watergate
Era" and list a number of the films which are analyzed
in this study.

the threat of their loss of identity as an art form. An
eclectic approach is needed which acknowledges what
Monaco has done in defining the business of American
film in the seventies, examines the social and cultural
history of the decade, yet also looks closely at the films
themselves as the final, most important, evidence of the
existence of a relationship between the art form and the
society within which it expresses itself.

What this book desires to do is catch the temper of
a decade, the 1970s, both in America and around the
world, as exhibited in the most perceptive of its
contemporary art forms-- the movies. The eclectic
approach to this task will employ the combination of
social history, film history and film criticism with the
last, the criticism of the visual/verbal meanings of the
individual films, being the dominant voice. This
approach is dependent upon a number of underlying
assumptions which bond the social/historical/critical
connections. First, the trends in seventies film proved to
be closely tied to the social, political and historical
events of the decade, principally Watergate and Vietnam.
Secondly, the events of the decade changed the
consciousness of the country and those changes in
national psychology were, in many instances, more
important themes in seventies film than were the straight
realistic portrayals of the historical events themselves.
Thirdly, film (both American and foriegn) in the
seventies was a reactive medium. Film was not
"reactionary" in the derogatory sense of that term, but
"reactive" in the sense that the films of the seventies
reacted directly in social and political ways to the
major historical, social and political events of the
decade. Fourthly, film in the seventies became a conduit
for analysis and interpretation of the realities of
seventies life; the movies dramatized, commented upon,
and made the news of the decade understandable by
means of conceptual film metaphors. With its highly
political and social concerns, this approach might
perhaps be considered "radical" in its definitions and
interpretations not only of the trends in American film

of the seventies but also of the American society which produced those trends. As the film editor said to the worried director whose set had been struck, "we have to make do with what we've got." Vietnam, Watergate, OPEC and Three Mile Island are what we've got and what the movies made do with in the seventies.

The approach, then, is thematic with an emphasis upon the visual and the verbal aspects of film as the means of metaphorically representing theme. The central concern of this approach is to relate the central themes of the major films of the seventies either directly to the major historical events of the decade which inspired them or to the social attitudes (the temper of the times) which those events caused to form in the general population and within the narrower sphere of the film industry itself.

An especially interesting case of the rela- tionship of the movies and society in regard to contemporary history can be seen in the interaction between the society's attitudes and the film industry's attitude toward the Vietnam War in the 1970s. From the start of American involvement in the war in 1962 to the end of that involvement in 1973, only one major American production-- John Wayne's military propaganda piece, The Green Berets (1967), fully assisted by the Pentagon for obvious reasons --dealt directly with the war. John Milius wrote the first script for Apocalypse Now in 1968 but he and Francis Coppola couldn't get the film made until 1976. Why? Because the film industry was heeding the signals of society, guaging the temper of the times. Vietnam was too troubling a theme for the people of America. They needed time to prepare themselves for their attempt to understand this war which had opened such raw wounds in the society. They needed time to heal. After a period of convalescence, in 1976, two films, Taxi Driver and Coming Home, which explored Vietnam War themes, were released and, more importantly, were accepted by the American movie-going public. Those films made America realize that it was finally time to start thinking and talking about Vietnam again. Those

films made Americans look at themselves. A spate of
even better Vietnam War films followed in the late
seventies and the society moved forward with exploring
and taking steps to cure the effects upon a society full
of all types of Vietnam veterans.

The second concern of this approach is to provide
closely text-related criticism of the major films of the
period: 1966-1983. Thus, the approach fully intends to
look not only at the social motives behind the films of
the period but also at the films themselves. The film
critic's task is one first of TRANSLATION, second of
CONNECTION and third of ANALYSIS. The good film
critic first translates the images on the screen into words
then connects those images to all that is relevant in the
world surrounding those images (including the sources
from whence those images come) and then analyzes those
images so as to define and understand the meanings they
offer. The good film critic consistently moves from the
VISUAL to the VERBAL to the SOCIAL to the
SYMBOLIC.

Pursuant to this thematic approach, parts of this
book will focus upon films which are grouped
thematically, such as the corporate villain films and the
Vietnam War films. Other sections of the book will deal
with film movements or even national cinemas such as
the Australian film industry. And finally, some chapters
will focus upon a single, highly important film which
proved especially prophetic or purposeful or articulate in
its connection to the social attitudes of the time.

The seventies is in this book's title, but it became
clear rather quickly that the themes which control film
in the seventies all started with films in the late sixties
and were still relevant and active three years into the
eighties. Useful as it may be for the purposes of book
titling, it is unrealistic and imprecise to take very
seriously the definition of periods of film history which
are codified within the rigid parameters of a decade.
There is also an unpredictability about the relationships
which movies establish with socio-historical events. In
some cases, the movies actually predict the themes of

social history as with the Blow-Up movies and their relationship to Watergate or the eerie timing of The China Syndrome to the Three Mile Island incident. In other cases, as with the Vietnam War, there is a lag time between the historical or social event and the movie reactions/portrayals/interpretations of that event.

This book also differs somewhat from the other available surveys of the films of the decade in its conscious attempt to be different in its style, its delivery to its audience. Jonathan Rosenbaum writing in American Film (December 1982) defines three audiences of film history today and three accompanying styles of writing film history:

> At least three distinct (if overlapping) publics now read about film, each accustomed to a distinct jargon. Filmmakers and other industry people have one way of talking about movies, journalists another, and academics a third. General readers sometimes find themselves bouncing back and forth between all three kinds of discourse. For book publishers, this triad is reduced further to two markets-- the scholarly and the mass market. (76)

This book is not written for any one of those three audiences but rather for all three. How can a book zero in on this sort of eclectic aim? By taking care with its style. By carefully avoiding (or at least restricting to only occasional intended use) any of what Rosenbaum calls the "distinct jargon" which has accrued to each of the three distinct audiences. This book's style, for example, is consciously unacademic yet it raises questions and defines themes of immediate interest to academics. It is not designed for classroom use yet it contains the pertinent material which any teacher dealing with this period of contemporary film history will find useful. It is not a popular movie magazine essay yet it deals with all the major popular movies of the seventies and offers a mainstream audience a great deal to think about through the discussion of their favorite films and the society which produced those films.

This book aims, then, at all three audiences simultaneously primarily by means of its film selection. Academic criticism usually focuses on a small number of technique distinctive films often with a heavier emphasis on foriegn films. Filmmakers and industry people lean to the Monaco "how-to" approach which focuses on how movies are getting made with heavy emphasis on the business angle. Journalists spend their ink on all sorts of films which appeal to the varied tastes of a highly diversified mass audience. This book deals with films which fall into all three categories of interest-- from The Conversation to The China Syndrome to TRON --and, more importantly, defines relationships between those films which are the darlings of the academics, such as Blow-Up and Chinatown, and those films which people lined up around city blocks to see, such as Star Wars and Shampoo.

Thus, with its questions posed, its influential socio-historical events chosen and described, its approach defined without discomfiture, the state of the art of the films of the seventies is ready to be assembled in much the same way that one might assemble a "state of the art" stereo system. All the components have been shopped, proven compatible, plugged into each other and now stand ready to play the films of the seventies through the whole system, deliver the clear strains of their art and meaning. The purpose of this system is a straightforward one: to show how the movies took the events of our times and made them into metaphors. In this book, the metaphor not the medium is the message.

2. MOVIE VILLAINS: THE SEVENTIES LOOK

In 1967, a B-movie starring James Coburn entitled
The President's Analyst appeared. It wasn't much of a
film, a spy comedy with Godfrey Cambridge playing a
CIA agent, but little did it know what a serious
Hollywood trend it was starting. Its plot might have
been lifted out of Kurt Vonnegut's novel Sirens of Titan
(1959). The kicker of that plot was the inability of
anyone to figure out who the villain was. That villain
turned out to be not a man, not a creature from some
black lagoon, not even an agent of some foreign power,
but . . . the phone company.

In that time before Watergate, The President's Analyst
was eerily prophetic. Its plot turns on a conspiracy by
the phone company to bug the brain of every human
being in America. Old Ma Bell/AT&T/GTE wants the
President to force Congress to pass legislation outlawing
names and turning everybody into their telephone
number.

The President's Analyst prefigured the bugging frenzy
of the late sixties and early seventies alright. At one
point, the Russian spy has this conversation with the
American CIA agent:

> RUSSIAN: Are you trying to tell me that
> every phone in America is tapped?
> CIA: What can I say?
> RUSSIAN: This is America not Russia.
> CIA: (shrug)!

Although The President's Analyst was a pretty dumb movie, nevertheless it was very influential. The President's Analyst became the germ for an idea which would redefine the nature of the Hollywood villain for the next 15 years.

Remember the old villains from the William S. Hart, Tom Mix, George Raft days. They wore black hats or rode in black cars or carried black violin cases. At other times, they've worn black masks ala Darth Vader or black skins ala the villains in both The Birth of A Nation (1915) and The Deep (1977) or flew black helicopters as in Capricorn One (1978). Other villains twirled handlebar mustaches or brandished horsewhips or riding crops or wore sinister monocles or black leather coats.

Still other villains sported physical deformities: stumps, deformed hands, hooks, burns, terrible scars. Remember Liberty Valance (Lee Marvin) with that bulging mutant wen splitting his hairline or Long John Silver (Wallace Beery or Robert Newton, take your pick) who was probably handicapped more by his raspy voice than his wooden leg.

Some villains had psychological scars which deformed their existence. Remember Dr. Jekyll's face going slack then twisting into Mr. Hyde; Jack Palance's famous cheek bones flattening above his terrible feline teeth. No longer do easily identifiable villains walk into the frame and radiate personal malignance. There just aren't many Liberty Valances, Dr. Mengeles or Ming the Mercilesses left. In the James Bond series, these types of villains have become campy comical caricatures.

The Hollywood villain of the seventies and eighties is a whole new breed. Whether it takes the form of the public utilities as in The President's Analyst or The China Syndrome (1979) or private corporations providing specialty services as in The Parallax View (1974) or government agencies working out their tangled conspiracies as in Three Days of the Condor (1975) or Winter Kills (1979) or multinational global cartels threatening the stability of the western world as in The

Formula (1980), the new Hollywood conception of the villain has gone corporate.

The corporate villain movies don't form a genre (they cross all the established genres), but neither are they just a temporary fad or brief trend. Call the corporate villain concept a "megatrend." As an idea, it has obsessed Hollywood for the last fifteen years and it shows no sign of abating.

Of course, the whole idea was out there festering long before 1967 and The President's Analyst. There was an inkling of the principle when the commuters all turned into sheep in Charlie Chaplin's Modern Times (1936). It certainly was present in The Man In The Gray Flannel Suit (1956) and in the facelessness of the corporation office in Billy Wilder's The Apartment (1960).

The corporation life forced upon the employees in The Apartment was frenetic, faceless and demeaning, but it wasn't sinister. In The Apartment, the corporation was a passive, insidious threat to identity and individual humanity, but it wasn't a threat to life. Only in the films of the late sixties and seventies did the villain as corporation become actively threatening and deadly. What are the reasons that corporate villainy became the most dominant symbol of evil in American film?

There are many reasons for the change in Hollywood's conception of the villain. Some are obvious; others more subtle, more submerged. Some are historical; others are social; still others psychological. Some simply involved the timely decoding of the signals that the seventies culture was giving off; others involved attempts to objectify the traumas and complexes working within the psychology of the Hollywood community itself.

The most obvious reason for the relentless portrayal of corporate villainy in films of the seventies and early eighties is the relentless reality of corporate villainy in seventies and eighties America. It is a cliche to blame everything that is wrong in America's recent history on the Vietnam War and Watergate, but both of those events were striking examples of America's two largest corporations, the military and the government, run amok.

Vietnam and Watergate changed America's whole attitude toward dealing with evil. These two scenarios taught us that individual evil could be subsumed by the corporate villain. Nobody, no individual, could shoulder the blame for what happened to America in that short decade from 1963 to 1973, so the corporate villain allowed guilt to become collective. The problems of America were so large and complex that no individual could deal with them alone because there were no individual villains who caused them. Vietnam could be blamed on the "military-industrial complex" and Watergate on perhaps the most appropriate acronym ever coined, CREEP.

Hollywood has always kept its finger clamped on the pulse of American society. In the late sixties and seventies, that society provided, besides Vietnam and Watergate, more than enough spectacular models of corporate villainy: the big oil companies tampering with the American and world economy; huge agribusiness conglomerates disenfranchising a whole new generation of Tom Joads; the tremendous irresponsibility of public utilities and private industry which allowed Three-Mile Island, Love Canal and the Silkwood affair to happen; the computer explosion which made corporate life possible by replacing individual identities with numbers. And finally, it was in the sixties that organized crime finally really got organized . . . along corporate lines.

Hollywood makes it its business to monitor the pulse of the American moviegoer. The movie industry, itself rapidly conglomerating, quickly realized that Americans were becoming more and more suspicious, fearful of, even hostile toward the corporate entities which were running the United States. Of course, this burgeoning hostility wasn't a secret that only Hollywood was in on.

In the mid-seventies, the corporate image became perhaps the major generator of national media advertising. Bob Hope with golf club started doing "Love your friendly oil corporation" commercials. "Creeping

Iacoccaism," corporate spokesmen putting out the party
line, embodying the corporate image, cluttered the air
waves. The talking heads of Eastern Airlines' Frank
Borman, Schlitz's Frank Sellinger, and, of course,
Chrysler's Lee Iacocca were direct attempts to personalize
corporations afflicted with bad reputations in the
consciousness of the American public.

However, at least one of the reasons for the rise of
the corporate villain in American films was more subtle,
almost psychological or self-reflexive. Sometimes
Hollywood doesn't directly imitate society. Sometimes
Hollywood imitates Hollywood.

The seventies was the decade when Hollywood, the
movie industry, went corporate. The power in the major
studios shifted from the film-making executives of the
past like Thalberg, Zanuck and Disney to accountants,
agents and bottom-line men. By the start of the eighties,
Hollywood had passed almost totally into the control of
major corporations. Movie studios had become diversification ventures, mere tentacles dangling from the
hungry bodies of the corporate octopi.

The people who made films-- writers, directors,
actors, technicians --were not blind to the structural
change and the change in the temper of the industry. In
reaction and resentment toward the corporate structures
which they saw as restricting and intruding upon their
work, they created the new faceless corporate villain of
the seventies and eighties. The corporate villain was in
part a subliminal expression of the Hollywood
experience-- the facelessness of collaborative art, the
cynicism of commercial motive, the impersonality of an
art form controlled by lawyers and accountants. Francois
Truffaut and Ingmar Bergman have never felt the need
for corporate villains, but in Hollywood, for now, the
auteur has been spindled by corporate decision-making.

What is interesting is that the corporations who own
the studios allow their films to portray corporations in
this way. What is also interesting is that the motive
resentment of writers, directors, et al, seeing their medium
being taken over, took form in movies so quickly.

Movie-makers   immediately   vented   their   resentment
through their art. What is finally interesting is how
broadly based the concept of the corporate villain has
become, establishing its presence all across the board in
every type of motion picture. The films of the seventies
all go to the same data bank for their versions of the
corporate villain. Perhaps the best indicator of a
"megatrend" in American film is the lining up of all
the genres behind that trend.

One genre which down through American film
history has always presented the most individualized yet
stylized and iconic of screen villains, the western, in the
seventies offers three-piece-suited corporation men. In
Sam Peckinpah's classic The Wild Bunch (1969), the
snarling villain who arranges for the pursuit of the
Bunch into Mexico is a respected, well-dressed member
of the community. "We represent the law," says Mr.
Harrigan the railroad executive to the cutthroats,
murderers and bounty hunters whom he has just allowed
to massacre half a town in a chaotic attempt to ambush
the Bunch. Deke Thornton (Robert Ryan), the leader of
the scuzzy gang of mercenaries hired by the corporate
villain to stalk the Bunch, confronts Harrigan and states
the exact facts of the moral and social power of the
corporate villain in American capitalistic life. "How's it
feel to be getting paid for it?" Deke hisses at him.
"Sitting back and having others to do your killing. How
does it feel to be so goddam right?" But Thornton's
moral indignation means nothing to the corporate
villain. He knows exactly what he is doing. He knows
full well that morality has no application in this world.
"You're my Judas goat," Harrigan spits back at
Thornton.

The Wild Bunch lashes out with images of
Vietnam-era America. Surrogate killers are hired to fight
for the corporation, the industrial complex. The opening
symbol of the film-- thousands of ants on an ant hill
overwhelming and killing two large scorpions while the
children watch --points to the corporate takeover of the
world. That image says immediately that the age of the

individual is gone, that all the little people are banding together into faceless power structures in order to tear down individuality, that the members of the Wild Bunch are anachronisms.

The opening scene of The Wild Bunch takes place in a village. It could be a village on the Mexican border or a village on the Cambodian border. Soldiers in uniform move into the village and fields of fire are established. People in religious procession are caught in a deadly crossfire. Children stand frozen in the lines of fire. When the firefight ends, body counts are taken, corpses stripped. "You used our town as a battlefield," one of the village elders screams at Harrigan.

Images of children pepper the scenes in The Wild Bunch. They are the helpless generation caught in the middle of the corporation's war. They are the same children's faces that appeared in so many photographs in LIFE magazine between 1964 and 1973. The people in the Mexican village who give the Bunch shelter are like the Montagnards of Vietnam, of Apocalypse Now (1979). They are caught between the outside corporations who want to take over, who violate their boundaries with impunity, and the corrupt government which plunders their lives for its own corporate sustenance. Mapache is the Chairman of the Board. He is always filmed sitting at the heads of tables and riding in big cars. He even has Nixonian jowls and is surrounded by a cabinet of bright young men including a German advisor.

The Wild Bunch ends with lines of refugees fleeing the decimated battleground. Neither corporation has won. The people have been driven from their village. The soldiers who dared to be individuals have died. The world has been defoliated and left a smoking wasteland where vultures flutter. The point is clear. The corporate villains, whether it be America in Vietnam or Harrigan's hired killers in Mexico or Mapache's corrupt government, accomplish nothing but destruction in the name of greed.

Even Peckinpah's handling of the violence in the film imitated (perhaps parodied) the American media's handling of the Vietnam War, slowing it down, distancing it, graphically analyzing it. The Wild Bunch bristles with historical, political and social metaphoricality. Its corporate villainy powerfully portrays the state of the American adventure circa 1969.

In Sergio Leone's Once Upon A Time In The West (1969), Henry Fonda's Frank may be the scariest personification of the amoral, unfeeling, totally impersonal representative of the corporate will in any recent film. He is certainly the coldest, most brutal corporate tool ever to appear in a western. One shocking scene crystalizes the lengths to which the corporation (again the railroad) will go to consolidate its power, feed its greed. In The Wild Bunch, children are everywhere, always in the line of fire but never getting shot. In Once Upon A Time In The West, the corporation sends Frank and his hired guns to kill a family that owns the land where the next railroad town is going to spring up. First the daughter is cut down by a rifle shot from long range then the father and eldest son are killed in the same way. Only a small boy of five or six is left. Gliding like ghosts in their white dusters, Frank and the corporation killers materialize out of the desert scrub as the small boy watches them. Frank walks within five feet of the wide-eyed child and, point-blank, blows him away. It is a single scene of chilling violence, but throughout the rest of the movie, in the name of the corporation, Frank kills men, women and children, rapes, plunders and tortures in one of the best portrayals of an emotionless killer ever to appear on the screen. The film begins with the destruction of the institution of the family and continues to destroy every institution that exists except the one institution which has commissioned the destruction, the corporation.

All of this destruction is done in the name of "business." When Frank reports to the corporate villain, Mr. Morton the crippled owner of the railroad, about the massacre of the McBain family, Morton informs him that "a Mrs. McBain has shown up. I hadn't counted on that. It happens in business." When Frank proposes to

Morton that they form a full partnership, Morton sits
Frank down behind the corporate desk in his private
railroad car:

> MORTON: How does it feel sitting behind
> that desk, Frank?
> FRANK: Almost like holding a gun.
> (Frank draws his gun and Morton holds up a
> sheaf of $100 bills)
> MORTON: The only thing that can stop that
> is this.
> FRANK: My weapons may look simple to you,
> Mister Morton, but they can still
> shoot holes big enough to take care
> of our problems.

It is a discussion of two kinds of power in the
world of the Western: the old traditional power of the
sixgun versus the new corporate power which has already
taken over most of America and is now moving west.
The difference between Frank and Morton is most clearly
defined in the last conversation between Frank and
Harmonica (Charles Bronson) before their final
one-on-one shootout:

> HARMONICA: So you found out you're not a
> businessman after all?
> FRANK: Just a man.
> HARMONICA: An ancient race. Men like
> Morton will keep coming along and
> finally they'll kill it off.

Frank is certainly rapacious and emotionless enough to
qualify to be a businessman but he is too much of an
individual, too proud of his evil identity to ever
become like Morton.
    The comic outlaw Cheyenne (Jason Robards) expresses
in one clear incisive image what Deke Thornton was
trying clumsily to express about Harrigan in The Wild
Bunch. Cheyenne's single inspired verbal image captures

brilliantly the insipid, emotionless nature of this new corporate villain which is leaving its mark on the American West. "Hey Mister Choo Choo," Cheyenne taunts Morton. "It's not hard to find you. I don't have to kill you now. You leave a slime behind you like a snail. Two bright shiny rails." Earlier Hollywood Westerns had employed the railroad as a corporate villain swallowing up the American west, but never had the theme been so explicitly presented both visually and verbally until The Wild Bunch and Once Upon A Time In The West. By the end of that latter film, even Frank-- baby killer, rapist, torturer --is given a dignity and identity which sets him, in his personification of personal evil, one level above the lowest circle of evil in the film, that of the corporate villain.

A more modern western, Sometimes A Great Notion (1971) which was retitled Never Give An Inch, adapted from Ken Kesey's fine novel about a lumber strike in the 1960s Pacific Northwest, like Once Upon A Time In The West and The Wild Bunch (in a symbolic sense), also examines the theme of a pioneer family under attack by organized corporate forces which would take away their rugged individuality. In this film, the theme of the individual (the Stamper family) versus the corporate villain (the union) is ironic because the film examines how even a group ostensibly formed to protect the individual can infringe upon the existential rights of the individual. In one of the funniest, most ironic scenes in the film, Hank Stamper (Paul Newman) cuts out the very heart of the corporate villain (the union) which threatens the freedom of his family. Carrying his logger's chainsaw, he marches down the main street of town at high noon and into the union representative's office where he proceeds to cut the union leader's desk in half. The scene is a marvelous ironic parody of the isolated cowboy hero (a Shane perhaps) standing up in the main street to the corporate hired gun.

At the end of the decade, in the brilliantly conceived and casted The Long Riders (1980), the villains, all dressed in the same black suits, hats and string ties, work for an incorporated law-enforcement agency, The Pinkerton Co. All of these westerns are, by definition, counterculture films because the heroes are criminals and the villains turn out to be the representatives of social institutions.

But the main point of the metaphors of these westerns is that individual evil-- the Wild Bunch's holdups, Cheyenne's outlaw life, the bank jobs Jesse (James Keach) and Frank (Stacy Keach) and the Younger boys (the Carradine brothers) pull --is much less a threat to the American way of life, to a society based on individual freedom, than is the hypocritical corporate evil which destroys humanity in the name of law and order. In each of these films, the corporation makes no distinction between the killing of the innocent and the killing of the guilty. For the corporation, who gets killed is of no consequence. Only the bottom line-- success, power, profits --has any meaning.

Science Fiction films and Westerns have always had a great deal in common. Their characters survive on somewhat different frontiers; their guns load and fire a bit differently; they ride somewhat different steeds; but their actions, their motives, their rugged individualism remain much the same. Predictably, as in the Westerns of the seventies, the villains of the Sci-Fi genre have a whole new corporate look.

Outland (1981) is a prime example. It is a stylish Sci-Fi remake of High Noon (1952). Sean Connery talking to a computer screen replaces Gary Cooper talking to skittery deputies and spineless townspeople. In Outland, earth corporations have franchised and sub-contracted the solar system. Planets on the far edges of space are being mined and stripped the way the monster coal companies once tore into West Virginia and Kentucky.

Labor sub-contractors, in order to increase production and keep the corporate accountants happy, sell volatile dope to the miners. What we've got is a major Angel Dust problem out there on the far reaches of the nebula.

The chemical stimulants help the workers to double their piecework as well as their wages. Increased production makes the company happy. More money makes the workers happy. In fact, everybody is happy in their greedy little way until the cumulative effects of the drugs start to surface. It seems that after nine months or so of mainlining the worker's friend, the worker suddenly goes paranoid, psychotic, schizophrenic, and launches into a highly violent form of deep space DTs which tend to badly mess up the rather cramped confines of the interplanetary space station.

When Space Marshall O'Neil (Sean Connery) tries to clean up this situation, the on-site corporate Manager, bearing the highly ironic name of Shepherd (the ever villainous Peter Boyle), beams to the parent company for help. The corporation sends out three of their best troubleshooters (literally) to get the Marshall off the company's back.

Unlike the menacing presences in its Western precursor High Noon, the professional gunmen in Outland possess no personal identities whatsoever. They simply disembark from a space shuttle and commence firing. They have no names, no motives, no emotions--their sole reason for existence is their corporate employment.

The world of Outland has been formed by the dark side of the corporate mentality with its productivity ethic, its profit motive, its competitive obsession. The villains who represent that corporate mentality are no more than industrial robots programmed to kill for the good of the company.

Another major recent Sci-Fi movie, Blade Runner (1982), actually examines what happens when industrial robots, called "Replicants," which exactly resemble human beings, run amok, rebel against the corporate mind that conceived them. A similar rebellion within the very camp of the corporate villain occurs in Star Wars (1977). Around the Empire's boardroom table sit gray-tunicked corporate executives with one exception, Vader. Vader's alliance with the uniformed rulers of the Death Star is tenuous and tense because Vader, by his dress and by his flaunting of the Force, signals that he is uncomfortable aligned with the corporate influence. Yet, Vader needs their power and numbers to spread his personal version of evil throughout the universe. That doesn't stop him from opposing Grand Moff Tarkin (Peter Cushing), the Chief Executive, at every turn.

TRON (1982) is Sci-Fi of a different ilk, but how similar are its villain and his minions to the villains of Outland and Star Wars. TRON's head villain is a power-mad executive in a computer/communication conglomerate. In the world inside the computer, this executive becomes a huge, powerful, vicious electronic warrior wielding an imposing electronic sword. Sound familiar? TRON has co-opted both of Star Wars' villains. In the world outside the computer, the executive villain is played by the established English villainous actor David Warner just as the Empire's Grand Moff Tarkin was played by the established English villain Peter Cushing. The helmeted warrior who rules the electronic world inside the computer is direct kin to Darth Vader in stature, costume, military utensils and temperament.

Only one of the recent Sci-Fi offerings chose to employ a classical villain instead of the modern corporate version. Star Trek II: THe Wrath of Khan (1982) takes the form of revenge tragedy. Khan's (Ricardo Montalban) obsessive malevolence stems from no other motive than his own personal revenge. He is a human, malignant, crazed, vulnerable, impetuous villain with a face, a personality and a range of emotions which are all absent in his brother villains all across the Sci-Fi galaxies. Khan may be in the vanguard of corporate villain backlash. We'll have to wait and see.

Of all the genres, the suspense thriller has become the most corporate villain conscious. Most suspense thrillers of the last decade, except for the various forms of Nazi movies which continue to be popular, offered striking images of corporate villainy emanating from the American public sector, from the halls of the U.S. government, or from the Byzantine world of international finance.

A little-seen film, The Parallax View (1974), may be one of the best written and most visual of all the thrillers which stalk that protean monster, the corporate villain. Corporate conspiracy is the film's subject; the helplessness of the individual no matter how smart, tough or tenacious in the face of corporate conspiracy is the film's theme. "Grim" is the only word for the message The Parallax View delivers.

That grimly realistic (and pessimistic) message probably accounts for the fact that The Parallax View is the only Warren Beatty starred movie of the seventies that wasn't a spectacular box-office hit. However, that grim symbolic realism of The Parallax View's ending is also what makes it so much better and so much more powerful a movie than two later films, Capricorn One (1978) and The China Syndrome (1979), both of which are strikingly similar to The Parallax View in characters and plot, both of which attempt to explore the same shadowy, elusive world of conspiracy, cover-up and corruption within America's largest corporations.

The central character in each of these films is a reporter trying to unravel the facts of a powerful corporate conspiracy. Kimberly Welles (Jane Fonda) in The China Syndrome and the Investigative Reporter (Elliott Gould) in Capricorn One both succeed in getting their stories, understanding the conspiracies they encounter, defeating the corporate villains, and seeing justice done. In other words, both films opt for sentimental resolutions. Joe Frady (Warren Beatty) gets no such satisfaction in The Parallax View. He goes undercover, infiltrates to the very heart of the corporate conspiracy, yet still never understands it, never sees its real intent, never realizes that instead of him penetrating the secrets of the corporation, all along the corporation is only using him as a pawn in their own much more complex game. Never in the whole film (and that is the source of the ultimate grimness of the ending) does Joe Frady realize that he is being set up for the role of the corporation's fall guy. The corporate conspiracy is so complex, so layered, that Joe Frady, acting totally alone, acting as a classic existential individual, can never hope to understand it much less expose and defeat it. The fact of the matter is that in The Parallax View the corporation simply has got Joe Frady outnumbered and he is not Wyatt Earp or Audie Murphy who could triumph over such uneven odds. The fact of the matter is that corporations are going to win 9 times out of 10 because they are simply bigger, richer and more powerful than the individual.

The Parallax Corporation is an international broker in assassination. In effect, the Parallax Corporation is what Murder Incorporated would have grown up to be if the Feds hadn't stunted its growth in the thirties. The film opens with the assassination of a Senatorial candidate in the futuristic Space Needle in Seattle and ends with the assassination of another political candidate in a huge Texas convention center. What is most interesting about the portrayal of the Parallax Corporation is the film's handling of the corporation's methods. The employees, whether they be assassins or simply messengers, are never given the slightest trace of humanity. They rarely speak, never show emotion, remain faceless throughout. Their methods are purely pragmatic and awesome in terms of overkill: a bomb planted in a full airplane to kill one man; a huge dam opened to drown one snoopy fisherman. The Parallax Corporation, in its utter disregard for human life, its systematic elimination of any obstacles to the success of its operations, its methodical recruitment and deployment of its deadly employees, embodies the furthest possible extension of bottom-line corporate mentality.

Huge futuristic corporate buildings dominate the visual imagery of The Parallax View. The characters walk, ride Sci-Fi elevators, ascend on escalators through geometric figure after geometric figure. In the same way that the Monument Valley used to dwarf men in John Ford's westerns, the towering skyscrapers and the dizzying layered atriums in The Parallax View emphasize how small and insignificant man is in the world of the corporation. The camera lingers on the ways in which the cold steel of the corporate edifice freezes humanity, the ways in which the converging mathematical lines imprison humanity, the ways in which the empty maws of the buildings swallow men up.

Perhaps the most visually interesting and frightening scene in The Parallax View is that moment in the film when Joe Frady must take a recruitment test for employment by the Parallax Corporation. He is seated in front of a large movie screen and wired with body sensors. A striking montage of images ranging from happy to loving to natural to violent to Fascistic to sexually perverse to utterly depraved are flashed before his eyes while his bodily reactions are monitored. The Parallax test sequence is strikingly reminiscent of the "treatment" which "cures" Alex (Malcolm McDowell) in Stanley Kubrick's A Clockwork Orange (1971).

The montage is riveting, but the comment that the whole sequence makes is also highly ironic if not comically satiric. The sequence is a direct parody of widespread American corporate recruitment methods. It is common practice in most corporations nowadays to give IQ tests, psychological and temperament tests, occupational aptitude tests as well as physical exams to every candidate for executive employment. The Parallax Corporation test is an interesting variation on this practice. The Parallax test isolates psychopathic killers rather than good salesmen or bank executives or supervisory personnel.

It is no accident that the corporation name, Parallax, means the "apparent change in direction of an object caused by a change in observational position." Every major suspense thriller of the seventies deals with the theme of a "parallax view." Both The China Syndrome and Capricorn One, for example, are based on the concept of the illusory nature of television's view of reality. In The China Syndrome, a TV station, under pressure from the public utility corporation which is one of its heaviest advertisers, refuses to air real news footage of a near-miss nuclear power plant accident. In

Capricorn One, the National Space Administration executives actually fake a moon landing for TV, feed their own parallax view to the networks not from 200 million miles out in space but from an abandoned airplane hangar 200 miles out in the desert.

The China Syndrome is not nearly as complex, tough-minded or realistic a movie as The Parallax View, but what the two films share is a common vision of the source of evil in contemporary American society. Like its early kitsch predecessor, The President's Analyst, the villain of The China Syndrome is a public utility, the electric company. While Kimberly Welles fares better in her confrontation with corporate conspiracy than Joe Frady does in The Parallax View, nevertheless her adversary is every bit as depersonalized, shadowy and elusive as the Parallax Corporation.

The corporate villain lurks in shadow on the periphery of the action in The China Syndrome. When the power company executives find out that Kimberly Welles has actual tape footage of a near nuclear disaster and is intent on investigating for further malfeasance at the nuclear plant, they start the wheels of corporate conspiracy turning. Bad publicity is a tangible threat to this particular corporation. It could not only shut down the already operating nuclear facility, but also delay licensing of a new nuclear power plant. The Chief Executive, the PR man and the nuclear plant Supervisor meet in a highly symbolic corporate boardroom. They conspire in almost total darkness in a glass-enclosed penthouse overlooking all the lights of the city of L.A., the lights which they control from their dark circle on high.

In the climactic scene in which Jack Godell (Jack Lemmon), a nuclear engineer, has taken over the control room of the reactor, once again the sinister Executives in their gray suits hover above the action, silently scowling down from behind the glass of the observation mezzanine into the prison of the reactor control room. They say nothing, but their emotionless faces radiate evil and threat.

Finally, the Executives give the order and their minions storm the control room. Like the faceless assassins in The Parallax View, the corporation looses the black-uniformed, black-masked SWAT team on the one scared individual who dared to stand up to the corporation and expose the truth. The corporation succeeds in killing the individual in the end just as it succeeded in The Parallax View, but in The China Syndrome the truth does emerge and proclaim itself whereas it never surfaces in The Parallax View.

The black-garbed apparitions that enforce and preserve the corporation conspiracy in The China Syndrome take a much more threatening, mechanistic shape in Capricorn One. Two black helicopters piloted by black-tunicked, black-helmeted storm troopers systematically, like relentless birds of prey, track down and kill those individuals who seek to expose the corporate conspiracy.

The corporation Chief Executive in Capricorn One (played by an unctuous and sinister Hal Holbrook) is the head of a government agency as is the corporate villain in Three Days of the Condor (1975). In both movies, the corporate villains are running covert operations within their own government agencies. When civilians stumble upon their corporate schemings, the executives are forced to orchestrate elaborate cover-ups. Sound familiar? Whereas The Parallax View takes its descendence directly from the Kennedy assassination legends and the widespread dissatisfaction with the Warren Commission, Capricorn One and Three Days of the Condor are explicitly Watergate offspring.

The government is America's biggest conglomerate under whose corporate umbrella hundreds of smaller corporations operate. Because of the staggering diversification of the government conglomerate, all control is lost. America's biggest conglomerate has simply outgrown the limited system of checks and balances installed at the outset in its original charter, developed too much complexity for any individual to understand or regulate. That is, ultimately, what all of these movies are about. All are statements of how the incorporation of America has outdistanced the concept of individual rights, has subsumed the basic concept of democracy. The people don't rule, votes don't count is what these movies are all saying. All we are doing is voting meaningless proxies, handing over our stock options to executives who have already gained majority control, have already decided what is best for the corporation and its stockholders. Remember the corporate slogan on Milo Minderbinder's stock certificates in Catch-22 (1970): "What's good for M&M Enterprises is good for the country"? Not really so!

The Formula (1980) goes one step further in its perception of the corporate villain and its examination of corporate intrigue. In its melodramatic odyssey into the intricacies of the "Big Oil" cartels, it expands the concept of the corporate villain into the realm of international geopolitics. In the world of The Formula, businessmen literally control the world, can do anything they want, and are totally immune to punishment for their crimes.

In fact, the cartels have no nationalities, no political identities. The Chief Executive of the international cartel, Adam Stiefel (Marlon Brando), scoffs at the idea of international competition between nationalities. When one of his sub-executives, Arthur Clements (G.D. Spradlin), argues for a twelve cent increase at the pumps saying, "We can blame it on the Arabs." Stiefel looks at him with disbelief and answers with irritation: "Arthur, you're missing the point. We are the Arabs." In another exchange, a Swiss executive says: "Adam, I always thought you were Swiss." Stiefel answers: "Well, in business we're all Swiss, aren't we?" An ex-Nazi describes the French in these terms: "The French will sleep with anyone for a profit. They are a nation of whores." And finally, the central and ugliest truth of the international corporate conspiracy, the reality of just how far back this particular corporate villainy goes, is revealed by another ex-Nazi: "During the war not one German hydrogenation plant was hit. You know why? Because certain American oil companies shared patents with the Third Reich. They were in business with the Third Reich!"

Barney Kane (George C. Scott), the L.A. cop who is trying to follow his slender thread through the complex international labyrinth of The Formula, calls the world of international corporate conspiracy the "overworld."

"What the hell's the overworld?" his Chief asks.

"Big oil. OPEC. International cartels," Barney Kane answers.

No longer is it his job to track underworld gangsters like Little Caesar and Scarface Capone down those mean streets. The cop of the seventies must enter a much more complex white-collar game, must travel to Germany, France and Switzerland just to understand, must never expect to make a good old-fashioned collar.

The overworld. Sounds very transcendental, very Emersonian, doesn't it? As Adam Stiefel sees it in The Formula, that is exactly what it is. He presents a highly convincing argument for corporate conspiracy being the life blood of America. Here's how the argument goes:

> KANE: "You've had the formula since '45, why all the masquerade?"
>
> STIEFEL: "In '46 we bought up the formula . . . . That was the time that this cartel started buying up all the coal fields. This cartel now owns 90% of all the coal in the United States . . . If you're gonna try to dispense with us as little men trying to hang on to their Swiss bank accounts, forget it . . . . Human beings are a paradox. They don't want to be leaders. They want to be followers . . . . I just wish I could get you to understand."
>
> KANE: "What is there to understand? You trade lives and human dignity for profit. You're the reason their money's no good, their kids get

STIEFEL: killed in bull shit wars. Christ, I
wish I could nail ya!"
STIEFEL: "You'd be nailing the American
dream, Barney. It was oil that
nourished the American dream. It's
the great American tit, Barney.
Without it there's no America."

Barney Kane's only answer to this cold and
passionless argument is a defeated outburst of gutteral
bravado: "If I didn't have a son who still loved me, I'd
blow your fuckin' brains all over that Venetian blind."
At the end of The Formula, as in The Parallax View,
the corporate villain triumphs over the individual and,
scott free, continues business as usual.

Of all the films of the seventies and early eighties in
the suspense thriller genre, The Formula presents the
fullest and clearest portrayal of the world and motives
of the corporate villain. Brando's portrayal of the world's
most powerful businessman is so disarming yet chilling,
so matter of fact yet exasperated yet sinister that it is
almost charming. Turning the Stanislovskian Method on
full blast, Brando plays Adam Stiefel as Porky Pig
chewing milk duds in a grey three-piece suit. In other
words, he plays him as a friendly, harmless, familiar face
which fronts for forces, interest groups, powers so
complex that they can't even be understood.

At the end of The Formula, Barney Kane takes his
only out. Standing on a bridge overlooking the 5PM
parking lot which is the Los Angeles freeway, he reverts
to being "Just another customer!" He goes back to being
plain old citizen Kane taking his beating at the pumps
while the fat corporate villain leans back in his leather
chair, rests his expensive brogans on his polished desk,
and surveys the world which he will always control as
long as the terrorists don't get the upper hand.
Ironically, another film, Fun With Dick and Jane (1974),
does a comic variation on the corporate villain thriller
yet the result is the same. The title characters (played by
Jane Fonda and George Segal) succeed in ripping off the

giant aerospace corporation (represented by Ed McMahon) but the corporation simply swallows its loss and continues to carry on business as usual.

Those first three genres-- the Western, Science Fiction, the Thriller --totally succumbed to the lure of the corporate villain in the 1970s. In some of the other genres, such as the Horror film, the Sports film and the Musical, this particular concept of villainy was not nearly so dominant, appeared much less frequently and was portrayed in less strident tones, yet it was present.

Though the Horror genre was one of the most active in the late seventies, few suspenseful classic Horror movies were made. The overwhelming majority followed the monotonous slice-n-dice formula. In fact, the Horror film became a new form of adolescent-targeted pornography.

There has always been an elegant impulse to eroticism in classic Horror movies from the sexual obsession of the original Murnau Nosferatu (1922) through the Dracula movies of the thirties through films like The Cat People (1942) with Simone Simone and The Phantom of the Opera (1943), House of Wax (1953) and The Phantom of the Rue Morgue (1954). In the seventies, however, the Horror film genre moved to wholehearted imitation of the structure of the pornographic film. Horror movies became essentially plotless, non-verbal formula movies whose whole structural intent was to simply string one violently dehumanizing slice-n-dice scene to the next. The Directors of all the Halloweens (1978) and Friday the Thirteenths (1979) must have done their apprenticeships making MagicKnife or Cuisinart presentations in the center aisles of department stores. Their characters were interminably nubile teenage girls; their villains were inexorably oversized clods wearing panty hose or ski-masks or Halloween masks over their faces. As with the conventional porno film, the audience was in the theater to see only one thing and cared little what came between those bloody slash and filet and impale extravaganzas.

When Poltergeist (1982) came along, it broke the

boringly repetitive pornographic mold of the genre. It
presented fresh characters, new sources of evil, a total
change in tone. It turned the whole Horror film genre
inside out. Most significantly however, it redefined the
source of evil in modern-day America. It identified
corporate greed as the new evil force which replaces the
individual motives to evil-- revenge, psychological
derangement, humiliation, sexual inadequacy --of the
conventional movies of the seventies in the Horror
genre.

Poltergeist is set in a California housing development
built by a large real estate corporation. The land upon
which the corporation parcelled out its lots was
previously the site of a large cemetery. Because of the
expense of moving each individual grave to make way
for the housing development, the corporation didn't
move the cemetery. Claiming to have relocated all the
graves, in reality the corporation has disturbed the dead
in the interest of a higher profit margin. Viewed in
those terms, Poltergeist is a metaphor for the many ways
in which corporate greed has tampered with the
American ecology, has violated the spirits of nature by
brutally rearranging the American landscape. In other
words, Poltergeist is one of the most thoughtful and
symbolic films to come along in the genre in quite a
while.

When the corporate villain looses that whole
cemetery of demons upon that tract community in
Poltergeist, we see the evil which lurks beneath the
artificial facades of American life striking back. What
Poltergeist is saying is that the incorporation of America
has violated the land, destroyed the American dream, and
that we are living in the ashes of that violated dream.
In essence it is the same message that F. Scott Fitzgerald
offered as a warning in his novel The Great Gatsby
(1925), except in Poltergeist it isn't a warning but rather
a metaphorical statement of entrenched fact.

The Sports film in America has always been a
harmless, sentimental little genre. Few Sports films, with
the possible exception of some of the boxing movies

like Champion (1949), The Harder They Fall (1956),
Requiem For A Heavyweight (1962) and Raging Bull
(1979), have ever pretended to make any kind of social
comment or to carry any kind of metaphorical
significance.

In the seventies, however, two quite serious Sports
films appeared which expressly explored the contemporary
theme of the plight of existential man imprisoned in a
world controlled by the corporate villain. Like all
Sports films, these two tell the story of an individual
hero battling against heavy odds to win. However, Bang
The Drum Slowly (1973) and Rollerball (1974) are much
more symbolically complex films than those simplistic
triumphal odysseys of the Rocky (1976) ilk.

Both Bang The Drum Slowly and Rollerball employ the sports metaphor (i.e.: winning at games =
winning at life) to comment upon the nature of
contemporary life as it exists under corporate control.
The sporting heroes in these films must rebel against an
entrenched corporate establishment in order to affirm
their own dignity and the humanity of people in
general as represented by their teammates. It is
significant that both movies are set within the milieu of
team sports rather than individual sports (like boxing).
Team sports metaphorically represent the relationships,
roles and responsibilities of individuals forced to exist
and function within the social structure. The tension
arises in these two films not from the rebellious
personality of the individual (both Henry Wiggin and
Jonathan E. have spent years in contented conformity
with their roles in society and have risen to positions
of success and eminence through that conformity), but
rather from the growing oppression and dehumanization
of those individuals by the corporate villains who rule
their sports. Both films follow a structure of
enlightenment leading to alienation. Both Henry Wiggan
and Jonathan E. realize that they are in danger of losing
their identities to the allure of corporate greed and both
take on the responsibility of rejecting money for the
less tangible rewards of friendship, dignity, and,

ultimately, their own humanity.

Anyone who even glanced at the newspaper sports pages during the seventies knows that the whole context of world sport changed. Nowadays, lawyers, agents, owners, corporation executives, labor negotiators get more sports page ink than the players. Of all the sectors of life, none has gone more publicly or chaotically corporate than the wide world of sports. Individual sports heroes like Pele, Mark Spitz, Bruce Jenner, Arnold Palmer and Jack Nicklaus have metamorphosed into instant conglomerates. In the realm of team sports, the Dallas Cowboys are the paradigm. A faceless team run by a faceless coach under the aegis of banks of faceless computers, their success, as chronicled in a mediocre sports novel and film entitled North Dallas Forty (1979), attests to the powerful inroads the corporate mentality has made into sports in the 1970s. Perhaps our only consolation comes from the phenomenal successes of the blue-collar Pittsburgh Steelers against those corporate automatons over the course of the decade.

Henry Wiggin (Michael Moriarty), star pitcher of the New York Mammoths in Bang The Drum Slowly, is a very contemporary sports hero whose main concern is not his won-lost record, but rather his financial statement, his next year's contract and his tax situation. At the beginning of Bang The Drum Slowly, Henry is a bottom-line, money-conscious ballplayer. His wife Holly is pregnant and he has already nicknamed his unborn child "six hundred dollars," claimed him as a kind of fetal tax deduction. The only chink in Henry Wiggin's corporate image is his stubborn humanity which is awakened when his roomie, a "plumb dumb" catcher named Bruce Pierson (Robert DeNiro), is diagnosed at the Mayo clinic as terminal with Hodgkin's Disease.

Henry decides to jettison his corporate image in order to give Bruce one last season as a ballplayer. The most expressive symbolic scene of the film occurs when Henry and the owners of the New York Mammoths sit down in the Executive Suite to negotiate his contract. The corporate battle lines are drawn. The owners start at

$60,000 and Henry starts at $125,000. The owners go to $75,000 and, suddenly, to everyone's surprise, Henry accepts their money figure. The owners do a double take then smirk in triumph. But then Henry hits them with the catch.

"I want something more than money," Henry says.

"Nothing's more than money," the grey pin-striped General Manager barks back at him.

Of course, what Henry wants "more than money" is a contractual clause which says that Bruce Pierson cannot be cut from the team for any reason. To get that clause, Henry looks the corporate villains right in the eye and bests them at their own game. As he puts it in his own quaint baseball diction, he gets everything he wants "wrote in" in nice corporate contractual legalese.

Rollerball offers a much more powerful and sinister portrayal of the corporate villain. Set in a corporate utopia in the Science Fiction future, Rollerball is a brutal, mechanized, chauvinistic, militaristic game (a hybrid of motocross, roller derby, hockey, basketball and full contact karate) which the Executives have established and nurtured as the religion, national pastime, central social ritual and major identity totem for the workers in the corporate utopias of the world. In the time and place of Rollerball, the world is no longer organized along national or ethnic or continental lines. The world has simply been divided among the ten most dominant corporations. On a small scale, it's not so hard to visualize. Just imagine the state of Michigan being renamed GM or Saudi Arabia being renamed EXXON or California being renamed IBM.

Jonathan E. (James Caan) is the finest player in this fanatical international game. He is the Pele of rollerball. The only problem is that the Executives of the Houston Corporation which owns Jonathan E's Houston rollerball team realize that Jonathan's individual identity is outgrowing the team identity which they are nurturing by means of rollerball fanaticism in their society. Jonathan is so good, so powerful, such a virtuoso, that the people in the stands actually chant his name,

recognize him as an individual. As the fans in the
stands chant "Jon-a-than, Jon-a-than" worshipfully, the
Executives sit in their glass-enclosed boxes and scowl.

For the Executives who govern the world of
Rollerball, the slightest trace of individuality is
something to be feared. The Executives decide that it is
time for Jonathan E. to retire. The only problem is that
Jonathan E. not only is at the top of his game but also
loves the game itself, the competition, the power it gives
him.

In one of the most chilling corporate villain scenes
ever filmed, Jonathan E. is summoned to the Chief
Executive's (John Houseman) suite to get the bad news
about the Executives' plans to end his rollerball career.
The decor of the suite itself is cold and sharp and dead
as an ice palace. Thousands of rectangular shards of
thin, sharp glass hang in the air to form transparent
partitions. Jonathan, moving across the room, touches one
of the hanging shards and cuts his finger. His blood
flows throughout the rest of the scene.

In this glassed-in world Jonathan E. faces the
emotionless cold countenance of the Chief Executive who
tells him that it has been decided that he must retire
for the good of the corporation. Jonathan is clearly out
of his element. He is a non-verbal jock, a thug, in the
presence of this grey-suited, persuasive, highly articulate
Executive. Yet he knows that he doesn't want to quit,
that the fans don't want him to quit, that his finger is
bleeding. In other words, he knows that he is alive and
he has the awakenings of a vague sense of rebellion
against the arbitrary role which the Executives want him
to play.

It is a marvellous scene. Because Jonathan E. is an
essentially non-verbal character, the visual setting and the
business, the gestures, of the scene become all-important.
The slashing coldness of the glass setting defines the
utopian world of the Executives. Jonathan's non-verbal
squirmings under the quiet cross-examination and
cajoling of the Chief Executive represents his alienation
as a purely physical man in this cuttingly cerebral

world. And the cut finger is a masterful symbolic touch. It focuses all the attention in the scene on Jonathan E's humanity as opposed to the cold, bloodless existence of the Chief Executive. If that Executive reached out and touched a shard of hanging glass, would he bleed?

Sports, one of the major opiates of the people, thus became another duelling ground where the corporate villain and the individual could clash. The same confrontation was also occuring in another unlikely place. Music, another of the peoples' major opiates, underwent revolutionary changes in the late sixties and seventies.

The genre of the film Musical participated in this revolution. It took on a whole new tone and structure and look. Thematically, the clash between individuality and the corporate villain took center stage amongst the many changes in the conventions of the movie Musical genre. Movie Musicals pre-1970 never took themselves very seriously in dramatic terms, in social terms, in terms of the realistic presentation of their worlds. They never paid much attention to the believability of their plots, the depth of their characterizations, the realism of their settings or their visions of society.

For example, movie Musicals rarely shot on location. If they did indulge themselves in any location shooting, it usually took the form of picture-postcard travelogue background shots of famous vacation spots such as the Alps in The Sound of Music (1965) and Waikiki Beach in Elvis's Blue Hawaii (1961) or mythic American scenes such as the amber waves of corn in Oklahoma (1955) and the Currier and Ives still lifes of White Christmas (1954). The overwhelming majority of movie Musicals were shot on studio lots and soundstages with painted backdrops of Caligari-esque surreality.

You could count the movie Musical's standard plot lines on the valves of a coronet. The most popular was "Boy-Meets-Girl-Loses-Girl-Finds-And-Wins-Girl" closely pushed by "Let's put on a show" not to forget "Governess wins hearts of household" or "Chorus girl/boy steps in for big star." The characters were all pretty much the same and the social comments offered were as downright corny as Kansas in August.

All of that unreal sentimentality and painted backdrop moviemaking changed in the early seventies. One film, a big-budget Musical which was so unconventional that it stunned audiences, changed the direction of the movie Musical genre. That film was Bob Fosse's Cabaret (1972). It proved that the movie Musical could be more than just a clothesline upon which songs and dances and elaborate production numbers could be hung. Cabaret redefined the subject matter, the characters, the tone and setting of the movie Musical.

First, Cabaret stressed realism in its setting, both historical (Nazi Berlin) and visual (the streets, alleys and grotesque cabarets; location shooting), and in its characterization (flawed characters whose lives are realistically motivated). Characters didn't burst into song at the drop of a cue or dance down city streets swinging from lampposts and riding on the tops of trolley cars. All the songs and musical accompaniments were given realistic on-screen sources, were very carefully integrated into the story, the setting, the moods of the characters.

Second, Cabaret consciously confronted social, political and sexual themes. It portrayed a vulnerable degenerating society. It vividly examined the political confrontation between the individual and the Fascist state. It laid bare the inner lives and tangled sexual relationships of its characters with a complex Freudian psychoanalytic understanding.

Finally, Cabaret totally rejected sentimentality. Its ending was neither sad/romantic (the West Side Story approach) nor happy/escapist nor epic/tragic. Its ending was human and credible and open.

Cabaret, in redefining the conventions of the movie Musical, also showed the first touches of awareness in the genre of the concept of the corporate villain. Corporate villainy, however, is little more than an off-stage shadow hanging over the world of Cabaret. Hitler could be considered a corporate villain perhaps.

All of Sally Bowles's psychological frustration can be traced to her father's neglect because he is too busy in his diplomatic career to pay any attention to her. Certainly, the cabaret song "Money" with its telling lyric "Money makes the world go around" intimates where the responsibility for society's confusion lies. But despite these intimations, the corporate villain doesn't really raise its ugly head in this film. Following the success of Cabaret, however, other Musicals of the seventies clearly and consciously identified the corporate mentality as the major destructive force in contemporary life.

Robert Altman's Nashville (1975), a realistic Musical fully dependent upon synchronous sound, examined three corporate themes: the impersonal manipulation of a political campaign; the debilitating competitiveness of the country music industry; and the personal fragility of individuals caught in the complementary vortexes of either politics or Country&Western success. Perhaps more than anything else, played against its backdrop of country songs, Nashville is a movie about how the corporate world (whether it be politics or the music business) takes individuals and deceives them, exploits them, humiliates them, twists them, and ultimately destroys them.

Almost every character in Nashville is subject to malign corporate influence. Sueleen (Gwen Welles), waitress and aspiring Country& Western singer, is given the opportunity to cheapen and humiliate herself by John Triplette (Michael Murphy), advance man for the Hal Phillip Walker political campaign, and Del Reese (Ned Beatty), music industry corporate lawyer. They need a stripper for a political fund raiser and Sueleen ends up sacrificing herself for their sleazy little show. Barbara Jean (Ronee Blakley), the hottest new female Country singer, is being pushed to the edge of a complete nervous breakdown by Barnett (Allen Garfield), her business manager husband, and is ultimately led to a rendezvous with an assassin's bullet because of the combination of Triplette's ambition which will exploit anyone in any way and Barnett's greed which will exploit his own wife despite her failing health.

Cabaret was the breakthrough film, but Nashville totally reversed the traditional movie Musical structure. Whereas in the past the story had served only as a backdrop for the staging of the songs and opulent production numbers, in Nashville the music serves as backdrop for the story, the characters, the realistic social themes. The first words in Nashville's soundtrack emanate from a soundtruck and construct an image of America as a corporate entity: "Fellow taxpayers and stockholders in America. On the first Tuesday in November we have to make some vital decisions about our management." Later in this political diatribe which serves as audio background for the film when the music isn't playing (as did the PA announcements in M*A*S*H), the Presidential Candidate, Hal Phillip Walker, declares: "Now, I know something about money . . . I know something of what money can do, and more important, I know of what it can't do. In time I did become President of the Corporation . . . Chairman of the Board." In Nashville, Hal Phillip Walker, a disembodied voice, is simply running for the Presidency of a bigger, more powerful corporation.

A whole sub-genre of seventies movie Musicals, the rock star films, present central characters whose individual creativity is being stunted, corrupted and, in some cases, destroyed by the insensitive franchising instincts of music industry corporate minds. In A Star Is Born (1976), John Norman Howard (Kris Kristofferson) is helped along the road to self-immolation by his moving-on record producer (Paul Mazurski) and the leader of his back-up band (Gary Busey) who is on the look-out for a better deal. In The Rose (1980), the title character comes apart under the same kinds of pressure to appear, to deliver, to put out for the realization of corporate profits. Everybody wants a piece of the Rose (Bette Midler) but nobody cares about the Rose herself, only the profits she generates. In One Trick Pony (1981), a moderately successful rock singer (Paul Simon), rebels against the music company which wants to change his

songs, change his arrangements, change him into the kind
of commercial star they can make big money on. For a
while he goes along with the sentimental string section
they keep adding to his arrangements, but in the end he
destroys the master tape which is going to make some
singer he isn't into a star. A brilliant punk rock film,
Breaking Glass (1981), in much starker, more vivid, much
more exciting visual terms stresses the overriding theme
that corporate management inevitably destroys the
creativity, the freedom, strangles the individuality of the
rock star. In each of these films, the record company
executives play sinister roles as the "possessor," roles
usually reserved for Satan in occult films. The record
producers possess the souls of the rock stars, turn them
into beings they are not, split their personalities, and,
when the inevitable nervous breakdown comes, callously
abandon them. The punk rock world of Breaking Glass,
so brilliantly captured in the rebellious lyrics of the
film, ultimately is swallowed up by the corporation,
franchised into meaninglessness, defanged, rendered
impotent because it has become that which it set out to
vilify and tear down.

One other movie Musical, All That Jazz (1979), offers
a characterization of the corporate villain more subtle
and ironic than all the rest. When Joe Gideon (Roy
Schieder), the central character in All That Jazz, has a
heart attack in the middle of rehearsals for an innovative and provocative new Broadway Musical which he
is directing, the play's producers and corporate angels all
sit down around a conference table to compute how
much money they are going to lose as a result of their
director's incapacity. The accountant consults his balance
sheets, tap dances on his pocket calculator and reports
that they are going to lose a lot of money, unless . . .

There is one ray of hope, one possibility that could
rescue them and actually turn the blood red ink on the
bottom line of their balance sheet into warm reassuring
black. If they would get lucky and Joe Gideon would
die from his heart attack, the insurance they have taken
out on him would not only cover all of their losses

but actually return a tidy profit on their investment.

When this news is broken to the gathering of corporate money men, a momentary hush falls over the conference table as they all revolve the possibility in their minds, try to decide whether they want to root for Gideon to live or die. That brief moment of hesitation as the camera pans the corporate faces around the table is ironically eloquent. It crystallizes the astoundingly flawed value system within which these men are operating. They are actually weighing profit on the same scale as human life and the camera forces the audience to wonder how many of them are tipping the scales on the profit side. The whole situation is briefly reminiscent of (and goes one step further than) the "win if we lose/lose if we win" situation of "Springtime For Hitler," the absurd Broadway Musical in Mel Brooks' The Producers (1968).

Movie Musicals are no longer just energy and bouncy songs and gorgeous dance numbers. Many of the movie Musicals of the seventies frontally assault some major social issues, including the corporate strangling of individual creativity and expression.

Film Noir remained alive and well during the seventies and early eighties and two films especially distinguished themselves: Roman Polanski's Chinatown (1974) and Lawrence Kasden's Body Heat (1981). Significantly, both focused upon the concept of the corporate villain. In Body Heat, the beautiful and mysterious Mattie (Kathleen Turner) is married to a very rich lawyer turned businessman with syndicate connections (Richard Crenna). In Chinatown, Noah Cross (John Huston) at one time owned the whole water supply for the city of Los Angeles. In the time of the film, Cross's corporation is trying to buy up all the valuable land in the San Fernando valley and it doesn't bother him in the least to bribe, to frame, to torture, to kill anyone who gets wind of his corporate machinations. Not only does Noah Cross indulge in all of this corporate villainy (as well as some very intimate personal villainy) but he gets away with it.

The War movie genre also acknowledged the corporate villain syndrome. Milo Minderbinder's "M and M Enterprises" in Mike Nichols' Catch-22 (1970) directly mirrored the multi-million dollar skimming, kickback and black marketeering scandals of the military PXs in Vietnam. Milo (Jon Voight) actually contracts with the Germans to bomb an American airfield. For Milo, the profit motive overshadows love of country, the sanctity of human life and any personal relationships. When the Army enters Rome in triumph, Milo is in the lead jeep. As a businessman he will be the very first to exploit the opportunities the war offers. Apocalypse Now (1979), however, portrays the military corporation realistically, without satiric exaggeration as was the technique of Catch-22.

Apocalypse Now is the story of six individuals caught in a web of expedient logic woven by America's most entrenched, hierarchical, inflexible, powerful, emotionless, conformist, faceless and necessary corporation, the military. The "military-industrial complex," built and nourished during the Eisenhower years of the fifties, threw its biggest trade show in Vietnam, put all of its hardware and software and human-ware on display. Apocalypse Now vividly captures that sense of Vietnam as a corporate testing ground for new technology, new methods of marketing war.

The only problem was that the onslaught of all that marvellous new technology took a lot of the fun out of war. Computerized bombing from 30,000 feet can't have given Air Force personnel the same kinds of satisfaction and excitement that the flyers portrayed in Catch-22 and Twelve O'Clock High (1949) must have felt. Similarly, when Colonel Kilgore of the 1st Air Cav (Airmobile) asserts that napalm carries "the smell of . . . victory," it is not the same kind of human victory that Patton's and Rommel's and MacArthur's men must have felt in World War II.

Machines dominate Apocalypse Now. Hovering, flying, burning, exploding, firing, they are photographed in such

a way that their beauty, their grace, their sculpted lines
can be viewed from all angles as if we were circling a
display of modern objets d'art in a gallery. In the epic
helicopter assault sequence, the camera lingers lovingly
on a "naming of parts." The assault helicopters' machine
guns, rockets, psyops speakers, rotors are all isolated for
study before the whole squadron of technological
sculptures is hung above the waves like a huge mobile
by Sikorsky. Coppola's camera brilliantly focuses upon
what Conrad in his novel Heart of Darkness (1899)
called "the fascination of the abomination" and the
abomination is the corporation which unleashes this
murderous hardware on the world.

But Apocalypse Now, like all of these other
corporate villain films, also presents human embodiments
of corporate villainy. Captain Willard (Martin Sheen), the
first individual entangled in this web of military
expediency, is given his mission at an archetypal
Executive luncheon. As the food is passed, the deal is
laid out on the table and the contract signed. Willard
signs on as a company troubleshooter (literally) assigned
the job of going out and curing an ailing franchise. The
Chairman of the Board in this scene is a General (G.D.
Spradlin, who had already played a similar executive role
in North Dallas Forty and would go on to play the
same role again in The Formula; Spradlin's consistent
type casting made him the cold executive King in the
movies of the seventies just as Marthe Keller's consistent
casting in movies like Marathon Man, Black Sunday, The
Formula and The Amatuer made her the terrorist Queen
of the decade). The General goes about his business of
commissioning assassination in a cold, matter-of-fact,
conscienceless way. The Executive Secretary (Harrison
Ford) stumbles about the boardroom fumbling folders
and uttering stilted, fragmented sentences like some
not-yet-perfected office robot.

As Willard travels up the river, he reads through
Kurtz's personnel file. "They were grooming him for a
top spot in the corporation," is Willard's evaluation of
Kurtz's career on paper. Later, when Willard finally

confronts Kurtz, a corporate executive who has run
amok, left the corporation, gone into business for
himself, Kurtz knows who Willard is right away:

>   KURTZ: Are you an assassin?
>   WILLARD: I'm a soldier.
>   KURTZ: You're neither. You're an errand boy
>   sent by grocery clerks to collect a
>   bill.

Apocalypse Now is one of the most important films of
the seventies for many reasons not the least of which is
its symbolic portrayal of individual men caught in the
toils of corporate villainy.

Of all the genre films of the seventies, however, one
stood out as the most complex, detailed, psychologically
and visually compelling portrayal of the ascendence to
power of the corporate villain in American life. Frances
Ford Coppola's two-part The Godfather gave the most
powerful expression of all to the concept of the
corporate villain as the new source of American evil. As
Apocalypse Now would do later in the decade, The
Godfather films penetrated to the depths of the American
heart of darkness, revealed the American business world
in its most elemental yet complexly structured form,
showed (as Conrad did) that the underworld is not that
far removed from our world, in fact may well be our
world.

The Godfather films were certainly gangster genre
films but they went far beyond the bounds of that genre
into a much wider context. That context is the way in
which those films brilliantly, at exactly the right time in
exactly the right place, caught the temper of a changing
America on film.

By the early 1970s, the gangster film had become all
but defunct. Bonnie and Clyde (1967) had been a
tremendously popular and critically acclaimed gangster
film of the late sixties but in no way was Bonnie and
Clyde a typical representative of the genre. In the
thirties heyday of the gangster genre, the hoods all came

from the same urban ethnic background. Even later
gangsters like Johnny Rocco (Edward G. Robinson) in
Key Largo (1948) were big city boys forced to hide out
in small towns. In Bonnie and Clyde, the Barrow gang
are a bunch of clodhoppers as far removed from Scarface
and Little Ceasar as Willie Nelson and Waylon Jennings
are from Peter Duchin and Dave Brubeck. The Barrow
gang rides through a different landscape, talks a different
language, commits different, more flamboyant, types of
crimes. If anything, Bonnie and Clyde are closer kin to
Butch Cassidy and the Sundance Kid (1969) than they
are to Al Capone and Dutch Schultz.

   The Godfather films returned the gangster to his
urban (New York, Las Vegas, Miami, Havana), ethnic
(Italian, Irish, Jewish) milieu but even in doing so
redefined the scope, the motives, the professional image
of the American gangster. Coppola turned the American
gangster into a businessman operating under the same
competitive pressures, business ethics and corporate
mentality as the Chairmen of the Boards of GM, AT&T
or Proctor and Gamble. As Hollywood was going corporate, as America had gone corporate, Coppola showed
how the Mafia also was representative of the society
within which it operated.

   In The Godfather (1972), the first installment of the
Corleone family saga, Don Corleone (Marlon Brando) is
a dinosaur in a changing world. He rules like a feudal
lord with his private army and his distribution of fiefs
to his loyal retainers. He is a man of the past, his life
tied to ethnic family loyalty and ancient ritual (the
wedding feast). But the times they are a changin'.

   Tom (Robert Duvall), the Consiglione, the lawyer,
deals with a soft Hollywood corporate executive using
the old methods, but those old methods can't work
forever. Back in New York, a very businesslike Sicilian
drug dealer named Sollazzo (Al Lettieri), personally
bodyguarded by one of New York city's finest crooked
Irish Police Captains (Sterling Hayden), is attempting to
negotiate a city-wide drug distribution deal with the five
syndicate families. Sollazzo is the first of the new breed

of corporate gangsters to show up in The Godfather. He
talks the corporate language. His sentences are peppered
with "percentages," "territories," "middlemen." When Don
Corleone refuses to go along with Sollazzo's corporate
prospectus, kills the merger, the mergees try to kill Don
Corleone.

It is this personal assault of the corporation upon
his father which catalyzes Michael Corleone (Al Pacino)
to act. When he kills Sollazzo, the battlelines are drawn
but they are a new kind of gangland battle lines. In the
earlier underworld legends of the twenties and thirties,
gang wars were always between individual families for
clear reasons of either revenge or territorial imperative.
The gang war in The Godfather is something completely
different. All of the other New York families have
banded together against the Corleones. As was the case
in American society during the sixties and the seventies,
the institution of the family is under attack by a
corporate, communalizing impulse in society.

At first Michael Corleone, the new Godfather, tries to
hold to the old way, the old methods, the isolationism
of family solidarity. Using the same method he used to
deal with Sollazzo, the original corporate threat, he
assassinates the Board of Directors of the newly formed
corporation. In the final scenes of The Godfather, each
of the Executive Officers of the families which have
incorporated receive very pink slips as Michael completes
his own version of a corporate takeover.

In The Godfather, Part Two (1974), Michael Corleone
has mastered the new corporate role which society
demands. The ethnic family wedding which began The
Godfather has given way to a very country clubby Las
Vegas cocktail party in which canapés, hors d'oeuvres and
thin-stemmed champagne glasses have replaced the sagging
tables of bread, pasta and blood red wine. Michael and
his assistants, in grey sharkskin suits, hobnob with
politicians in grey silk suits. The Corleone family indeed
has incorporated with a vengeance. Where the old Don
took pride in his ability to control the votes of state
representatives in Albany and aldermen in the Bronx,

Michael now deals with United States Senators. Not only
has Michael organized crime nationwide along corporate
lines but he is getting ready to go international.

With the help of Hyman Roth (Lee Strasburg) of
Miami, Michael is forming an international cartel which
plans to become majority stockholder in the Caribbean
nation of Cuba. Unfortunately, as Adam Stiefel of The
Formula could have told him, the only thing which
stands in the way of any international business deal is
political instability. Enter Castro. Adios the Corleone
cartel.

The central drama of the whole Godfather saga
comes from the change from generation to generation in
the Corleone family. Michael changes from loving human
being to cold, emotionless corporate villain; the family
changes from a close-knit unit to a faceless corporate
entity in which brothers kill brothers and outsiders call
the shots; the two Godfather films mirror the social
changes that America has undergone in the mid-twentieth
century. Of all the corporate villains, Michael Corleone
is the most interesting because we are allowed to follow
his development from beginning to end. Most of the
corporate villains of the seventies either are totally
depersonalized as in The Parallax View and Rollerball or
are totally one dimensional as are Harrigan in The Wild
Bunch and Adam Stiefel in The Formula. But Michael
Corleone is the exception. We follow him every step of
the way as he changes from a normal human being into
a cold, isolated, ruthless corporate villain.

Thus, all the genres have retooled. Unanimously they
have acknowledged that evil conspiracies and violent
threats to both individuals and society are coming out
of corporate boardrooms every bit as frequently as they
always used to come out of outlaw strongholds, prisons
and mental institutions.

Within this cross-genre "megatrend," specific types of
corporate villains can be isolated. The corporation as
VENGEFUL PUNISHER appears in The Wild Bunch and
Apocalypse Now. These corporate villains will not allow
any deviation from or rebellion against their methods of

organizing life. They take immediate steps to crush or
"terminate with extreme prejudice" any rebellious
factions which rise against them. A second type is the
corporation as SINISTER CONSPIRATOR as in The
Parallax View and Three Days of the Condor. This form
of corporate villainy tends to be the most
depersonalized, robot-like and shadowy. The sole
function of the cold war corporate villain is to
eliminate anyone who threatens to expose, bring out into
the light of day, the machinations of the corporation
which wishes to remain submerged beneath the surface
of American life. The third type is the corporation as
PUBLIC UTILITY as in The President's Analyst,
Chinatown, The China Syndrome and Rollerball. This
version of the corporate villain fits most closely the
failed Utopia visions of classic novels (and movies) like
George Orwell's 1984 (1949) and Aldous Huxley's Brave
New World (1932). The technique of these corporate villains is more subtle. It involves the insidious attempt to
discredit or ruin the reputations of those who stand in
the way of or rebel against the corporations's rules.
Invariably in these films, the public utility aligns itself
with the rational, sane, "what is best for society" role
and casts those individuals who question or challenge
the corporate line as insane, disturbed, socially deviant
or subversive. A fourth form of corporate villainy can be
designated the UNIFORMED FASCIST ARMY type. The
Pinkertons in The Long Riders and the ironically
white-uniformed storm troopers in Star Wars and The
Empire Strikes Back best represent this type. The last
major type of corporate villainy to assert itself across the
genres is the ultimate BOTTOM LINE MEN. These are
the most singular and focused of all the types of
corporate villains because they are interested, quite
simply, in only one thing-- making a profit. They have
no political, philosophical or historical motives. Their
sole interest is to bathe in black ink. All That Jazz and
Outland portray this type which is perhaps most
extravagantly represented by Catch-22's Milo
Minderbinder. The sanctity of human life isn't even

considered by these villains when their profit margin is at stake.

If the genre films provide this much ammunition in support of this "megatrend" in film, do the mainstream, non-genre films also support the generalization? Without question, they do. Villainy in any motion picture arises out of some sort of conflict: between individuals; between individuals and society or social institutions; within the individual. Conflict, in either simple or complex form, is at the heart of every good film's structure and appeal whether that film be a genre or a non-genre film. And, film usually sticks to the most basic of conflicts, that between good and evil. The definition of "good" rarely changes. It generally involves right-thinking, productive action taken by a strong and decisive individual following his own existential prerogatives. The nature and definition of "evil," however, is a definite variant in non-genre films.

In genre films, conflict is always <u>objectively</u> definable. Two objective factions face off for social, political, financial or moral reasons. In non-genre films, however, conflict is not always so easily definable or straightforward. In fact, many non-genre films focus directly on the frustration of the individual's ability to clearly define the antagonists in the conflict. In many of the films, the forces of "good" spend the whole film trying to track down the forces of "evil" and never succeed.

Francis Coppola's <u>The Conversation</u> (1974), Hal Ashby's <u>Shampoo</u> (1975) and Sidney Lumet's <u>Network</u> (1976) are perhaps the best examples of this frustration. At the end of each of these films, the central character is left isolated and alone, more confused, less in control than he was when the film began. In each of these films an individual observes then tries to penetrate the secrets of a corporation as part of his own personal quests for understanding of both the world and himself. However, by the end of their quests, they are still right where they were when they began, on the outside looking in. The ironic flip-side of this "isolated anti-

hero" dillemma appears in Robert Redford's "winning"
trilogy of the early seventies composed of Downhill
Racer (1969), The Candidate (1972) and Jeremiah Johnson
(1972). In each of these films, the isolated, non-verbal
anti-establishment hero ostensibly wins yet is puzzled by
the value of the prize he has won, sees the terrible
fragility of his "winning." Because non-genre films are
based on ideas rather than upon objective oppositions,
conflict between good and evil takes a much more fluid
form. The heroes of non-genre films are more often
anti-heroes. Instead of being perceptive, persistent and
strong in their individuality, they are often timid,
tentative, confused, and sometimes, as in the case of
George Roundby, the hairdresser in Shampoo, not even
very bright. Almost universally in non-genre films
conflict simultaneously moves in two directions from the
central character-- outward and inward. Harry Caul (Gene
Hackman) in The Conversation, Max Schumacher (William
Holden) in Network and George (Warren Beatty) in
Shampoo are individuals who find themselves questioning
the operation of society. However, simultaneously, they
are also constantly questioning their own motives,
exploring their own interior landscapes as they move
through the exterior worlds of their respective films. At
the end of both The Conversation and Shampoo, the
anti-hero is left alone, defeated, puzzled, frustrated.
Network ends apocalyptically but shares the same sense
of non-resolution for the individual which is so strongly
underlined in the final sequences of The Conversation
and Shampoo.

Of all the Directors to emerge as major forces in the
film industry in the seventies, Francis Coppola is the
most corporation conscious. In the two Godfather films
and Apocalypse Now, the corporate villain is fully
delineated, but in Coppola's maverick character study,
The Conversation, the concept of the corporate villain is
given its most ironic and labyrinthine treatment.

The two Godfather films are a biography of the
insidious corporate takeover of American life. They are
developmental films interested in exploring "where" the

corporate villain comes from and "how" the corporate villain develops, gains power and influence to the point where he can take over. Apocalypse Now is an expose of the hypocrisy and ruthlessness of the corporate villain in a situation, the Vietnam War, so fluid, unregulated, out of control, that power brokers can employ any methods they choose to carry out their corporate schemes. Imagine the stock market functioning without any FTC regulation whatsoever. That is the kind of corporate situation Vietnam offers in Apocalypse Now. It is a situation so unregulated that every crime becomes merely a misdemeanor. As Captain Willard (Martin Sheen), the voice-over narrator, says: "Charging someone with murder in Vietnam was like handing out speeding tickets at the Indianapolis 500." But The Conversation is the most ironic and the most complex of all of Coppola's films in its vision of the intricacy of corporate takeover.

In The Conversation, Harry Caul is a man whose whole life is an on-going attempt to capture reality: record it, piece it together, reconstruct it, interpret it, understand it. He is the best in his business, yet he never succeeds. He can't grasp reality, define reality, no matter how "state of the art" his equipment, no matter how many operatives he uses, no matter how often he plays and replays his high-quality Memorex tapes.The fact of the matter is that Harry Caul never really knows what is going on because he is an individual who persistently resists incorporation in a world where everything, even bugging, has gone corporate.

Harry is in trouble because he won't sell out to one corporation which wants to acquire control of his expertise and franchise it, and he won't go to work for another corporation which wants to acquire his exclusive services. His individuality makes him a target for corporate malice while at the same time Harry is raising all kinds of interior questions about the ethics of his life and his life's work. Harry Caul in The Conversation is the first of a series of isolated obsessive heroes to surface in the Existentialist films of the late seventies and early eighties. The angst-ridden protagonists of

<u>Taxi-Driver</u> (1976), <u>Thief</u> (1980) and <u>Tattoo</u> (1982) follow similar obsessive drives. In a much more social, less pathologic vein, the Redford "winning" trilogy aligns well with this "isolated obsessive character" theme in seventies non-genre American film. Thus, the conflict of the external corporate threat with the internal personal threat is established. Both external corporate pressure and internal psychological pressure disrupt Harry Caul's attempt to live his life on a purely "business as usual" basis.

Two different types of corporate villain intrude upon Harry Caul's peace of mind. One is simply a BOTTOM LINE MAN while the other is a VENGEFUL PUNISHER. In both cases, the corporation involved-- the first, the biggest surveillance equipment company in the growing bugging industry; the second, a much more shadowy and diversified multi-national corporation --is represented by a real character whose personal motives are dramatized. However, that character's actions are invariably motivated by the corporate mind set (or world view) for which that character is either the spokesman or the executor.

When Harry attends a wiretapper's convention and trade show, he meets the founder and executive officer of the major personal surveillance equipment corporation in that burgeoning industry (Allen Garfield). He is a sort of sleazy evangelist spreading the gospel of wiretapping and invasion of privacy (the joys, virtues, techniques and "state of the art" accessories of buggery) nationwide. He wants Harry to join the corporation. He wants Harry to sign over his name as the most successful and creative bugger in the business as an endorsement for the corporation's line of bugging devices just as the superstars of sports, stage and screen endorse corporate products. Harry, who likes to maintain a low profile in his work, refuses to become the surveillance corporation's talking head, opts to remain a hand-made, self-employed loner rather than an assembly line shill.

But Harry's dealings with the other corporation in the film are not so easy to resolve. Hired by a huge corporation, he has taped a conversation that took place in Ghirardelli Square. He initially thinks that the man and woman conversing privately in this public place are simply having an affair and he has been hired by her corporate executive husband to gather divorce court evidence. The more he listens to his tapes, however, the more he suspects that the reality is more than it seems to be. He suspects that something else is going on that he can't pin down. In fact, the two conversants may not be discussing an illicit sexual affair at all. They may be discussing a corporate takeover.

His own inability to know exactly what he's got on his tapes and the attendant inability to predict what his tapes are going to be used for after he turns them over to his corporate client bothers Harry. He is in the bugging business because the technical challenges, the problem-solving, fascinate him but at the same time he is starting to consider the ethical questions of his business. Those ethical questions are what are causing all of Harry's problems. They are the same ethical questions which caused many of America's problems in the seventies.

Everyone knows that business and ethics have no connection with each other. Harry realizes that it is no longer good enough just to be "professional." He has to be not only involved with recording and reconstructing the "cause" but he also must try to exert some control over the "effect." No longer is it possible for him to just do his usual professional job and then walk away.

Harry Caul finds himself alone in a world in which both the murderers whom he works for and the buggers who want him to work for them are under corporate organization. There is nothing he can do because he can't wiretap a whole conglomerate. The Conversation raises a single fundamental question about life in 1970s America: Is it possible to live as an individual with a private life attuned to a traditional set of moral ethics in a world which has gone totally corporate? Harry Caul finds out that it isn't possible. He cannot control the effects of his work. He must face the fact that the fruits of his genius and professional expertise when passed out of his hands and into the hands of the corporation become evil, threatening, actually murderous. Harry can gain great interior satisfaction from the high quality and intricacy of his work but the exterior influence of his work is evil and destructive. He realizes that he can never again reconcile the interior/exterior conflict in his relation to the seventies world.

The final scene of The Conversation is a sequence of socio-political symbolism right up there with the symbolic commentaries made by such memorable endings as James Allen's (Paul Muni) "I steal!" at the end of I Am A Fugitive From A Chain Gang (1932) or the empty looks on Benjamin and Elaine's faces in the back of the bus at the end of The Graduate (1967). In the final scene of The Conversation, Harry has found out that he, the master bugger, has been bugged all along. In a fit of obsessive paranoia, Harry totally dismantles his apartment, tears up every floor board, pulverizes every inch of plaster in walls and ceiling, splinters all the furniture, trying to find the bug which has invaded his privacy as he has been invading the privacy of others all his life. He fails to find the bug. Once again he has failed to exert control over a reality which he feels his professional expertise should be able to handle. The last shot of the film shows Harry alone and defeated in the rubble of his world.

The "bugger bugged" irony of that last sequence of The Conversation represents the fact that America is in danger of becoming a society much like Russia's (remember that exchange between the CIA and KGB agents in The President's Analyst) where no one's privacy is safe, where no one is immune to the threat of corporate control. The whole scene symbolically comments upon the desperation of the individual who reaches the point where he feels it absolutely necessary to tear apart his world, his society, in order to understand it. The greatest irony working in the symbolic context of this radical symbolic scene is that even after the world has been torn down, dismantled, there is still no guarantee that full understanding, much

less control, will be forthcoming. The fact of the matter
is that the corporation can control and manipulate the
individual, can outdo the individual in every way. Harry
may be a virtuoso bugger yet the corporation with all
its wealth, manpower and technical resources can best
him at his own game, bug the world's greatest bugger.

Like Harry Caul in The Conversation, George
Roundby in Shampoo has a bothersome ethical problem.
He is, as Harry was with listening devices, the most
talented hair stylist in Beverly Hills, the class of his
profession. Fatiguingly however, most of the women in
that serendipitous community want him not only to
"do" their hair but also to "do" them morning, noon
and night.

In playing George, the roving, loveless, spiritually
impotent stud of Shampoo, Beatty has not moved that
far from his 1967 characterization of Clyde Barrow. Where
Bonnie caressed the barrel of Clyde's gun in the phallic
giveaway scene in Bonnie and Clyde, George wears a
blow-dryer on his hip instead of a six-shooter, rides a
motorcycle instead of a horse and works out of a salon
instead of a saloon. George and Clyde are similar types
of gunslinger-hustlers time-machined out of the old west
into much more bizarre but equally predatory worlds.

George wants to open his own hairstyling salon-- as
he describes it to an incredulous loan executive at a
bank: "I've got the heads!" --but the banks just laugh at
him. His only chance at investment capital lies with
Lester Karp (Jack Warden), an extremely powerful corporate tycoon who has his fingers in every pie, including
the 1972 world of Republican politics, and is reputedly
dangerous toward those who cross him. George's
connection to Karp is a complex and potentially
dangerous one. He has been doing Karp's wife's hair and
body for years. It is, in fact, Karp's wife Felicia (Lee
Grant) who suggests that George hit up her husband for
the money to start his salon. Simultaneously, George
finds out that Jackie (Julie Christie), his old girlfriend
whom he still kind of loves, is the kept mistress of
Karp. Therefore, the plot is a basic case of "George

loves Jackie kept by Karp married to Felicia who fucks George who needs Karp," just your basic Beverly Hills daisy chain romance with one final twist, all along Karp thinks George is a homosexual.

All of the tension and intricacy of these tangled sexual relationships pivots on the character of Karp. He has what all the others need or want or depend upon. As the corporate tycoon, he controls the purse-strings of the whole society of the movie. All of the others need him and seem willing to do what he wants in order to gain or keep his patronage. It sounds like your common squalid Hollywood sex comedy of manners, right? Wrong! Because of the texture of the film, the labyrinthine sexual entanglements of the characters present meaning on a symbolic level which asserts itself over the steamy sexual level of the plot line. This symbolic level involves political, social and existential comment on the situation of people in seventies America.

Shampoo is a film about the temptation to prostitution of the self that seventies corporate America holds out to the individual. The texture of the film is filigreed with visual images and verbal references to the hypocrisy, deception and emptiness of Nixon's America where exploitation and prostitution-- sexual, finan- cial, political --are the accepted ways of living and doing business. George and Jackie have to decide whether they want to prostitute themselves to Karp and thus reap the benefits of selling out to the corporate world. Jackie chooses to market herself; George chooses not to.

At the end of the film, the audience is left with the unsettling sense that perhaps Jackie made the smarter choice. George has been brilliantly portrayed throughout the film as confused, slow to understand, just not very bright. In the last shot of the film, he stands on a bluff overlooking Beverly Hills and watches Karp's tiny blue Mercedes, which is taking Jackie away for good, weave through the meticulously manicured streets below. As he watches the car cruise past luxurious lawns, wind under overhanging palm trees, George is still confused, still alone, nothing really has changed. He is still an

outsider in corporate America but he still isn't really
sure that he wants to be the outsider. He isn't a strong
existential anti-hero like McMurphy (Jack Nicholson) in
One Flew Over The Cuckoo's Nest (1975); he is a
confused, ineffectual stud who has a vague sense that his
best chance to be somebody, to love somebody, is
driving away from him and he is powerless to do
anything about it. His only satisfaction is totally
ephemeral. He didn't sell himself out but he isn't really
sure why he didn't. He can't really define any particular
ethic or motive upon which he has acted. Like Benjamin
Braddock (Dustin Hoffman) and Elaine Robinson
(Katherine Ross) staring straight ahead from the back of
the bus in The Graduate, like Redford's skier in
Downhill Racer and young politician in The Candidate,
he has fought a battle with himself and won but he
doesn't have the slightest idea what he has won.

George, at the end of Shampoo, represents the
helplessness and incomprehension of individual
Americans in the face of the "BIGNESS" which has taken
over the country. Business, the government, even sexual
relationships, have grown too big, too complex, too
corporate for us to grasp anymore. What Shampoo says is
that we either submit to that "BIGNESS" or we will be
left like George-- alone, confused, on the outside
looking in with no ties to all the people on the inside
who have chosen to submit.

George is like Harry Caul. He realizes that he has
lost control of his own life. His relationships with the
external world are a shambles: he hates working for his
hair-dresser boss who treats him as a chattel; all his
women customers want is for him to make them look
good and feel good; the banks laugh at his loan
applications; Karp thinks he's a flaky homosexual and
uses him as a decoy; Jackie won't take him seriously
because he's a nobody. His relationship with his own
internal life is vague and confused: he wants to be his
own man but he sees no way to do it unless he sells
himself for Karp's money; he feels cheapened and
exploited and betrayed by the society in which he lives

yet he is totally unable to say "no" to anyone. The fact
of the matter is that George, like most of us, comes to
recognize the dehumanizing nature of corporate society
but is in no way smart enough, in no way possesses the
weapons, to act effectually on that shock of recognition.
So what does he do? What can he do? He scratches his
head and wonders what the hell he ought to do. And,
that is as far as it goes.

Network goes one step further than either The
Conversation or Shampoo. It elevates the corporate
villain to the level of God in society. Standing at the
head of a boardroom table which seems as long as the
deck of an aircraft carrier, God appears in the shape of
Arthur Jensen (Ned Beatty), the world's greatest salesman
risen from rags to riches to become the Chief Executive
of a huge communications conglomerate. Ned Beatty
plays this corporate deity as a patois of Ted Turner and
Billy Graham with a dash of the department store
MagicKnife demonstrator thrown in.

Howard Beale (Peter Finch) works for the United
Broadcasting System (UBS), one of the four major TV
networks, as an anchor man on the Evening News. Told
that he is going to be fired because of low ratings,
Howard has a nervous breakdown which changes his
whole on-camera style. Instead of the news, Howard
starts delivering Jeremiads on America and his Nielsen
ratings soar. Howard becomes "a latter-day prophet
denouncing the hypocrisies of our time." Listen:

> This tube is the Bible!
> When the twelfth largest company in the
> world, CCA, the Communications Corporation
> of America, controls the most godless industry
> in the world, God knows what you'll get for
> truth.
> CCA is being sold to Western World
> Trading Corporation which is owned by the
> Arabs.
> The Arabs own half of America!
> Send telegrams to the White House saying

'Stop the CCA deal!'

Beale, with his "We're mad as hell and we aren't going to take it any more" battle cry, speaks out against the corporate stranglehold upon individuality which has changed the face of American life. Even though his maniacal ravings garner top Nielsen ratings, the subversive anti-corporate message that Beale is spreading makes the conglomerate executives so nervous that they are forced to bring in their number one heavyweight to change Beale's point of view. In the boardroom scene, Jensen in his three-piece-suit is the corporate God who delivers His Sermon on the Mount, imparts His corporate vision of the world to a receptive eager prophet, a resurrected Lazarus, Howard Beale.

In the deranged mind of Howard Beale, the world's greatest salesman is transfigured into God, or at least the voice of God. Howard feels himself being commissioned, inspired, as the new prophet of the corporate millenium. "Are ya with me, boy?" Howard's new God asks in a slow South Georgia drawl which intrudes right in the middle of his unaccented, fast-talking, Yankee sales pitch. This corporate God's dialect combines both the North and the South. He is both fast-talking carpetbagger and "good ol' boy." He is a deity for the whole country, a real All-American.

He delivers a speech about what makes up America. It is almost exactly the same speech that Stiefel in The Formula and Karp in Shampoo deliver-- a persuasively cynical argument detailing how the corporation has already inherited the earth and how all people, if they know what's good for them, ought to pack up all their existential cares and woe and become disciples in the new corporate religion. I mean, you sinners, we're talkin' stirring EEEEvangelism here! The boardroom table becomes an altar, Howard Beale receives the gift of tongues and the chubby corporate deity weaves a mesmerizing spell so powerful that if the devil were listening he could probably be convinced to give himself a hotfoot. As the voice-over narrator says when the scene ends: "And thus Howard Beale went out to preach the corporate cosmology of Arthur Jensen."

But this new God that appears to Howard Beale is really the Anti-Christ: A vengeful villain God who has replaced truth, love and integrity with power, exploitation and ratings numbers as the dogma of his religion. He has Howard Beale killed for getting bad ratings! In the free-wheeling late seventies days of the legendary Freddie Silverman, whole network schedules were cancelled no more than six weeks into the TV season, shows "got the ax" without warning despite excellent reviews seemingly at the whim of any Chief Programmer who could decode the voodoo of a Nielsen ratings sheet. But even in that sort of volatile atmosphere, assassination is still a bit extreme. Evidently not too extreme however for corporate villains like Jensen or Frank Hackett (Robert Duvall) who sneers "the business of management is management" and is described as "a corporation man body and soul. His loves, lusts and allegiances are all directed at becoming a CCA board member."

In another crucial scene in Network, Max Schumacher (William Holden) and Diana Christiansen (Faye Dunaway) make love. He is a retired TV executive; she is the new TV executive who has taken his place in the corporate structure. In bed, she assumes the dominant active position on top, he the passive. She never stops talking during their sexual bout which is OK if you're talking sexy, but all she can talk about are numbers, ratings points, audience shares and commercial rates. "All I want out of life is a 30 share and a 20 rating" Diana describes her goal. Her corporate obsession has turned her into a robot and she achieves orgasm to the sound of her own voice chanting the litany of the network's future successes. Grabbing Max's job the night after she has slept with him, she changes the whole Evening News show into a show-biz extravaganza with soothsayers and terrorist stringers all leading up to Howard's ranting Jeremiads delivered in front of a stained-glass window. Max Schumacher can't believe what Diana has done to his news show and his close friend Howard. Raising one of the few human voices in the film, he protests: "He needs care and treatment and all you graverobbers care about is that he's a hit!"

Diana Christiansen graduates to corporate evangelist in another scene where she stands in a white dress before hundreds of network affiliates, extends her hands in priestly blessing and exhorts them to follow the prophecy of the Nielsen numbers. She is the Anti-Virgin who turns bank robberies, politics, even the weather, into a prime-time Black Mass and man's most fundamental expression of shared humanity and love, the sexual act, into a mechanical matrix of corporate emotions. The Anti-Christ kills a man for getting bad ratings; the Anti-Virgin gets off on corporate success. Her orgasm in the love scene is very similar to the machine-induced orgasm of the photographer's model (Veruschka) in that early scene in Antonioni's Blow-Up.

What Network has done with the American corporate institution of Television is, in many ways, quite similar to what The President's Analyst did with the phone company and The China Syndrome did with the power company. Each of these films shows how corporate institutions are seriously involved in a takeover of America; how the final goal of the phone company or the television industry could conceivably be to rule the world through mind control; how Communism is no longer America's greatest enemy but rather our own macro-conglomerates are the forces to be feared in our society. Our own home-grown social structures have mutated out of control, grown so large, so diverse, so powerful, that we no longer control them, they control us. Thus is the final truth of corporate reality revealed: Man does not control the structure, the structure controls the man.

But what is most important and distinctive about Network's version of the whole corporate villain concept is the presentation of corporate villainy in terms of a religious iconography. In all of these corporate villain movies, the boardroom conference table has come to symbolize conspiracy, threat, social evil in the exact same

way that a Colt Peacemaker or a Derringer became an
immediately identifiable icon in the old Westerns or the
violin case in the gangster films of the thirties and
forties. In Network, the conference table becomes the
altar of the Anti-Christ, takes on a Satanic implication
more sinister and Faustian than it ever carried in any of
the other corporate villain films. Network is about how
America has indeed sold its rugged individualist soul to
the lusty, fast-talking devil of corporate greed. A similar
boardroom table appears in a more recent movie, Sydney
Lumet's The Verdict (1982). Around that conference table
are gathered the thirty or so members of one of Boston's
largest law firms-- Concannon, Pierce and Stearns.
Around this massive table this corporation of lawyers led
by Concannon (James Mason) plot the firm's strategy for
winning a million dollar malpractice suit. Routinely they
plan to manipulate the media (both newspapers and
TV), plan payoffs to make witnesses disappear, try to
buy off the litigants, plan to turn people like Laura
Fisher (Charlotte Rampling) into whores and spies. Only
one weak man, Frank Galvin (Paul Newman), stands in
the firm's way.

The Verdict follows the same pattern of so many of
these corporate villain films. An embattled individual
goes up against all the power of the corporation. In The
Verdict, Frank Galvin wins, but in more realistic films,
like The Parallax View, the individual never really has
much of a chance against the powers that be. But what
all of these films are doing is recognizing and defining
who those dark powers are, where the most threatening
evil in our society resides. Mickey Morrissey (Jack
Warden) in The Verdict puts his finger right on it. When
Frank Galvin asks him to characterize the corporate
lawyer Concannon, Mickey answers: "He's the fucking
Prince of Darkness!"

3. BLOW-UP: THE GAME WITH NO BALLS

Since its release in 1966, Michaelangelo Antonioni's Blow-Up has emerged as a full-fledged classic. Arthur Knight writing in Film Heritage magazine in Spring 1967 rightly suspected "that future historians will recognize it as important and germinal a film as Citizen Kane, Open City and Hiroshima, Mon Amour." Knight was one of the few early critics to recognize what a prophetic and influential film Blow-Up would turn out to be. He sensed that Blow-Up's central themes, the impotence of the Existential impulse and the futility of man's attempts to grasp and understand reality, would become the central issues in the films of the whole following decade.Though the comparison is ludicrous, Blow-Up would go on to have the same germinal influence on a whole decade of films about seventies man's relation to reality that The President's Analyst had upon a decade of corporate villain films. Perhaps that ludicrous comparison is the best proof of Ian Jarvie's statement in Movies and Society that "one can argue that the best and the worst films come from the same social structure of production, enter the same mass market, present their particular views of the world, and have certain images in the public mind. Further, even a poor film may raise or explore an interesting social, moral, or personal problem (xv)."

Blow-Up puzzled its early critics. They may have sensed that it was an important film but few of them could put their finger on why. The film's "message," its techniques, its mysteries and unresolved questions may

have puzzled the critics, but in a number of vague ways
they were aware that the film "works" in both cinematic
and even literary ways. Thus Blow-Up became the
darling of film classes and academic film journals. But,
for all the attention paid it, discussions of its central
conceptual themes have always remained either tentative
or diffuse. Critics seem prone to the same puzzled
bewilderment that haunts Antonioni's central character
throughout his meanderings in the world of the film.
Blow-Up is a work that critics analyze parts of
brilliantly, but none (with the possible exception of
Charles Thomas Samuels in "The Blow-Up: Sorting
Things Out" The American Scholar, Winter, 1967) have
attempted to pull the whole thing together, define it as
an organized structure by means of discussion of
Antonioni's major thematic generalization. The Director
himself has confessed that Blow-Up was his most
ratiocinative effort-- "All of the other films I did with
my stomach, this one I did with my brain."[4] --and,
without arguing the relative values of duodenal and
cerebral genesis, clearly Antonioni had something in
mind. What?

Blow-Up is a film about impotence of all sorts,
ranging from the PHYSICAL (the inability to sexually
satisfy) to the MORAL (the inability to act
intersubjectively with other people) to the AESTHETIC
(the inability to create beauty, truth and meaning for
the world outside the self) to the EXISTENTIAL (the
inability to divine the direction of one's own life and
progress due to an inability to grasp and understand reality). It is all one theme operating on ascending levels
of meaning like an escalator in a big-city department
store that rises from lingerie in the bargain basement up
through housewares, books and art prints, to the
decision-making corporate boardrooms and billing offices

---

[4]Quoted by Carey Harrison in "Blow-Up," Sight and
Sound, Spring, 1967.

on the top floor. Past critics have stepped on this
escalator of the impotence theme but none have ever
risen very far with it, explored every level of the
thematic structuring of meaning in Blow-Up.

Charles Thomas Samuels comes close in shopping for
Antonioni's central theme when he writes in "The
Blow-Up: Sorting Things Out" that "the climax is
reached when the protagonist comes to face his own
impotence." Sounds a bit contradictory, that sentence!

John Freccero in "Blow-Up: From the Word to the
Image" in Yale/Theatre (Fall 1970) pursues the theme a
bit more articulately than Samuels:

> Until her [the woman-in-the-park]
> appearance in the film, Thomas' [the
> photographer] sexuality seems as dehumanized
> as his art, the sexuality of the voyeur (a
> metaphor for novelistic detachment at least as
> old as Chaucer), who so transcends his own
> mortality that he can achieve his satisfaction
> merely by observing, like some God, from a
> privileged perspective.

Freccero then goes on to briefly note that "the
parallelism that the film has established between the
artist's sexuality and his art, the failure of human love,
or at least human contact is exactly equivalent to the
failure of his work to achieve humanity."

Other critics notice the impotence theme in passing
and drop it a quick phrase or a backward glance. The
word "abortive" seems to roll handily off the points of
many pens: "the abortiveness" of the Director's and his
central character's "obsession with states of mind"[5] and
the repeatedly "abortive seductions"[6] of the film have

---

[5]Max Kosloff, "The Blow-Up," Film Quarterly, XX, 3.

[6]Roy Huss, "Introduction," Focus on "Blow-Up".

been glimpsed. Another hurried shopper has noticed how the protagonist becomes "morally impotent,"[7] and even the solemn experts of the National Council of Churches ordained that Blow-Up presented "perhaps the most cheerless sex"[8] ever. Generally, the critics skip quickly over this theme like women shuffling through racks of dresses on the King's Road and fail to see the thematic pattern in the quick-hitting scenes of anti-sexuality which lace Blow-Up and define its delicate structure.

Perhaps many critics reacted negatively when Blow-Up was first released because of the film's literariness. The presence of a brilliant cinematic talent is evident everywhere in Blow-Up, but it is Antonioni's combining of the verbal thematic statements with his striking visual images, his use of novelistic literary techniques such as scene-by-scene construction and image patterning which carries meaning in the film. Perhaps it is this aspect of Antonioni's art which causes Samuels to direct that "Antonioni's close-ups must be 'read'" like a text, just as the photographer-protagonist must 'read' the meaning in his photos. James F. Scott also serves as a courier of

> a special message from Antonioni to his critics, those who have looked askance at the seemingly arbitrary imagery in some of his earlier films. Watch closely, gentlemen; trifles are not always a trifling matter.[9]

Henry James would certainly agree.

---

[7]Andrew Sarris, "No Antoniennui," The Village Voice, 29 December 1966.

[8]Quoted by Arthur Knight in "Three Encounters with Blow-Up," Film Heritage, Spring, 1967.

[9]"Blow-Up: Antonioni and the Mod World," Cross Currents (Spring 1967).

Antonioni is as much thematic novelist as he is camera virtuoso. Interestingly enough, the camera virtuoso is the very person that Blow-Up condemns to impotence. The point is that Antonioni's masterpiece turns on literary symbols and symbolic juxtapositions as well as upon camera angles, narrative positioning and purely cinematic techniques of symbolism. What accounts for the artistic success of Blow-Up is the ability of its creator to form a symbiosis between the filmic and the literary, a relationship in which the visual cinematics support, frame, even spotlight the literary representations of meaning.

The theme of impotence in its different forms functions negatively in each of the major scenes as well as in the central image patterns of the film. The one major image cluster which defines impotence in Blow-Up is the succession of phallic symbols the presence of which in each scene comments upon the meaning of that scene. These recurring symbols' presence helps the viewer to focus upon the photographer's sexual, moral, aesthetic and existential dilemma.

Early in Blow-Up, in the first major picture-taking sequence, two distinct phallic symbols dominate. They define the motif's meaning. In later scenes, symbols of phallic impotence recur. In this highly erotic scene, in which the photographer-protagonist (David Hemmings) makes love to his model (Veruschka) with his camera, the symbolic significance of the camera has oft been noted, but a previous phallic symbol, the feathers, has never been mentioned. As the scene begins, the photographer, still grubby from his night in a dosshouse, advances toward his model holding a handful of feathered fans. The fans are the kind old-time burlesque dancers flourished to stroke themselves and play erotic peek-a-boo. As photographer and model meet in center screen, he fans the feathers out before him at groin level and forms a bridge between his and her pubic areas. The feathers, waving limply in his hands, are symbolically untumesced. As the model looks at the feathers fanning up between them, she moistens her lips

88   The Films of the Seventies

suggestively. The scene then moves to semi-tumescence as
the photographer mounts the fans on a metal stick to
form a huge feathered phallus which fills the entire
foreground of the screen and of the shot the
photographer has set up. The model arches and moves
seductively toward the stiffened plumes as the
photographer takes his tripod shots. The camera is
mounted on a tripod at groin level and in the midst of
a series of shots it is raised slightly before the
photographer returns to his masturbatory pumping out of
shots. Then, well warmed-up, fanned by this feathered
foreplay, the photographer advances on the model with
his hand-held camera, the hard, metallic machine of full
tumescence, and gets down to the real love-making.
When all of his film is spent, he rises from her. As he
pulls up, her leg seems to hang downward from between
his legs in center screen. The scene ends as he collapses
depressed on the couch with the still-excited model,
obviously unsatisfied, collapsing slowly, like a fan
folding up, in the foreground.

The scene is perhaps most reminiscent of a similar
scene in John Fowles' novel The Collector (1963), and
the subsequent film of that novel (1965), in which
Clegg, the pornographic collector who is impotent, rapes
Miranda, his kidnap victim, with his camera. Both scenes
clearly make the point that no human intercourse of any
kind is occurring. Rather, a strange and strained parody
of the sexual act, unfulfilling, mechanical, bizarre, is
being choreographed. The fan-dancers' fans with their
intimations of titillating pornography point to the
dehumanizing nature of this scene of technological
coupling. The feathers, the cameras, are the dildos of
impotent men, taxidermic tumescences, surrogates for a
dead sexuality. Both Clegg and the photographer of
Blow-Up are latter-day Popeyes fondling the
technological descendents of that infamous Faulknerian
corncob. In the techno-sexual seventies, this very kind of
parodying of the sexual act is in rancid evidence every
month when the slick girlie magazines in which models
open themselves completely to the penetration of the

camera lens hit the newsstands.

Throughout the film, in major scenes or just in offhand references, the phallic representations of the theme of impotence recur. "I'm fed up with those bloody bitches," the photographer says at one point, apropos of nothing. Later, when the woman-in-the-park (Vanessa Redgrave) has materialized at his studio, she stands against the wall as he approaches. Again, the feathers are between them. Then, in an enigmatic conversation touched off by an interrupting phone call, the photographer admits semi-sadly, "No. No kids. Not even kids." Later in the same scene, the camera lingers on the cigarette they pass between them. The photographer can't share anything with a woman except through some objective, external conduit, some phallic surrogate. He sees women only as objects to be exploited by his camera for his own aggrandizement and therefore he can only communicate with these objects through other objects. He can only deal with human beings objectively and therefore he closes off any possibility for an intersubjective relationship. The feathers, the camera, the cigarette, are cautionary devices for him, a means of keeping human emotion at arm's length, a means of distancing himself from feeling. Later in this scene, as the sexuality of the situation becomes more overt, the woman-in-the-park again retreats against the wall, the feathers between her and the photographer. The feathers screen her as she takes off her blouse and offers herself in exchange for the incriminating photos. The photographer's impulse surely is to take another snap of her.

Near the end of Blow-Up, another pivotal scene representing the theme of impotence occurs. The photographer, searching for the elusive woman-in-the-park, wanders into an eerie cellar-club where a rock band entertains a crowd of dull-eyed zombies.[10] Tubes connect the phallic guitars to their power sources, the speakers and amplifiers, which sit in the background, electronic testes spewing out sound. One of the guitar players' speakers breaks down leaving him

strumming away but producing no sound, impotent. No
one in the audience seems to notice, much less care. In
his frustration, the guitar player beats on his own
speaker to no effect. He goes berserk, ripping out the
wires that connect the guitar to the speakers, throwing
the guitar to the floor, stomping it, finally tearing its
neck off and throwing it, like some strange sacrifice in
an infertility rite, to the crowd. The photographer fights
for the severed guitar neck and flees. The adventures of
the   guitar   in   this   scene   are   symbolic   of
mid-twentieth-century castration, of what happens when
the machine stops and man finds himself cast adrift
impotent in a drugged, unfeeling world. For Antonioni's
photographer, this scene is a mythic descent into the
underworld, an Odyssean communing in the land of the
dead. Unfortunately, the photographer doesn't heed the
message that he carries out of the underworld. He
discards it and moves on, unenlightened. At different
times in the film the protagonist mindlessly discards a
propellor, an anti-war sign and the guitar neck. Each of
these phallic objects attempts to convey a message to the
photographer-- the propellor = "rise and fly"; the sign
says "GO AWAY"; the guitar neck = "Sing out in your
own voice" --and in each case he ignores and discards
the message.

     Though the propellor is recognized as an im-
portant symbol in Blow-Up, there is widespread
disagreement on what it means. F. A. Macklin writing in
December (1967) calls the propellor "the major symbol
of the early part of the film. There is a photograph of
a plane in the antique shop, and there is a photograph

[10]Hubert Meeker, "Blow-Up," Film Heritage (Spring
1967) briefly alludes to a proper interpretation of this
scene while Stanley Kauffmann, "A Year with Blow-Up:
Some Notes," Film 67/68 (New York: Simon and
Schuster, Inc., 1968) and Freccero completely misinterpret
the scene.

of a parachutist in Hemmings' room. While the latter picture may represent his leap or fall (his abandon in space), the propellor is tangible evidence of the disengagement." Freccero argues that it is "a symbol of flight." Marsha Kinder, however, in "Antonioni in Transit" in Sight and Sound (Summer 1967) offers the most perceptive interpretation yet: "It is the one item among all those antiques that is linked with the contemporary world-- with technology, with dynamic motion."

The propellor is perhaps the best example of the photographer's aimlessness. "I can't live without it," he says of this phallic totem when he spots it in a junk shop. His desire for the propellor signals a momentary realization that he needs to somehow rise above the meaninglessness of his unsatisfying and mundane life. In his acknowledgement of the importance of the propellor as symbol, the photographer shows a desire for human potency. He shows this desire many times throughout the film. But, he can never sustain his impulse in the face of the technological sirens that always call. Almost immediately upon taking up the propellor, he discards it. This distracted throwing-off of the just-attained is typical of the photographer's short attention span throughout the film. A motif of literal and metaphysical coitus interruptus punctuates the action.

Whenever the photographer seems to be getting involved with someone or something-- a woman, a sexual act, a mystery, a work of art (his book of photos with text) --he is always interrupted. The photographer's impotence-- sexual, moral, aesthetic --in these situations could be overcome by an act of will. But never does he resist the distractions. In the studio, he sits the woman-in-the-park down on his sofa. He is fascinated by her, wants to know more about her. Naturally, the phone rings. He hesitates. He doesn't want to answer it. He wants to follow through with the seduction he has begun. He tries to ignore the insistent, invisible ringing. But, instead, he dives for the phone desperately like a man leaping to smother a grenade. The moment is shattered. The fledgling relationship is blown apart. Immediately after hanging up the phone, he can only talk about himself.

Later in the same scene as the two of them are actually entering the bedroom, having touched for the first time only moments before, both on the verge of overcoming impotence, the doorbell rings. Again, the photographer considers resisting the interruption, but he can't. He answers the door and is rewarded with the already rejected propellor. Machines always intervene in the photographer's attempts to establish human contact. He hasn't the will to ever reject society's call or ring. Whenever he stands on the verge of establishing some kind of sexual or moral potency, some kind of touching with another person, he opts to be interrupted.

His movement toward aesthetic potency is interrupted in precisely the same way. In the central scene of the film, the "developing" scene, just as the photographer is getting to the heart of the mystery, just as his art photos are starting to come to life through the phenomenology of interpretation, just as the mid-twentieth-century artist is becoming _engage_, the doorbell rings again and the two young "birds" swoop in on him.

This playful orgy scene should dispel any questions about the photographer's sexual potency. Yet, ironically, he leaves the young "birds" whose tails he has salted unsatisfied. He hasn't proven his real potency to them at all. "You haven't taken any photos," they coo in Cockney disillusion as he shoos them from his nest. The meaningful intellectual _coitus_ between the photographer and his mysterious pictures has been interrupted by a meaningless interlude of ricocheting romance which leaves the participants exhausted yet still unsatisfied. The young "birds" walk out of this scene as morosely as did the sexy model in the earlier picture-taking sequence.

The phallic imagery and the scenes of literal and metaphorical _coitus interruptus_ help to define the LITERAL, MORAL and AESTHETIC levels of the impotence theme. The central, most suspenseful, most fixating, scene in Blow-Up, the "developing" scene, gives definition to the EXISTENTIAL level of Antonioni's major theme. From the very beginning of the film, during the opening credits, the conceptual idea of the difficulty of seeing reality clearly, of grasping reality whole, is presented by means of clever cinematurgy. During the credits the scene is fragmented because it is viewed through cutouts in a black foreground. Seen in moving pieces as if through a wandering keyhole is a scene of a voluptuous woman dancing on a roof above a cheering crowd in which one middle-grounded figure is waving a camera. As the credits flash, changing the image with each new cut-out, the viewer strains to catch a full view of the dancer's sexily undulating body, but all the viewer gets are fragmented views through the peek-a-boo cutouts, teasers. The effect is frustrating yet fascinating, like trying to piece together a voyeuristic jigsaw puzzle. The technique of the opening credits foreshadows the "developing" scene: reality can never be seen whole, only in fragments, and even then one has to strain to find meaning.[11] This theme of the difficulty of grasping, controlling, understanding reality will become one of the central themes which will dominate the films of the seventies.

Other intimations of this same fragmentation, this difficulty in seeing and understanding life in its changeableness, reverberate in small symbolic details throughout the film. These details are all echoes of the foreshadowing of the opening credits. The photographer's realities are always filtered and oblique as when he shoots his fashion lay-outs through smoky, transparent

---

[11]Not all of the prints of Blow-Up presently in distribution present this "cut-outs" version of the opening credits. Some simply roll the open ing credits over a high angle long shot of an empty expanse of grass which is also the final shot of the film.

screens. In his studio, the beams and angular equipment
cut people into parts by means of foregrounding. The
painter's wife, as she tries to explain to the
photographer her inability to act, wears a wide-crocheted
peek-a-boo dress. That dress forces the viewer to lean
forward as he tries to distinguish her body beneath it,
tries to put together the curve of her breasts, the
protrusion of her nipples, but she is fragmented like the
dancer behind the opening credits. This concept of
reality-fragmented is what gives such suspense, tension
and mystery to the pivotal "developing" scene. The
pictures taken in the park which the photographer first
develops, then sections, then blows up are fragments,
cutouts, of a larger drama which he must strain to put
together and see clearly.

Five major photos and two minor ones (in which
the lovers first, notice the photographer, and second,
watch him retreat) dominate the "developing" scene.
Those five major photos present the following views:

> WOMAN LURING-- the woman seems to be
> tantalizing her lover, moving toward
> him then away, leading him to a
> particular spot in the peaceful park;

> EMBRACE/SHOCK-- in the midst of an
> embrace, the woman is startled,
> looks with shock toward the bushes;

> FENCE/BUSHES-- the photographer blows up
> the area of the bushes that the
> woman is staring at in the
> EMBRACE/SHOCK still;

> FENCE BIGGER-- the photographer further
> blows up a section of the
> FENCE/BUSHES blow-up;

> WOMAN, HAND RAISED ACCUSINGLY-- the
> woman, at the top of a flight of

steps in the park, looking directly at the photographer with an expression on her face similar to that in the EMBRACE /SHOCK photo, accuses him of spying on them, shooting pictures of them.

The photographer's (and the audience's as the camera takes to the subjective first person) viewing of these photos throughout the "developing" scene takes the following sequence:

1) WOMAN LURING
2) EMBRACE/SHOCK
(photographer uses the magnifying glass, then blows up a section of bushes)
3) FENCE/BUSHES
4) EMBRACE/SHOCK
5) FENCE/BUSHES
6) EMBRACE/SHOCK
7) FENCE/BUSHES
(photographer further blows up section of bushes)
8) FENCE BIGGER
(at this point, the photographer mixes the blow-ups of the bushes and the startled woman with a picture of the woman looking accusingly at him)
9) WOMAN, HAND RAISED ACCUSINGLY
10) FENCE BIGGER
11) WOMAN LURING
12) EMBRACE/SHOCK
13) FENCE BUSHES (he sees a face in the bushes)
14) FENCE BIGGER (he sees a gun)
15) Lovers see him
16) Lovers stare at him
17) WOMAN, HAND RAISED ACCUSINGLY

At this point in the sequence, the two young models break in on the photographer and all meaning that has been developing in his mind disintegrates.

The sequence of the stills as they are arranged in the photographer's mind raises the most important question about this "developing" scene. The HAND RAISED ACCUSINGLY photo has no relevance whatsoever to the mystery that the photographer is trying to unravel. That photo violates all of the sight-lines upon which the photographer's construction of the mystery are based. For him, the key to solving the mystery has been concentration upon where the woman in the pictures is looking. In turn, she looks at her lover, then at the gunman in the bushes. But finally in the HAND RAISED ACCUSINGLY still, she is looking at the photographer. Why does he include this HAND RAISED ACCUSINGLY still in the sequence at all? He certainly hasn't become confused with the sight-lines. Therefore, he must be thinking that her looking at him has some meaning, that he has become part of the reality he has tried to capture. Ironically, in the HAND RAISED ACCUSINGLY still, the look of shock on the woman's face is almost identical to that same look in the EMBRACE/SHOCK still when she is looking at the gunman in the bushes. In fact, in terms of what this sequence which the photographer constructs intimates, the inclusion of the HAND RAISED ACCUSINGLY still is the most impor- tant inclusion of all. It says that he, the photographer, is the real killer lurking in the bushes. He has shot them, destroyed their idyll, interrupted them in their touching. He has im- posed the repeated coitus interruptus of his own existence upon them. The gun in the bushes, the camera in the bushes, both lurk ready to violate from long range. They are both hard, metallic symbols which coldly mimic life and art.

Ultimately, Blow-Up becomes highly existential, Sartrean, Camusian. The photographer becomes like Meurseult in Camus' The Stranger drawn into something he does not understand by the sun pounding on his jangled nerves and his fraying sense of reality. As in The Stranger, the murder plot loses its relevance in direct proportion to the amount of analysis the photographer and, by identification, the audience (in Camus' novel, the lawyers and the jury) give to it. The murder mystery becomes only a shadowy vehicle, a metaphor, for the central character's introspection upon his own guilt of uninvolvement. In Sartrean terms, the photographer in Blow-Up never becomes an "engage" artist.[12] This inability on the photographer's part causes all the different kinds of impotence which parade through his life from the very beginning of the film until finally his camera, like Clegg's in Fowles' novel, becomes an instrument which brings death to both life and art.

In the process of blowing things up, the closer one gets to an image, the more illusory it becomes. When the photographer finally sees what he thinks is the body of the murder victim in the final blow-up, it is just an outline, its molecules dispersing into incomprehensibility.

The photographer's artist friend, painter of abstracts, says of his own paintings:

> They don't mean anything when I do them. Afterwards I find something to hang onto. Then it sorts itself out. It's like a clue in a detective story.

The blow-ups become like those abstract paintings and, for a while, even participate as clues in a literal detective story. But the artist can only find meaning in his art by imposing it himself, by getting involved with that work of art. That is precisely what the photographer attempts with his inclusion of the WOMAN, HAND RAISED ACCUSINGLY still in the "developing" sequence. But, he cannot sustain his

---

[12]What Is Literature? (New York: Harper and Row, 1965).

momentary involvement with himself, with his own role in his own art. He is interrupted. He loses it, as he always has.

One small scene early in Blow-Up both defines the path the photographer must follow in order to find identity in life/art and crystallizes his total lack of direction. Immediately after the words of the song "Did You Ever Have To Make Up Your Mind" play in the background, the photographer picks up the old clothes he had worn as his disguise in the dosshouse, carries them outside the studio and drops them in the trash. Like a chameleon, like his models who constantly change their costumes and make-up, he changes identities thoughtlessly. Because he does not heed the existential advice of the song, he discards identities at random. He never gives himself the chance to become "engagé" and his opportunities for humanness and both moral and aesthetic potency are repeatedly lost.

All this considered, the final scene, in which the mimes play tennis with no balls, is strikingly appropriate. This scene is both an end-symbol (or coda) which ironically comments upon all that has gone before and an optimistic statement of the possibilities of the photographer finding his humanness and selfhood even if he can't grasp and understand reality in the ways that he would like. When the not-yet-existent (because it has not been acknowledged by any agent of the real world outside of the mime troupe) tennis ball flies over the fence, the photographer, a detached observer, significantly puts down his camera and picks it up. He tosses it in his hand, looks at it with a sheepish grin and puts it back into play. Only then does the game with no balls come to life as the sound of human intercourse, the mimes rallying, breaks the impotent silence.

4. BLOW-UP MEETS RICHARD NIXON

Antonioni's Blow-Up became a cult film of the late sixties but the film's themes and images which so captured the imagination of those late sixties audiences have, over time, proved more complex and ambiguous than they were first considered to be. It seemed a very "hot" film photographed in bright reds and blues, but, in fact, the greys of the London slums and the photographer's black and white blown-up photos overshadow the Director's pop-art exteriors. It seemed a film about the free-wheeling spirit of "swinging London" yet the most important scenes take place not on the King's Road or in Soho but inside the photographer's studio and dark room or in a tiny deserted park far from the neon lights, mini-skirts, rock guitars and madding crowds. It seemed a film which threw itself headfirst into the sexual revolution, but Blow-Up really dramatizes the emptiness and insecurity that the sexual revolution caused. All of Blow-Up's images of impotence announce what would be the sixties' legacy to the seventies, announce that all of the revolutionary excess is leading nowhere, that human beings are confused and wandering in a world which mirrors their own emptiness, that reality is no longer graspable, comprehensible, controllable.

In fact, none of the themes which so attracted Blow-Up's sixties audiences is of much interest any more. The "Swinging Sixties" are long gone and seem almost caricatured in the film. Blow-up's orgiastic scenes of sexual revolution nowadays get yawns from audiences

desensitized to sex by relentless movies like <u>Deep</u>
<u>Throat, Behind The Green Door</u> and <u>Debbie Does</u>
------- (fill in your favorite city, country, continent,
solar system, sporting event, national monument or
institution of higher learning). What wasn't immediately
recognized was that <u>Blow-Up</u> wasn't a <u>paeon</u> to the
sixties but rather an epitaph, not a play-by-play of an
exciting game but an expose of a dying game being
played without any balls. All the while, <u>Blow-Up</u> was
making the statement that the sixties game of sex, dope,
revolution and freedom was all an illusion.

What <u>Blow-Up</u> is really about is the ephemeral
nature, thus the kinship, of both illusion and reality. In
the world of <u>Blow-Up</u>, nothing is ever what it seems to
be. But the realization that what appears to be real may
be only an illusion is but the first step into the post-
modernist wasteland, the beginning of a descent into a
cynical underworld where reality can never be anything
more than a flickering shadow projected on a cavern
wall.

What <u>Blow-Up</u> declares is that when post-modern
man attempts to grasp the reality of his world, to
capture it, analyze it, understand it, he is doomed to
failure because reality is only an illusion infinitely
subject to the changing processes and perspectives of
Einstienian relativity. One can never look at reality
whole. One can only view reality from one's own angle,
from one single limited perspective. A major point which
<u>Blow-Up</u> makes is that man can choose to play the
game without any balls but, perhaps like Camus'
Sisyphus, he should derive his joy only from the illusion
of the game itself; he should never expect to experience
any success in his face-offs with reality.

But, not only was <u>Blow-Up</u> an expose and an
epitaph, it was, like <u>The President's Analyst,</u> a highly
prophetic movie. Instead of being a film whose intent
was to capture the texture of the sixties, <u>Blow-Up</u>
predicted the social temper of the seventies, introduced
the central theme which would define the politics, the
corporate ethic, the war and the movies of the seventies.

That theme stated that "nothing is ever what it seems to be." That theme represented the INSECURITY of everyone with things which people had always believed in, such as our Presidents, our Generals, and our Captains of Industry. Blow-Up predicted a decade in which even water and air couldn't be trusted. Blow-Up imaged a world resistant to man's intellectual power to understand and control. Blow-Up imaged reality as a fragmented mystery which multiplies its resistance to understanding in direct proportion to man's attempts to understand it, which becomes more distorted the more it is blown up. Blow-Up's images for the theme of man's attempts to capture and analyze and understand reality predicted a heavily populated set of movies which appeared in the seventies. Blow-Up's images sired the thematic concerns of this particular set of motion pictures but it was the social history of the seventies, particularly the Watergate affair, which played midwife to these films.

Francis Ford Coppola's The Conversation (1974) is the most important of the Blow-Up/Watergate offspring. In plot, in major scenes, in central character, The Conversation is Blow-Up for the ears. Where Antonioni's photographer captured the images of a couple flirting playfully in a small park, Coppola's Harry Caul (Gene Hackman), a professional bugger, captures on audio tape the words of a couple walking in a small city square. Where in Blow-Up's developing scene the photographer enlarged the photographs again and again trying to establish their relation to each other and the story they seemed to want to tell, in The Conversation's dubbing scene Harry Caul plays and replays, turns up the volume and magnifies the words, meticulously juxtaposes and mixes the sounds picked up on each of the microphones in the attempt to capture and analyze not only the words themselves but their proper sequence and inflection in order to understand what has actually been said. Like the photographer in Blow-Up, Harry Caul, after trying to magnify and interpret the reality he has captured with his high-tech equipment, chooses to become a detective, to pursue reality as far as he can in the attempt to understand. And the protagonists of both Blow-Up and The Conversation are strikingly similar. Both are bachelors, loners, observers of life extremely wary of involvement. Both are high-tech virtuosos, the best in their respective businesses. Both are adrift in their complex worlds, quizzical about who they really are and what their world and reality in general really is and means. Both function under the impulse of a vague, tired, out of shape moral sense which is not strong enough to be effective yet which cannot be ignored. At the ends of both films, both protagonists find themselves alone, on the outside looking in, having failed in their quests to understand and subdue the reality which they captured.

In fact, both Blow-Up and The Conversation owe much of the conception of their plots, their protagonists, their central theme of capturing, collating and trying to understand reality to the influence of Alfred Hitchcock's Rear Window (1954). Rear Window is the original voyeur film, the original dramatization of a weakened, impotent, aimless man's attempts to piece collected fragments of reality together to give them meaning. As in both Blow-Up and The Conversation, when Hitchcock's wheelchair immobilized Peeping Tom (James Stewart) does seem to have found some meaning in his collection of realities, that meaning proves to be threatening and dangerous, something that the protagonist can't really control.

But the genesis of The Conversation involved more than just the cloning of Antonioni's earlier film or the influence of Hitchcock. The Conversation was the first major filmic reaction to the Watergate affair, the central event of the social history of the 1970s. An earlier underrated film, The Anderson Tapes (1971), had examined the ethics of the national bugging frenzy but The Conversation was the first major film to have "Watergate" written all over it. Blow-Up first stated the "nothing is ever what it seems to be" theme, focused upon the concept of the relativity of reality, presented

the characters and the contexts for the presentation of
that theme, but The Conversation took those characters,
contexts and that theme and gave it Watergate relevance.

Where Blow-Up and The Conversation are character
studies focusing upon the act of an individual trying to
understand the confusing realities which he has captured,
The Anderson Tapes is a much more clinical film, its
narrative point of view much more aloof and
unsympathetic. It is the story of Eddie Anderson (Sean
Connery), a small-time burglar recently paroled from stir,
who wants to pull one big heist (of all the apartments
in a posh, supposedly impenetrable apartment building).
Unbeknownst to him, as he puts together his gang and
irons out all of his logistical details, his every move is
being taped and recorded by federal surveillance teams
who have no interest in him but are squirming on every
word of the mob leaders who he must visit in
preparation. The film is a lattice of point of view shots
through surveillance zoom lenses of Eddie entering and
leaving his connections' buildings and of spools of tape
spinning out Eddie's conversations with the bigwigs who
are the real objects of the Feds' surveillance. The
crowning irony of the film comes at the end when it is
revealed that the Federal investigators have Anderson's
every move on tape yet don't know its meaning, don't
realize that they have the evidence to convict him.
Reality in all its elusiveness triumphs once again.
Anderson is a small fish caught in a net so much bigger
than him that he manages to swim out through the
webbing.

After The Anderson Tapes, the reality of Watergate
(whatever that was) and The Conversation in that order,
the wiretapping motif became, in a steady stream of
seventies and early eighties films, a dominant symbolic
tool for the representation of man's attempts to
understand the reality of his world. The most prominant
of these Blow-Up/Watergate films were Coming Home
(1978), Prince of the City (1981) and Sharky's Machine
(1982). In each, the wiretapping becomes an emblem of
the government's or the police's distance and impersonal

detachment from the subjects of their surveillance. In each, the buggers listen in on the sexual lives of their subjects and react by making off-color remarks, passing judgement negatively and impersonally upon the private acts of individuals. The buggers act as voyeurs, Peeping Toms, invading the privacy of others to collect information which they think they understand but which they invariably find to be too complex or wide-ranging to comprehend.

In Coming Home, the government wiretap on Luke Martin (Jon Voight), a Vietnam vet/protestor, is used for purposes totally different than originally intended. In the course of bugging Luke, the tapes reveal that Sally Hyde (Jane Fonda), the wife of a Marine Captain on duty in Vietnam, is having an affair with the original subject of the surveillance. Since this sexual betrayal of the war effort is the only real crime this bugging operation turns up, the prurient little men in Marine Intelligence dutifully deliver all the evidence of his wife's infidelity to Captain Bob Hyde (Bruce Dern) as soon as he makes it back from the combat zone. He commits suicide as a result! Stalking one reality yet finding a different reality barely stalled the zealous buggers of Coming Home. It made no difference to them how they used their tapes as long as they used them.

In Sidney Lumet's Prince of the City, a detective, Danny Aiello (Treat Williams), a member of New York's elite narcotics investigation unit, sickened by the corruption he sees all around him in the police department, becomes a walking wiretap for the special task force on police corruption. As the tapes pile up, are numbered and filed, and the evidence accumulates, Danny realizes that he is just a machine that the men who run him turn off and turn on whenever they wish. He realizes that he is losing himself, his identity, his friends and his mind. Prince of the City is a brilliant study of a man allowing himself to be turned into a machine, all the while thinking that he is in control. When he finally realizes that the machine, the wire taped to his chest, his back, his groin, controls him, it is too late; the machine has taken over his whole existence.

The title Sharky's Machine is an especially ironic one which parallels the theme of dehumanization and loss of identity in Prince of the City. Sharky's (Burt Reynolds) "machine" is both the conglomeration of high-tech spying equipment (wiretaps, cameras) which he employs to watch the apartment of Domino (Rachel Ward), the highest class call girl in Atlanta, and it is the name Sharky uses to describe his team of narcotics surveillance specialists. In this film, the machines and the human cops collect segments of reality and feed them all into the main machine in hopes of coming to some understanding of what is going on. Sharky's Machine is a cross between The Conversation and Hitchcock's Rear Window. As in Rear Window, Sharky is a temporarily paralyzed man (professionally, due to his bungling of a big narcotics case) forced to sit in a small room and spy on the world outside his window. He is trying to catch reality and reconstruct it out of a collection of sensory fragments-- sounds, conversations, photographs, images --but there is always a barrier-- a curtain, a window, a closed door --between the reality and Sharky who is trying to catch that reality, analyze it, understand it.

But Sharky doesn't stay paralyzed long. Like Harry Caul in The Conversation, Sharky gets involved with the subject of his surveillance. In fact, the similarity between Sharky and Harry Caul is uncanny. Both are loners and losers though highly adept professionals. Both reject their positions of detachment from the reality which they are trying to capture; both attempt to get closer to reality, become personally involved with it in order to better understand and control it. Both fail or think that they have failed because "nothing is ever what it seems to be." The wiretapping motif that appears in so many of these films of the seventies and early eighties is quite predictable considering the Watergate obsession of that era, but that motif can also be viewed as an outgrowth of another social theme of seventies America, the rise of the corporate ethic. The dehumanization and loss of identity, the separation from human reality so endemic to all of those films of corporate villainy is also metaphorically embodied in the imagery of distance, detachment and dehumanizing objectification of the wiretap. The imagery of wiretapping stands for intrusion into private human realities without any intendant involvement in those realities.

Three other films of the decade-- Capricorn One, The China Syndrome and Eyewitness (1982) --extend this imagery one step further by combining the visual emphasis of Blow-Up with the audio emphasis of The Conversation by means of the use of videotape. In these films, videotape captures reality or what seems to be reality and the plots of the films turn upon very Watergate-like attempts by opposing factions to either uncover or cover-up the seeming realities captured on the videotapes.

In Capricorn One, reality via videotaped transmissions from a space mission is certainly not what it seems to be. In fact, the pictures and sounds from outer space are being transmitted from a studio in order to hoax the American people into continued funding of a faltering space program. The whole plot of Capricorn One is built upon the violent attempts to cover-up this hoax when the word starts to leak out. NIXON'S PLUMBERS MEET THE BOYS WITH "THE RIGHT STUFF."

In The China Syndrome, a maverick TV cameraman (Michael Douglas) secretly videotapes a near accident at a nuclear power plant. As soon as he goes public about the existence of the tape and tries to get his exclusive footage on the Evening News, the plumbers start coming out of the woodwork and the cover-up is on. Because the power company is a major advertiser on the TV station for which the freelance cameraman was working when he shot the controversial tape, the initial showing of the tape is stalled. Because the power company is in the midst of licensing hearings for a new nuclear power plant, its executives order a full-scale cover-up which includes employee harassment, attempted murder and even putting back on-line a faulty power plant which threatens to go into nuclear meltdown at the slightest strain. The possible consequences of the cover-up in The China Syndrome make Watergate look like a group of six-year-olds trying to cover-up a foray into a cookie jar.

Of these three cover-up movies, Eyewitness is the weakest and the least metaphorically expressive. In fact, in terms of plot it is a real mess. Nobody ever really knows (or cares) why the Vietnamese importer is killed or what the Vietnam vet/building janitor (William Hurt) was an eyewitness to (if anything). The videotape which comes into play in the plot is neither part of the hoax which the dark powers wish to cover up (as in Capricorn One) nor of the event which occasions the cover-up (as in The China Syndrome) but is just a goofy TV News interview in which the janitor leads everyone to believe he has seen something because he wants a date with the pretty TV anchorwoman (Sigourney Weaver). The social metaphor of cover-up is at the heart of Eyewitness but the film's plot is so confused and the film's imagery so bungled that the audience never gets any sense whatsoever that the film has any social conscience or carries any historical message. The audience doesn't even know what is being covered up until the very end. As Hitchcock might have said: "What's the use of having a McGuffin if nobody knows what it is they don't care about."

Throughout the seventies, films exploited the Watergate affair metaphorically as a means of examining the Blow-Up theme of "nothing is ever what it seems to be" or the political themes of corporate dehumanization and cover-up. Two other important films, however, didn't turn Watergate into a metaphor at all. They dealt with it overtly. They either recreated it head-on in the form of slick and accurate docu-drama or satirized it so transparently that there was no mistaking it. All The President's Men (1976) and a witty British satire entitled Nasty Habits (1977) are the two films which (aside from a number of TV mini-series) deal with Watergate as Watergate and recreate reasonable facsimiles of the zany participants in Watergate from Richard Nixon and Henry Kissinger to the immortal "Deep Throat."

What is somewhat ironic about All The President's Men is that the drama and tension of that film comes not from its documentary-like presentation of the reality of the Watergate event and the real people involved but from its presentation of the reality of being an investigative reporter on a contemporary big-city newspaper. All The President's Men's audience ends up caring little about what Watergate meant or how it happened or what its effect on American society turned out to be. Instead, All The President's Men's audience finds itself caught up in a starkly realistic contemporary film noir detective story like Body Heat or Night Moves (1975) or The Late Show (1977). The audience finds itself much more involved with how Woodward (Robert Redford) and Bernstein (Dustin Hoffman) get their story or meet with their sources or track down their facts than with the meaning of the whole affair. All The President's Men turns out to be a well-made how-to movie for journalism majors rather than a real document of social history. It succeeds in portraying the inner workings of The Washington Post, but it reveals little about either the factual or metaphorical inner workings of the Watergate Affair.

Yet despite its failure to deal directly with its ostensible subject, All The President's Men does dramatize that Blow-Up theme of "nothing is ever what it seems to be." It shows, in almost documentary fashion, how Woodward and Bernstein (dubbed "Woodstein" by their editor) develop a reality out of collected fragments of factual information. Like the photographer in Blow-Up with his series of photos or Harry Caul in The Conversation with his spools of tape, "Woodstein" splice and mix snippets of information, cross-reference their sources, liberate and match quarantined financial records and follow up anonymous tips until the elusive reality of the Watergate cover-up starts to take shape. The only problem is that the film makes all that meticulous developing of reality take

shape as nothing more exciting than a series of expose
newspaper stories as if the real significance of Watergate
was to simply give dogged Woodward and ingenious
Bernstein something to keep them busy.

All The President's Men gets carried away with its
docu-drama realism and, as a result, loses sight of the
more complex social and historical reality which it
purportedly set out to examine. All The President's Men
ends up as just another newspaper movie because it
underestimates the complexity and metaphoricality of
contemporary social reality. All The President's Men ends
up treating Watergate as a mere headline rather than an
event destined not only to metaphorically represent the
erosion of American idealism but to actually change the
whole direction of American society.

All The President's Men failed because it took reality
for granted. Nasty Habits is equally entertaining and
equally empty because it laughs at reality without any
ironic edge on its laughter. Nasty Habits is based on
Muriel Spark's novel The Abbess of Crewe (1975). It is
set in a convent which, under a new Mother Superior
and her cabinet of wimpled advisors, becomes a
microcosmic version of Watergate. The Mother Superior
(Glenda Jackson) supervises the tape recording of
conversations and runs the convent with a Nixonian
paranoia. One of her advisors is a globe-trotting,
publicity-seeking, fund-raising, Kissinger-like nun with a
foreign accent (Melina Mercouri). Another is a nervous,
goofy, yes-man nun in John Dean spectacles (Sandy
Dennis). The satire gently recreates the political and
social motives of the Watergate affair within the
supposedly sacred confines of the convent.

Unfortunately, Nasty Habits' satire gets old awfully
quick. It only operates on one rather obvious level. It is
witty for a while until you get done identifying the
parallels to Watergate, but then there just isn't much of
anything left to do. As in All The President's Men, no
real metaphorical conclusions are drawn. No social theme
pokes up its messy head. The bugging really comes to
no more than simply a quaint thing to do in either a

nunnery or a White House.

The factual attempts to deal with the fragile, erasable, labyrinthine realities of the Watergate affair fail because they don't make the proper connection between the factual event, that event's effect upon society, and the established symbolic (or metaphoric) modes for expressing that relationship between history and society. Of all the late seventies films which attempt to make this connection, certainly the clearest descendant of Blow-Up and The Conversation is Brian DePalma's Blow-Out (1979). DePalma is Hollywood's resident film historian and rip-off expert and there is little doubt that Blow-Out is simply Blow-Up and The Conversation run through DePalma's celluloid cuisinart. In the central developing scene upon which Blow-Out pivots, both photographic images and taped sounds of the captured event are reproduced and synchronized and puzzled over. The structures of the three films are exactly the same. They move from the capturing of a real event by a machine (the lovers in the park with the camera, the lovers in the square with the microphones, the lovers in the car going into the river with both camera and microphones) to the pivotal developing scene to the attempts and total failures of the protagonists to involve themselves with the realities which they think they understand and feel that they can control. In other words, of all the Blow-up/Watergate movie offspring of the seventies, DePalma's Blow-Out is the most elaborate and the most deliberately derivative.

However, Blow-Out is also competently written with an ironic sense fully comparable to both Blow-Up and The Conversation. Its characters, settings and images are every bit as symbolically expressive as their counterparts in those two films from which it is derived. Its treatment of the "nothing is ever what it seems to be" theme, the theme of modern man's tenuous relationship with reality, is every bit as politically, philosophically and socially meaningful as it was in those two earlier films. Brian DePalma may not be the most original of American filmmakers, but when he makes an imitation he makes a first-rate imitation. He elaborates on the themes of his imitation: that is, he adds new dimensions to the old images; recasts and updates the characters; adds new touches and twists to the symbolic meanings in the images and themes. Blow-Out may only be an imitation of the two earlier masterpieces, but it is a thoughtful, very well executed one.

Blow-Out is the story of Jack Terry's (John Travolta) quest for the perfect scream. He works as the sound man at an independent movie studio in Philadelphia which specializes in soft-core porno horror movies. One night, while out recording wild sound for the studio's latest slice-n-dice, T-n-A extravaganza, he tape records an automobile accident. A speeding car blows out a tire, careens through a bridge railing and plummets into a river. Jack gets it all on "state-of-the-art" audio tape before he dives in and saves a girl from drowning in the submerged car.

But, at the hospital afterwards, nobody treats Jack like a hero. The police detective investigating the accident keeps Jack away from the TV people. Sally (Nancy Allen), the girl he saved, just wants to get out of the hospital as fast as she can, concussion or no concussion. Jack finds himself totally confused by the reality he has plunged into. As it turns out, the man who drowned in the car in which Sally was riding was Governor McRyan, a straight-arrow, law and order, shoo-in Candidate for the Presidency of the United States. It further turns out that Sally is really a hooker paid to set up the pristine Governor for some incriminating photographs taken by Manny Karp, a small-time pimp and hustler conveniently stationed beneath the bridge with his camera to record the accident. Thus, Jack Terry finds himself in the middle of a burgeoning political scandal.

Lawrence Henry, Governor McRyan's campaign manager, shows up at the hospital to engineer the cover-up. He pays off Sally the hooker and appeals to Jack's sympathy for the Governor's widow to convince him to forget about Sally's presence in the car. Jack balks at participating in the cover-up of the real facts of the accident. "That is the truth, isn't it?" Jack, still confused by the snowballing momentum of events, asks Henry. "What difference does that make to you?" Henry snarls. The rest of the film examines, even more cynically than did Blow-Up or The Conversation, how much (and finally how little) difference the truth of what happened, the truth about the nature of reality, does make.

This central event of Blow-Out is exactly what Watergate was: a political dirty trick run amok; a political cover-up with too many holes in it. Just as in the Watergate Affair, the key to reality, the truth of what really happened, is on the tapes. Just as was the case with those phony transmissions from the moon in Capricorn One, this cover-up in Blow-Out is a deliberate attempt to falsify reality, reshape reality for political profit. Except that Jack Terry won't let it go. Like the photographer in Blow-Up and Harry Caul in The Conversation, Jack collects his captured fragments of reality, assembles them, and, in a developing scene identical to those which appear in both Blow-Up and The Conversation, tries to interpret and understand the reality he has captured.

Blow-Out's developing scene combines the high-tech methods of capturing reality of both Blow-Up (the visual) and The Conversation (the audio). If The Conversation is Blow-Up for the ears, then Blow-Out is Blow-Up for both the eyes and ears. Jack, with his access to the porno studio's film and sound lab, takes Manny Karp's still photographs of the accident, blows them up, transfers them onto movie film then matches his taped sound of the accident to the film. In essence, he reconstructs reality on film with sound; he takes the separate fragments of reality and orders them to prove that the accident wasn't an accident at all, that there were two explosive sounds coming in close succession, a detonation or gun shot followed by the blow out of a tire.

Throughout this developing scene, counterpointed to

the still photos and the taped sounds, are close-up
images of the tapes and spools and heads which form a
naming of parts of the high-tech sound equipment used
for this reconstruction of that momentary reality of the
event. When the whole reality is developed and Jack has
made his sound movie of what he now believes to be a
murder, he flashes back in his mind, exactly as the
photographer did to the park and Harry Caul did to his
point of vantage in the sound truck parked by the
square, to his own position on the footbridge that night
recording and watching the car crash into the water. In
this flashback, again the individual images present a
close-up naming of parts of Jack's portable sound
equipment-- his shotgun mike, the volume and tone
guages on his shoulder-slung tape recorder. As the car
speeds into view across the way from his position on
the foot- bridge, Jack, by reflex, aims his shotgun mike
at the sound. Just as in the developing scene in Blow-
Up when the WOMAN, HAND RAISED ACCUSINGLY
still is illogically included in the sequence of shots thus
pointing the finger at the photographer as the real
"shooter" in the park, the images in Jack Terry's
flashback to the scene of the crime suggest that Jack
stands in the same position to the reality he is trying to
capture as did the photographer in Blow-Up. The
shotgun mike in Jack's hand comes up like a gun barrel
aimed at the car as if he shot out the tire. Only Jack
knows if the tire blew out or was shot out. In trying to
prove what happened, Jack becomes responsible for the
whole event, becomes the guilty party simply because he
wants to tamper with reality. He is a Peeping Tom who
fails to keep his distance from the scene he has crept
up on.

     In fact, the whole film is shot through windows.
These Peeping Tom point of view scenes move from the
scenes in the porno film being screened at the very
beginning of Blow-Out to Jack electronically
eavesdropping on the two lovers below him on the
footbridge to a whole succession of scenes shot through
the windows of cars, of buildings, of phone booths, of

subway trains. Jack's guilt lies in the fact that he is a
practicing resident in a voyeur's world, a world where
people do not dare to involve themselves directly with
reality. When he rejects his Peeping Tom role in the
voyeur's world, tries to penetrate the barrier between his
ineffectuality and the reality on the other side of the
window-pane, he commits the original sin. In the crash
scene, when he dives down underwater to save Sally, he
must actually dredge up a rock from the river floor and
smash the car window which separates him from the
drowning girl. The photographer in Blow-Up, Harry Caul
in The Conversation and Jack Terry all commit a crime
against the laws of life in the anti-existential seventies
world; they break down the barriers and try to involve
themselves with reality. All of them must take
responsibility for their subversive act and all of them
must psychologically pay for their crime. In fact, like
Harry Caul (and like Jake Gittes in Chinatown), Jack
Terry has also had an earlier brush with reality in his
practice of the wiretapping profession. Ironically, neither
Harry nor Jack learned their lesson well enough the first
time around. They both come back for another bout
with reality and they both get floored.

Just as at the end of The Conversation where Harry
Caul sits in utter defeat amidst the ruins of his world, a
similar scene in Blow-Out demonstrates the fragility of
Jack Terry's attempt to establish his existential identity
by capturing and ordering reality on tape. In the sound
room of the porno movie studio, Jack has meticulously
labeled and filed all the sounds of reality he has
collected over the years. Whereas the developing scene
represents man's attempt to order reality as a means of
defining his relation to it, this particular scene (like the
final scene in The Conversation) is a scene of chaos
which represents the ungovernableness of reality, its
potential for grinding human identity into useless
fragments. Jack Terry returns to the sound room and as
he enters the camera takes his subjective point of view.
The room has been trashed. Every one of his tapes has
been erased. Strands of useless tape hang like tangled

vines from the walls, coil on the floor like nests of dead snakes. This scene is truly Watergate run amok. The intruders didn't just deftly erase the crucial soundtrack as Richard Nixon did with his notorious eighteen minutes, they erased Jack Terry's whole life's work, his whole collection of realities, his identity. By the end of Blow-Out, this scene of chaos (which is reprised as a backdrop for the final credits) comes to represent Jack's defeat in his quixotic jousting with reality. By the end of Blow-Out, Jack Terry's humanity has been totally erased and he has lost all touch with reality. His existence is simply the illusions he dubs onto the screen in his porno movies. Sally's real dying scream is no more than a usable sound which can make a movie image seem real.

Jack's cohort in Blow-Out, Sally the hooker, is much like Jack in her ambiguous relationship with reality. She is also a make-up expert, as adept at creating facial illusions as Jack is at creating sound illusions. Sally delivers the single most important thematic line in the film, a line which defines the tension that exists between illusion and reality and identifies reality as the more exciting and desirable state of existence. After Jack tells Sally about his past work as a wiretapping expert for the crime commission, Sally exclaims: "Movies are great, but, like, this is, like, real life on the streets." The irony of Sally's outburst on the side of "real life on the streets" is that by the end of Blow-Out both she and Jack learn that involvement with reality can be very dangerous.

Jack's real sin is against Sally. He uses her in his quest to capture and control reality just as he uses his microphones and tape decks. He turns her into a machine, a walking wiretap. He destroys her humanity and loses her to a reality that he simply can't control. She ends up a victim caught in the crossfire of man's attempt to subdue reality just as Evelyn Mulwray (Faye Dunaway) does at the end of Roman Polanski's China-town (1974). The climactic scene of Blow-Out is set in a citadel of American history, a Liberty Day celebration at

Penn's Landing with fireworks and flags and stirring
music all of which masks a psychopathic murderer's
strangling of Sally while Jack struggles desperately to
prevent it and fails. It is a scene of grim reality graphically choking off the American dream. It is a scene
which demonstrates the helplessness of man to understand
and control reality no matter how many high-tech
machines he has at his disposal. Jack has wired Sally for
sound but all he gets is her scream as she is murdered.
Sally simply becomes a scream, as if she never was real,
as if her existence has just been erased and all that is
left is her final scream on a piece of mechanical tape.

In the ironic and cynical coda scene of Blow-Out
the audience hears Sally's final scream once again. Jack
has used it on the soundtrack of his porno movie. He
has become the "shooter," a participant in the murder
of Sally. He has turned her into a pornographic object,
taken one piece of her existence and exploited it as the
pornographer cuts pieces off of the woman's anatomy by
filming them in graphic close-up. The sleazy producer
of Jack's movie defined the pornographic mentality
earlier in Blow-Out when he said, "I didn't hire her for
her scream, I hired her for her tits." By the end of
Blow-Out, Jack Terry has completed his quest for the
perfect scream but in the process he has learned that
man can never understand or control the dangerous
protean reality of the seventies world. Blow-Out ends
very much the way The Parallax View and Chinatown
end, with a disturbing coda defining the cynicism,
corruption and despair of man in the seventies world.

5.   CHINATOWN: A   WORLD   OF   INSCRUTABLE
                         REALITY
5.   CHINATOWN: A   WORLD   OF   INSCRUTABLE
                         REALITY
"You can't always tell what's goin' on."

Roman Polanski's and Robert Towne's Chinatown
(1974) is the quintessential 1970s movie. It embodies all
of the major seventies themes: corporate conspiracy, the
inability to decipher and understand reality, the failure
of the existential impulse. It metaphorically comments
upon Watergate and the American failure in foreign
(oriental?) neighborhoods. It is the ultimate Blow-Up
offspring because, like all the Blow-Up movies, it
focuses on a man's attempt to see reality, to grasp and
interpret the surface reality of his world, and it
chronicles man's failure to find meaning in the reality
he sees. It portrays reality as so multi-layered that man
can never see and understand with any clarity. Reality
becomes a fractured mirror, shards which reflect only
distorted fragments of a society complicated far beyond
any individual's ability to understand, shards of reality
which can be dangerous, can cut.

I
The Chinatown World

What Chinatown is about, its central theme and that
theme's non-resolution, is stated in the two most
important lines in the film. Appropriately, neither of
those lines is delivered by the film's central character,
Jake Gittes (Jack Nicholson), who, like the photographer
in Blow-Up, spends the whole film trying to capture and
interpret reality. Noah Cross (John Huston), the powerful

and dangerous corporate conspirator of this seventies film
set in a metaphorical thirties world, delivers the line
which tips off the whole thematic construct of the
movie: "You may think you know what you're dealing
with, but believe me you don't."   This line, delivered
with all the portentousness that John Huston's gravelly
voice can muster, is both a warning and a statement of
the obvious.   The line makes Jake laugh a knowing yet
incredibly naive laugh, the laugh of a man who thinks
he has heard it all before, has everything under control.
"Why is that funny?"   Cross asks in the voice of a man
used to being heeded not chuckled at.   "That's what the
District Attorney used to tell me in Chinatown," Jake
answers, sobering somewhat and wiping his mouth with
his napkin as if to clear that last sour word away.
Small scraps of innuendo about Jake's unsuccessful past
in Chinatown have already been dropped by the time
that Cross delivers his important line.   Jake's reaction
signals that he is not the kind of man who is good at
heeding warnings.   But Cross's line is not just a warning
to Jake, it is also a broad warning to the audience that
they oughtn't to feel so secure with this nice period
piece genre movie they are so comfortably settling into,
that they oughtn't to watch this movie with the same
smugness that Jake Gittes has just shown, that this movie
is stalking bigger thematic game than film noir usually
goes after.

The second important line-- "Forget it, Jake, it's
Chinatown." --is the last line of the film.   It is
delivered in a stunned whisper in the middle of a
neon-lit, forever foreign Chinatown street, by Walsh (Joe
Mantell), Jake's detective agency operative.   It is a line
that takes the whole movie and wraps it in one envel-
oping metaphor.   In fact, it is perhaps the one
metaphor from any film of the seventies which embodies
that whole decade. If in the sixties "we all live[d] in a
yellow submarine" as the Beatles put it, in the seventies
we all lived in a Chinatown world where nothing was
ever what it seemed, where reality was so layered and
complicated that it could never be grasped, where any

natural impulses were doomed to failure, where innocence was but a naive dream in the face of the sinister and brutal nightmare known as reality.

Walsh delivers that last line as consolation to Jake. "Forget it, there was nothing you could do," is Walsh's sentiment. But that last line also implies all of the futility and hopelessness of the film and of the seventies decade. In the course of the movie, "Chinatown" has become more than just a sinister L.A. neighborhood. It has become a way of life, a mode of thinking, a symbol of all that is opaque, sinister, and ultimately, dangerous. "Chinatown" becomes a symbol of the futility of attempting to grasp and interpret reality. Those who listened to what was left of the Watergate tapes, who sat in throughout those interminable Watergate hearings, must have felt the same frustration with grasping reality that Jake felt in Chinatown. Those who examined their conscience about Vietnam, either incountry or at home, faced the same problem of understanding what they were doing that Jake faced in Chinatown.

Walsh also delivers that last line as a prescription for Jake's sanity. You have to "forget it" he says, because if you don't back off, leave it go, resign yourself to the fact that you live in a world that you are simply unable to understand, you will go crazy. Walsh's advice is depressing and, coming as the last word in the film, gives terminal punctuation to man's existential failure in the real world, stresses that Jake, like Sisyphus, has pushed his rock just as far as he can. Walsh's advice to Jake is sound. It is the advice that every Vietnam veteran gave himself as he flew eastward across the Pacific after thirteen months of chasing the most elusive of realities. The only problem with that "forget it" advice is that it is much easier given than taken. Forgetting, especially forgetting a death in which you are intimately involved, is not an easy thing to do. Whether it occurs as part of a night scene in Chinatown or a war in Vietnam, reality is a difficult thing to avoid, an impossible thing to grasp, and an even harder thing to forget.

Therefore, the last line of <u>Chinatown</u> captures the whole spirit and mood of the film and of the country at the time the film appeared. "Chinatown" is our 1970s world where nothing is ever what it seems, where everyone's vision is always flawed, where any attempt to understand is doomed, where survival is dependent upon disengagement, walking away, forgetting.

In the last scene of <u>Chinatown</u>, after Walsh delivers that last line, Jake turns and walks away into the melancholy neon night. Walking away is his only option. Accepting reality without presuming to understand it is his only remaining alternative (as it turned out to be America's only option in Vietnam). But the most frightening lesson that lurks in that last line is that not only does existential action, moral questing after truth, intellectual struggle to see and understand reality, do no good whatsoever, it actually does harm, tells us things about ourselves that it would be better we didn't see because they can only ruin our lives, our outlooks, our perceptions of society. What good did Jake Gittes's pursuit of reality do? It caused a death. What good did protesting the Vietnam war do? What good did turning over the rock of Watergate do? The deaths in Vietnam continued. The nation's whole image of itself, post-Watergate, was changed for the worse. Would things have been any different if America had just done "as little as possible" as Jake Gittes advises himself too late in that last scene of <u>Chinatown</u>? Would the war have stopped sooner? Would the country have thought better of itself? Forget it, America, it's Chinatown.

"Chinatown": a metaphor for man's relation to reality; a metaphor for America's relation to its own history in the seventies. For 95% of the movie, the audience wonders where the title came from, wonders why the film wasn't titled <u>The Death of the Water Commissioner</u> or <u>Fathers and Daughters</u> or <u>Citizen Cross</u> or <u>The Big Landgrab</u>. There are intimations throughout that the movie's title means something, but the movie doesn't physically enter Chinatown until its last five

minutes. As is often the case with metaphors,
"Chinatown" does lurk enigmatically around the edges of
the movie's plot. The audience receives pieces in the
puzzle but becomes frustrated at its lack of success in
putting those pieces together.

The irony of this puzzle quality of Chinatown is the
same irony which develops out of the puzzle quality of
Orson Welles' Citizen Kane: all through both films we
receive the pieces to the puzzle. At the end of Citizen
Kane, Thompson (Everett Sloane), the intrepid newsreel
reporter, looks at the piles of puzzle pieces amidst all
the piled artifacts of Kane's life, throws up his hands
and walks away without ever finding out what "Rosebud"
really meant. At the end of Chinatown, Jake also walks
away, no wiser, understanding no more than he did when
he first began. "Rosebud" and "Chinatown" are both
metaphors for the mysteriousness of reality.

In many ways, "Chinatown" is the kind of metaphor that Kurtz becomes in both Conrad's Heart of
Darkness and Coppola's Apocalypse Now. It is a
metaphor kept in reserve, a metaphor waiting at the end
of a long, twisted, arduous journey. Just as Marlow and
Captain Willard (Martin Sheen) collect, piece by piece,
glimpses of Kurtz by means of which they construct (in
their imaginations) a ghostly shimmering image of the
man, so also does the audience of Chinatown collect
fragments of that title metaphor. Allusions to
"Chinatown" glide like ghosts through the film but
never is the metaphor made flesh until that final scene.

Though Chinatown is offstage throughout the film,
both visual and verbal allusions keep the mysterious title
in the audience's consciousness. Those allusions begin
with Jake's regaling of Duffy (Bruce Glover) and Walsh
with his long, involved joke about how Chinamen make
love. As Jake tells the joke, unbeknownst to him, Mrs.
Evelyn Mulwray (Faye Dunaway) listens in over his
shoulder. The scene ironically foreshadows the final
scene in Chinatown where Duffy, Walsh, Jake and Mrs.
Mulwray all come together again. In the joke scene as
in the final scene, Jake thinks he is in control, waves

off Duffy and Walsh's warnings and plunges blindly
ahead with his joke only to be embarrassed. This is a
trivial revelation scene which prefigures the later
revelation scenes where much greater stakes are on the
table and Jake is similarly deceived as to the amount of
understanding he possesses and the degree of control he
is exercising.

The second title allusion is visual. Khan, the
Mulwray's Chinese butler opens the door of the Mulwray
mansion for Jake and then slams it in his face. Khan,
like the title metaphor, always waits in the background
of the film. After gaining admittance, Jake waits in the
garden for Mrs. Mulwray and makes small talk with the
Japanese gardener who is working on Mr. Mulwray's
artificial salt water tide pool. The wordplay of this
seemingly throwaway conversation is ingenious. Pulling
seaweed and commenting on the salt water (a valuable
piece of plot information which will be put to use
later in the unravelling of the mystery), the oriental gardener complains, "Bad for glass. Bad for glass." Jake
mockingly repeats the man's mispronunciation: "Yeah,
bad for the glass." Ironically, the key to the whole
mystery of Hollis Mulwray's death, a pair of glasses, is
already submerged and waiting to be found in the tide
pool.

After these preliminary title allusions, "Chinatown"
takes on metaphorical character in verbal exchanges
which link it to Jake's past, image it as a dangerous and
sinister place, and define it as a world in which reality
is different, ungraspable, hard to control. Three specific
scenes delve progressively deeper into Jake's Chinatown
past. These three scenes define the meaning of the title
metaphor and prepare for the final scene of the film.

First, Jake meets his old partner Lou Escobar (Perry
Lopez) from the days working as an investigator for the
District Attorney. Escobar, police lieutenant in charge
of the Hollis Mulwray murder case, is less than happy to
see his old partner. "How'd you get past the guard?"
Escobar barks. Jake's talent for wordplay surfaces once
again: "To tell you the truth, I lied." Walking along

the reservoir toward the corpse of the Water Commissioner, Jake pursues his old less-than-friendly acquaintance with Escobar: "You still bustin' Chinamen for spittin' in the laundry?" "I'm outa Chinatown," Escobar snaps back. The linkage of the thus far enigmatic title to Jake's past is established.

Soon after, Jake meets Noah Cross at the Albacore Club and once again Jake's past in Chinatown dominates the conversation. Like the tracking two-shot with Escobar at the reservoir, this whole scene is composed as a long two-shot to emphasize how the dialogue is guarded and yet pointed like two cautious fencers testing one another:

> CROSS: This Escobar, you know him?
> JAKE: Oh yeah.
> CROSS: Where from?
> JAKE: We used to work together in Chinatown.

The title's link to Jake's past from that earlier scene is quickly reestablished but this exchange goes on to give that past its primary definition.

> CROSS: Mr. Gitts . . .
> JAKE: Gittes (correcting Cross's pronunciation)
> CROSS: You may think you know what you're dealing with, but believe me you don't.
> JAKE: (Laughs)
> CROSS: Why is that funny?
> JAKE: That's what the District Attorney used to tell me in Chinatown.

Cross's line sets the whole "reality is never what it seems" theme of the film. Jake's linking of that theme to the Chinatown of his past gives the first real definition to the title metaphor of the movie. "Chinatown" is more than just a sinister foreign neighborhood. "Chinatown" stands for a state of mind, an insecure paranoid vision of the world, an internal feeling that you can never really know what is going on. Even Cross's mispronunciation of Jake's name and Jake's correction of the error points to the instability of reality. As simple a fact as a man's name can take different forms for different people.

This whole scene at the Albacore Club is done as one long two-shot because Cross and Jake are fencing. Shooting the scene as alternating close-ups and reaction shots would not have worked. Not only would there have been little to work with in the way of exterior reactions due to the guardedness of the characters but the subtle interplay of both men simultaneously trying to guage each other and hide from each other would have been lost. Thus, the first shadowy definition is given to the title metaphor. "Chinatown" is a covert, mysterious place where reality constantly changes and is impossible to grasp.

A third scene gives much fuller definition to the metaphorical significance of that offstage, still mysterious "Chinatown" of the film's title. After a narrow escape, Evelyn Mulwray takes Jake home with her. Finally secure inside her mansion, the same cautious fencing that governed Jake's conversation with her father rules their conversation. Jake and Evelyn are moments away from becoming lovers, yet their exchange is guarded. Both hold things back. They are not ready to fully reveal themselves. Once again, the scene is shot primarily in two-shot as a means of capturing the nervousness and the guardedness of these two characters. Their dialogue moves from innuendo to inflection to irony to Jake's teetering on the edge of truthfulness yet never tumbling over:

> JAKE: Maid's night off?
> MRS. MULWRAY: I gave everybody the night off.
> JAKE: Easy, It's an innocent question.
> MRS. MULWRAY: No question from you is

innocent.
JAKE: This hasn't happened to me for a
           long time.
MRS. MULWRAY: When was the last time?
JAKE: Why?
MRS. MULWRAY: (coyly) It was an inno-
           cent question.
JAKE: In Chinatown.
MRS. MULWRAY: What were you doing
           there?
JAKE: As little as possible.

The scene, the dialogue exchange, once again brings
up Jake's past in Chinatown, but Evelyn's question
("What were you doing there?") is much more probing
than any question Jake has been asked about his
Chinatown past thus far.   His answer ("As little as
possible.") seems to be an evasion, but really isn't at
all.   It is a straightforward statement of the smart cop's
approach to survival in Chinatown.   Unfortunately, as
the film progresses, the audience more and more comes
to suspect that Jake Gittes is not as smart a cop as he
thinks he is.   The skeptical wordplay with "innocent" in
this exchange is also quite revealing.   As the film
progresses, the "innocence" of the characters escalates.
As one revelation follows another, Jake finds out just
how "innocent" he is in the ways of the Chinatown
world.   And, in the final scenes of the film, as Jake and
Evelyn attempt to protect Katherine's innocence, it
becomes clearer and clearer that their whole attempt is
futile.   Visual images of "innocence" become ironic
comments on the death of innocence in a world so
devious and corrupt.
     After their initial exchange, Jake and Evelyn go to
bed and, after making love, their conversation picks up
again.   The camera moves into its two-shot mode as
once again these two characters, who have just been as
intimate as two people can be, try to dodge and parry
each other and the reality of their own pasts.

MRS. MULWRAY: You don't like to talk about the past.

JAKE: I'm tired.

MRS. MULWRAY: You don't like to talk about the past.

JAKE: It bothers everybody who works there. It's just bad luck.

MRS. MULWRAY: Where?

JAKE: Chinatown.

MRS. MULWRAY: Why?

JAKE: You can't always tell what's goin' on.

MRS. MULWRAY: Why was it bad luck?

JAKE: I was trying to keep someone from getting hurt and I ended up making sure she was hurt.

MRS. MULWRAY: _Cherchez la femme_?

JAKE: What?

MRS. MULWRAY: Was there a woman involved?

JAKE: Of course.

MRS. MULWRAY: My father is a very dangerous man. You don't know how dangerous, how crazy.

JAKE: You trying to tell me he might be behind all this?

They ask everything of each other, yet they give no real answers. Jake tells of his past in Chinatown in a series of vague generalizations. Evelyn warns of her father's evil power yet avoids spelling it out. But despite their intentional guardedness, we have learned that Chinatown is truly a dangerous place where the expected never happens and helping can be hurting. Good intentions count for nothing in Chinatown because reality is blind to the intentions which touch it off, is as likely to explode in the face of an innocent child as in the face of a ruthless killer. But the real tragedy which lurks in the background of all of these conversations is that once the "Chinatown" reality explodes there is no way to protect the innocent bystanders.

As controlling metaphor of the film, "Chinatown" embodies the offstage inscrutability and unpredictable explosiveness of reality. Jake Gittes looks at the world through the chivalric lenses of the hard-boiled detective's code, but all he sees is . . . "Chinatown." In the last brief preparatory vignette before the film physically enters the world of its title metaphor, Jake, on the phone talking to Walsh, watches through a bamboo window shade as Evelyn and Katherine put their bags in that big white Packard and pull away, destination Chinatown. As they pull away, Jake gives Walsh the address:

> JAKE: You and Duffy meet me at 1712 Alameda.
> WALSH: Jesus, that's in Chinatown, isn't it?
> JAKE: (resigned, doomed) I know where it is.

Jake is scared of returning to Chinatown because he can see its threat if only through a glass darkly (a bamboo shade dimly), yet he has no choice. He must try to protect his charges even if it means returning to his own personal heart of darkness. The audience and Jake have waited the whole film to find out what the title means, have picked up and put down all the pieces in the puzzle. At last, the time has come to enter the metaphor.

Finally, the movie actually goes to Chinatown. Chinatown, where Jake used to work. Chinatown, where he lost a past love. Chinatown, where nothing is ever what it seems. Chinatown, where survival demands that you do as little as possible. Chinatown, where all is tangled, involvement dangerous, disengagement absolutely necessary. Chinatown, a metaphor for America in the seventies.

The title metaphor of Chinatown and the scenes which prepare that metaphor underline the major themes of the film (and of America in the decade of Vietnam

and Watergate): the danger of trying to penetrate inscrutable reality; the illusion of control in the modern
world; the death of innocence. These central themes are
presented throughout <u>Chinatown</u> by means of different
visual and verbal techniques.

First and foremost, <u>Chinatown</u> is an imagistic film.
Roman Polanski and Robert Towne weave elaborate patterns of visual and verbal imagery through the whole
fabric of the film. The film's metaphors are presented
by means of accumulating images which form meaningful
motifs which define the central themes. In <u>Chinatown</u>,
no detail in the frame is too small, no object in the
background too insignificant, no line a throwaway.
Everything contributes to the film's meaning.

Secondly, <u>Chinatown</u> achieves thematic impact
through visual allusion to past classic films such as
<u>Citizen Kane</u>, <u>Blow-Up</u>, <u>The Big Sleep</u> and <u>The Lady
From Shanghai</u>, its most influential genre ancestor.
Thirdly, its visual techniques-- principally its deep focus
composition and deep focus lighting, its use of
perspective to create tunnels of meaningful focus within
frame, its use of consistent camera point of view to
define the relationship of audience to images --support
the themes of the film. Fourthly, its tightly written
script employs verbal irony to comment upon the visual
imaging of theme.

Lastly, a meticulous lattice of prefiguration makes
this film move from scene to scene with a feeling of
connection and unity. This structural unity not only
encourages the audience to constantly remember earlier
scenes and connect, but also encourages them to come
back to the theater for a second look at the intimate
connection and relation of every scene of the film to
every other scene.

II
Flawed Sight

In plot, <u>Chinatown</u> is about the manner in which
the unraveling of the secrets of men's private lives

inevitably leads to the exposing of men's complex public
affairs. In Chinatown a private puzzle of tangled sexual
relationships leads Jake Gittes to the discovery of a
complex public corporate conspiracy to divert valuable
water from the city of Los Angeles to a real estate
development in the San Fernando Valley. As Jake
collects the puzzle pieces and attempts to assemble
them, he struggles to see what the whole image looks
like, but all he can manage is its vague outline.

   Chinatown is about the attempt to grasp and define
the submerged reality of the time and place by
collecting and analyzing all the separate surface realities
which can be found. Like Blow-Up, Chinatown is a
movie about seeing. Seeing clearly, seeing beneath the
surface, seeing the connections between private sexual
evil and public corporate evil.

   The theme of seeing takes a number of different
forms in Chinatown. An eloquent imagery of eyes and
seeing and lenses and photography accumulates.
Concepts involving the ways of seeing, the obstacles to
seeing, the limitations of sight are embedded in the
visual techniques which Polanski chooses for the
presentation of his images. Those images express themselves by means of deep focus composition and lighting,
by means of perspective, by means of consistent camera
point of view. Through the accumulation of images
into motifs and the expressive techniques by which the
images are presented, Polanski and Towne draw the
audience into the theme of seeing and link that theme
to the theme of inscrutable reality embodied in the
film's title metaphor.

   The theme of seeing begins in the opening scene of
Chinatown. The first images which appear on the screen
are blown-up photographs of Curly's (Burt Young) wife
enjoying nature with another man. As in Blow-Up,
photography in Chinatown becomes symbolic of man's
attempt to capture reality as well as man's accompanying
inability to interpret and understand the reality which
he has supposedly captured. In this symbolic motif of
photography, Chinatown becomes the ultimate Blow-Up

movie and points to the similar ironic use of the imagery of photography in the major Vietnam films of the end of the decade.

In The Deer Hunter, for example, the huge blown-up photos of the incredibly clean-cut Michael, Steven and Nick hang over the wedding hall. But those photos are already out of date. Michael, Steven and Nick will be so changed by Vietnam that those photos will never again have any relevance in their lives. The closest anyone ever comes to articulating the nature of reality in The Deer Hunter is when Michael (Robert DeNiro) holds up a single bullet and declares, "This is this!" He is immediately laughed at. Stash (John Cazale) scoffs, "What the fuck does that mean? This is this." Michael is ridiculed for making his futile, inarticulate attempt to define reality.

In Apocalypse Now, Captain Willard (Martin Sheen) pores over the shadowy photographs of Colonel Walter Kurtz (Marlon Brando) attempting to get some hold on the man. When Willard finally reaches Kurtz's stronghold, the first person to greet him is a crazy hippie photographer (Dennis Hopper) with a whole platoon of cameras slung around his neck (Coppola's modern version of Conrad's Harlequin man from Heart of Darkness but also perhaps Sean Flynn who disappeared into Cambodia in 1968 as recounted in Michael Herr's Dispatches). This photojournalist is supposedly trying to catch the reality of the war on film but his mind, if his words are any indication, already resides somewhere on the outer reaches of some distant star system.

In both The Deer Hunter and Apocalypse Now as was certainly the case in Blow-Up, photography attempts to capture reality for analysis. The problem is that the pictures never really define reality clearly. No matter how talented the photographer, the attempt to blow-up reality so that it can be understood is always futile. Jake's bumbling uses of photography in Chinatown make this futility abundantly clear. The imagery of photography in Chinatown forms a continuum with the other

major films of the decade which examine the theme of
the inscrutability of reality.

Jake spends most of the early moments of the film
trying to freeze and analyze reality by means of
photographs. He moves from studying the pictures of
Curly's wife to Walsh's pictures of Mulwray and Cross
arguing outside The Pig and Whistle to taking pictures
of Hollis Mulwray (Darrell Zwerling) and Katherine
rowing in the Echo Park lagoon and embracing at the
El Macondo apartments. As Jake perches on the El
Macondo roof focusing in on what he supposes are the
illicit lovers below, Polanski's camera switches to a
reverse angle and the reflections of Mulwray and
Katherine are caught in the lens of Jake's camera. The
inclusion of that reverse angle just at that moment is an
ironic comment on Jake's cavalier dependence on the
camera to freeze reality for him. That reverse angle
offers a photograph of the photographer caught in the
midst of his photography. Its ironic comment is that
photographs can turn on the photographer, can come
back to haunt the photographer, as in fact that very
photograph reflected in Jake's lens actually does. Jake
is simply too smug about the ability to interpet reality
through photographs. What Jake doesn't realize is that
his photos, taken from the spy's distance, can only
capture the surface of reality. They are only "facts"
which don't tell the whole "truth." Once again, even
with photographic evidence in hand, nothing is ever
what it seems.

How badly Jake misinterprets his El Macondo
photographs is revealed later when he finds out that
Katherine is not Mulwray's illicit lover but rather their
relation is much more tangled and layered than any
photograph could ever comprehend. Jake's dependence
on his camera is very much like Harry Caul's
dependence on his tape recording machines in The Conversation. With "state of the art" accuracy, both spies
capture versions of the reality they stalk, but for all
their technology they still cannot fully understand the
reality they think they have captured.

Photography is one way by which Jake attempts to see and interpret reality, but the theme of eyes and seeing is much more complex and allusive and takes other forms in <u>Chinatown</u>. Objects, visual details, even the key elements in the mystery plot itself form an imagery of eyes and seeing which is constructed and resolved in exactly the same manner as is the parallel theme of inscrutable reality. Just as that theme of "you may think you know what you're dealing with, but believe me you really don't" and "you can't always tell what's goin' on" is presented in a few key scenes of verbal exchange, so also is the imagery of eyes and vision defined in a crucial preparatory scene. Just as that theme of inscrutable reality is resolved (or inscrutably unresolved) in the film's last scene and last line, so also is the imagery of eyes and vision culminated in that same final scene.

The single preparatory scene which tips off the importance of all the imagery of eyes and seeing which has been accumulating throughout the film occurs in Evelyn Mulwray's bathroom as she administers to Jake's much abused nose. Once again, as was the Albacore Club scene with Noah Cross, this whole scene is shot in a tight two-shot in order to catch that probing/evasion mood which dominates all the major two-shot composed scenes. Evelyn Mulwray is swabbing Jake's nose when he looks into her eye and is startled:

MRS. MULWRAY: What's wrong?
JAKE: Your eye.   There's something black
           in the green part of your eye.
MRS. MULWRAY: It's a flaw in the iris.
JAKE: A flaw?
MRS. MULWRAY: It's sort of a birthmark.

Polanski and Towne bring this whole seduction scene to a dead stop to focus attention on this one small detail. Evelyn's tragic flaw?   Not really.   She is the one character who does see things clearly, who seems to understand all the tangled relationships. No, if anything,

Jake, looking into her eye, is only seeing the reflection
of his own flawed vision. He is the one who has failed
in every one of his attempts to grasp and control the
reality of the world around him.

What this key exchange does is draw attention to all
the eye imagery which has come before and alert us to
the mounting importance of this imagistic theme for the
scenes which follow. Remember the glass eye of the
camera lens catching the reflection of Hollis and
Katherine from atop the roof of the El Macondo and
how flawed its vision turned out to be? Remember the
magnifying glass that Jake finds in Mulwray's desk drawer
as he surreptitiously searches the office? Remember the
single eye of the fish on the Albacore Club flag and
the dead eye of the fish on Noah Cross's plate?
Remember Jake climbing out of his car after smashing
into a tree in the orange groves, his broken sunglasses
sitting twisted and askew across his already damaged nose
with only one black lens left intact? There are three
separate scenes of people in fleeing cars being shot at in
Chinatown and each is immediately followed by an
image of a flawed eye. After Jake and Mrs. Mulwray
flee the gunmen at the Mar Vista rest home, Jake first
notices the flaw in Evelyn's eye; the second such scene
is in the orange groves; the third is the final scene of
the film.

After Jake notices the flaw in Evelyn's eye, other
images of flawed sight surface. Jake breaks the lens on
the Packard's right rear taillight and follows that flawed
eye through the dark night in pursuit of the reality he
is trying to understand. Jake, finally back at his flat,
stares into his own blank tired eyes in the mirror. Ida
Sessions' wide dead eyes stare emptily up at her kitchen
ceiling. Curly's unfaithful wife opens the door and her
full black eye greets Jake. Jake finds a pair of broken
bifocal eyeglasses in Hollis Mulwray's tide pool and they
prove to be the key piece of evidence leading to
Mulwray's murderer. All of these images of eyes and
flawed sight accumulate throughout Chinatown in
preparation for the shocking irony of the final scene.

Evelyn Mulwray, the only one who has seen reality for what it really is, ends up with the most flawed sight of all. Her flawed vision rests in the mistake that while seeing the reality clearly she still believes that she can understand it, control it, change it.

In the final scene of the film, in one last desperate attempt to shelter Katherine from reality, Evelyn Mulwray drags Katherine into that big white Packard and flees down a neon-lit Chinatown street. Jake's hands are cuffed. There is nothing he can do when Loach (Dick Bakalyan), Lou Escobar's assistant, pulls a gun and fires off two wild shots at the fleeing white car. Down the street, the white Packard slows and rolls to a halt as its horn sounds a drawn-out mournful wail.

All of the visual and verbal images of eyes and flawed sight which appeared earlier in the film come home to roost (with ironic overtones) in this final scene. The horn moans relentlessly as Escobar and Loach, Jake and Duffy and Walsh, and Noah Cross run toward the car. Katherine's screams pierce the night as the horn wails on. That horn's mournful wail doesn't stop until Escobar pulls Evelyn's head off of the steering wheel. That head lolls to the side revealing Evelyn's face and in one brief shocking image all the previous images of eyes and flawed sight are united and defined. The flaw in Evelyn's eye, her birthmark, comes true. The ominous prediction of Jake's one black sunglass lens from the orange grove scene comes true. When Evelyn's head lolls sideways, the theme of the futility of trying to see is visually stated in an image so clear, so shocking, so eloquent, that its irony causes everyone from Escobar to Jake to the audience to recoil from its impact. Loach's wild bullet has entered through the back of Evelyn Mulwray's head and exited through her flawed eye. As her head lolls sideways, the black hole where her flawed eye had been gapes like the barrel of a gun leveled on the audience and fires off its single deadly imagistic shot, compresses all of the previous eye imagery into one shocking bullet of definition. It is an image of the emptiness of man's romantic impulse to see, to understand, to control the reality of the world in which he lives. That black empty socket says that in a "Chinatown" world man can never hope to see clearly, never hope to understand, in fact, as Jake advised the phony Mrs. Mulwray in the very first scene: "Do you know the expression 'Let sleeping dogs lie?' You're better off not knowing."

Other aspects of this final scene in that Chinatown street have also been meticulously prefigured earlier. The scene is an instant replay of Evelyn and Jake's earlier successful escape from the Mar Vista Nursing Home-- white car speeding away into the night, wild gunshots --with the single ironic exception that this time Loach the cop, supposed guardian of law and order, proves a better shot than were the threatening thugs. Evelyn has been able to deal with evil, stay one step ahead of it, but, ironically, it is well-intentioned good that does her in at the end. Good intentions are nothing more than romantic illusions in the "Chinatown" world. The final lesson that Jake learns is that good intentions can be more destructive than evil intentions.

One other specific detail of this final scene is an eloquent ironic commentary on Jake's attempt to see and understand reality. In an earlier scene, after Jake has followed the broken lens of Evelyn's white Packard through the night and spied on her and Katherine through a window of the safe house, he waits in the front seat of her parked car to confront her with his interpretation of the truth. It is another of those sustained two-shot scenes of probing and evasion and lies and misunderstandings. Evelyn gets into the front seat and is startled when she sees Jake sitting there. When she realizes it is him, her head falls forward in relief and inadvertently blows the horn. It is seemingly just a brief bit of business in the midst of a complex verbal exchange. However, in the final scene, that small detail from the earlier scene, that inadvertent blowing of the horn, makes its ironic return. Evelyn's head blows the horn again in that final scene and that horn's steady

mournful wail acts as a signal that Jake's attempt to
untangle all of the relationships of this "Chinatown"
world is futile.   The relentless wail of that horn is a
ghost's last scream against a world and a reality so
hostile that man should never presume to attempt to
penetrate it.

Chinatown's imagistic patterns of eyes, flawed sight
and photography are much more sinister than the same
images as they appeared in Antonioni's Blow-Up.   In
both films, the more you blow up reality and try to
interpret it, the more distorted and confusing it gets.   In
both films, after realizing that their attempts to capture
and understand reality are futile, the protagonists both
can only walk away.   But Chinatown's representation of
this contemporary dilemma is much more violent and
dark and hopeless.   The photographer in Blow-Up
doesn't even know in the end if the murder he thinks
he witnessed really happened.   Since he realizes that
possibly all of reality may exist only in his imagination,
he can blithely pick up the imaginary tennis ball and
lob it back into life's imaginary game.   Jake cannot
walk so blithely away.   He has looked a real death
right in its empty eye and, despite Walsh's advice, he
will not be able to forget it, ever.

III
Polanski's Camera Point of View

Chinatown's two major themes of "inscrutable reality"
and "flawed sight" are visually supported by three
aspects of Polanski's technique: the employment of a
consistent camera point of view; the use of deep focus
composition with emphasis upon tunneled perspective;
and the chiaroscuro lighting of his scenes with emphasis
upon the constant counterpoint of glaring white sunlight
to deep shadow.

The camera point of view which Polanski chooses
for Chinatown is consistent and especially appropriate in
terms of the relationship it defines between the
audience, the central character and the world of the

film. Polanski uses few subjective first-person point of
view shots of the sort that Robert Montgomery used to
make the audience become Phillip Marlowe in The Lady
in the Lake (1946). Instead, Polanski shoots his film
from a consistent third-person limited point of view.
The audience becomes the detached observer who
watches from a point of vantage quite close yet not a
part of the action. Polanski accomplishes this point of
view by consistently shooting Jake Gittes in over-the-
shoulder deep focus. As Jake moves through the world
of the film, follows his leads, spies on his suspect, the
camera is always just one step back looking over his
shoulder, observing yet detached.

This emphasis upon the over-the-shoulder shot rather
than the subjective point of view shot is appropriate in
terms of Jake's role in real life, his "meeteeyay" as a
detective. He is a keyhole peeper, a professional
middleman/spy for clients who want to keep a distance.
In Chinatown, the audience becomes that slightly distanced client. Jake is always between the audience and the
world of the film. He leads the audience through that
world, gets involved in that world as the audience's
surrogate. The audience identifies closely with him
because the audience is every bit as limited as he is in
its understanding of what it sees. Yet, all of the safety
and smugness that the audience feels as it looks over
his shoulder builds a false sense of security. The
audience's detachment generates the same false sense of
knowing what is going on that Jake nurtures throughout.
What is ironic about this over-the-shoulder point of view
which dominates so many of the scenes is that
invariably, as the audience is looking over Jake's
shoulder, Jake is looking through some other obstacle
which separates him from the reality that both he and
the audience are trying to observe. The audience is
constantly watching the keyhole peeper peep through the
keyhole. In other words, Jake is always between the
audience and the action while there is always some
other barrier between Jake and the action. Thus, the
audience is actually twice removed from reality.

Something, a camera lens, a windshield, drawn curtains, a
pulled bamboo blind, always stands between Jake and
reality.   He spends the whole movie looking through
things, attempting to penetrate the barrier between him
and the world.   The audience spends the whole movie
looking over his shoulder through the barriers and
having no more success than he.

This third person limited point of view is established
for the first time in the Los Angeles County Courthouse
hearing room as the audience reads about Seabiscuit in
the Racing Record over Jake's shoulder. By far the most
consistent expression of the third person point of view
takes the form of a shot which repeats so often in the
film that it forms a visual motif.   In this shot, the
camera is placed in the back seat of Jake's car and
shoots over Jake's shoulder, through the windshield to
finally, in the deep focus background, reveal the object
of both Jake's and the audience's attention.   The
audience first sees this "over-the-shoulder/windshield"
shot as Jake follows Hollis Mulwray to the ocean. The
first shot of this sequence is through the windshield of
Jake's car.   Then a shot exactly similar in composition
yet with a final twist is intercut as Jake turns and
parks.   The camera moves outside the car and in the
foreground of the frame Jake's elbow and hand rest on
the door frame of the car's open window.   As the
audience looks over his shoulder, Jake's hand adjusts the
side mirror and picks up the reflection of Mulwray
parking and leaving his car.   The next shot repeats the
same "Jake-barrier-object of surviellance" composition.
Jake squats in a corrugated drain pipe which serves as a
shield between him and Mulwray on the rocks below.
Jake is always in the foreground of these deep focus
point of view shots.

The "over-the-shoulder/windshield" shot or variations
on it dominate the rest of Chinatown. In the boat on
the lagoon in Echo Park, Jake, cigarette and camera in
hand, lounges with his back to us looking through his
camera, first at Duffy and then at Mulwray and
Katherine rowing past them in another boat. Later, after

seeing the notation "OAK PASS RES. - 7 channels"
scrawled on the back of one of the engineering blue-
prints in Mulwray's office, Jake drives to the reservoir in
broad daylight with the top down. The audience rides
along in the back seat and sees the uniformed cops
guarding the gate through the windshield as Jake drives
up. Later that night, in the same shot through the car's
windshield, Jake returns to the reservoir to have a look
around. When Jake gets out of the car, the audience
stays right on his shoulder as he walks along the chain
link fence. By his repeated use of this shot, Polanski
has managed to further extend the composition of the
deep focus frame. Instead of just three planes of image
within the frame, this shot's repetition suggests that there
are really four planes: The background where the
object of surveillance waits; the middleground occupied
by the barrier which the spy must penetrate; the
foreground where Jake, the spy, or at least part of him
(the back of a neck, a shoulder, an elbow), is always
present; and the fore-foreground where the audience
strains to look over Jake's shoulder. Another important
mid-seventies film, Martin Scorsese's Taxi Driver (1976),
takes its cue from Chinatown and chooses the same
"over-the-shoulder/windshield," four-plane, deep focus,
point of view for its presentation of Travis Bickle
(Robert DeNiro) the New York taxi driver's relationship
to his world. Like Jake, Travis is always an observer
watching the world move and smoke and neon shimmer
through the windshield of his cab. The audience of
Taxi Driver also occupies that fourth plane, that
fore-foreground, as if they were perpetual passengers in
the back seat of Travis Bickle's cab.
    This same technique is used for Jake's entrance to
the Albacore Club, the chase through the orange groves
before he crashes his car, and the night scene where he
follows the broken taillight of Mrs. Mulwray's big
Packard to the safe house. The reason this
"over-the-shoulder/windshield" point of view shot motif
is so important is that it visually supports the themes of
"inscrutable reality" and "flawed sight."

This point of view shot does two things. First, it consistently redefines Jake's role as spy, separated from reality, forced to always look through barriers which stand between him and the truth. Despite the barriers which always separate him and distort his view, Jake continues to foster the illusion that he understands what he sees, that he is in control of reality, when, in fact, the things he sees are never what they seem.

The second way in which this visual approach to presenting the narrative supports those two central themes is that by repeatedly forcing the audience to look over Jake's shoulder, by accustoming the audience to a consistent viewpoint, Polanski gives the audience a definite identity closely linked to that of Jake yet also detached and perhaps more suspicious, more skeptical. Because the audience receives exactly the same information as Jake and analyzes that information from the same point of view, the audience always misinterprets reality in the same way that Jake does. Yet, because the audience is still detached, it comes as a double shock when the audience finds itself no more capable than Jake of penetrating reality or seeing clearly. Polanski violates this third-person limited point of view only once. When Jake is telling the Chinaman joke is the only time Polanski gives the audience more information than he gives to Jake. The consistent point of view of Chinatown makes the audience a full participant in the experience of the central themes of the film. Like Jake's, the audience's sight is flawed and, as it is for Jake, reality is inscrutable.

Of all the scenes in the film in which it appears, the most masterful and expressive use of the over-the-shoulder, four-plane, deep focus, point of view technique occurs in the scene in which Jake follows Evelyn Mulwray to the safe house where she is keeping Katherine incognito. The scene begins with a low angle establishing shot from across the street. The shot presents a modest house with a modest yard which is gently banked up to the front porch. The angle and point of view of the shot is that of a man keeping watch while crouching or kneeling behind a low bush or fire hydrant on the grass strip across the street from the house. Mrs. Mulwray's big white Packard rolls down the street, pulls into the banked driveway next to the house and parks. As she gets out of her car and enters the house, the huge front fender and hood of Jake's car, engine already cut, rolls to a stop in the extreme foreground of the frame completely blocking the point of view.

At this point, Polanski's use of camera point of view as a means of involving the audience as detectives on their own stakeouts is most clearly defined. Instead of cutting to a different angle, perhaps showing Jake getting out of his car, the camera maintains its connection with that fourth plane, that fore-foreground. Instead of a cut to another angle, the camera slowly raises up until it can see over the hood of the parked car as if that man kneeling behind the bush had crept closer and stood up to get a better view of Jake getting out of the car, crossing the street and darting up the driveway to check out the house.

When the cut finally does come, it is to the exact same position looking over Jake's shoulder and tracking with him as he moves along the side of the house. When he stops to look in the window, the classic relationship of the four planes of Chinatown's recurrent point of view is reestablished. The shot looks over Jake's shoulder through the gauzy-curtained window at Khan, the sinister Chinese butler, and Mrs. Mulwray forcing pills on a helpless, disturbed young girl. Polanski's moving camera is us. It does exactly what we would do if a car hood obscured our view at a critical moment. It stands up to get a better look. It follows along out of curiosity. It spies through the window and it sees everything just as Jake sees it. It views the action from behind a barrier. It takes in the information. It thinks it knows what it is seeing, but it doesn't at all. It misinterprets the reality in the same way that Jake does. What this brilliant use of point of view visually states underlines the two central themes again: the barriers to

The Films of the Seventies

reality are never as easy to penetrate as we may think they are; our sight is not something that we can always trust.

In a later scene, this point of view shot over Jake's shoulder offers a textbook demonstration of how to set a _film_ _noir_ mood. The shot is from the darkness of the verandah at the Mulwray mansion down through the dim tunnel of the entry hall and out through the open front door to the waiting night. At first the audience doesn't realize that this is an over-the-shoulder shot, but then a puff of wispy cigarette smoke floats across the foreground of the scene. Seeing that smoke, the audience realizes that even though Jake is not seen within the frame he is still there, even though the audience can't sight over his shoulder or down the length of his arm as he holds his binoculars or adjusts his car's side-view mirror he is still there, leaning in the verandah doorway, looking down through the hall to the open front door, smoking while he waits. When the front fender of Noah Cross's car pulls across the open front door in the deep background, the object of Jake's waiting in the shadows is announced and the audience, by purely visual means, has been put on full alert for a crucial confrontation scene.

Remember the front fender of Jake's car pulling across the foreground in that night scene at the safe house? In this night scene at the Mulwray home, the same prop, a car, is used again but its function in frame is reversed. Instead of obscuring the full foreground and thus forcing the audience to react by raising up and looking over that fender, it fills the empty waiting background forcing the audience to connect Jake waiting in the darkness at one end of the house to Cross's car filling the darkness at the other end of the house. What Polanski has done with this shot is expand the deep focus planes of the frame even further, adding a fifth plane to the four planes of the over-the-shoulder shot which he has employed throughout the film. The car fills the waiting background, the tunnel of the entry hall waits to be crossed in the middleground, the smoke from Jake's cigarette hangs in the foreground, Jake waits just offscreen in the close fore-foreground and the audience tenses in the before-foreground waiting to see what is going to happen. The whole atmosphere of anticipation has been brilliantly established by means of Polanski's total extension of the point of view possibilities of deep focus.

When Cross does finally cross the middle-ground, Jake steps up into the frame and the audience also moves up one plane to look over Jake's shoulder as he confronts Cross with the incriminating evidence. After all of this visual preparation, when the confrontation scene finally begins, it verbally leaps immediately to the thematic concept of "flawed sight."

> JAKE: I've got something I've gotta show you, Mr. Cross.
> CROSS: What is it?
> JAKE: An obituary column. Can you see alright in this light?
> CROSS: I'm fine. I've got these (taking out his bifocals).

What this scene reveals is that Jake is just as much a Director as Polanski is. Jake has chosen his setting, has set his lighting, for the purpose of making Cross reveal himself. Jake's politeness aims only at matching the damning evidence of the broken bifocals fished from the backyard tidepool to the new bifocals of the murderer. In this scene, the visual point of view prepares for the verbal revelation.

IV
Deep Focus Composition

Polanski's use of deep focus composition in Chinatown is not, however, restricted only to the establishing of the film's audience participatory point of view. Deep focus composition, with its ability to juxtapose and connect objects and actions which occur in different sectors of the frame, is one of <u>Chinatown</u>'s major visual means of revealing theme. For example, in a number of scenes Polanski employs two of the three planes of his deep focus frame, usually the foreground and the middleground, to play the action of the scene and to reveal the theme of the scene, whether it be the theme of "inscrutable reality" or the theme of "flawed sight." While presenting the action and themes in his foreground and middleground, Polanski reserves the background plane as a symbolic space in which objects or action can offer commentary upon what is going on in the other two planes of the frame. Remember the stuffed birds of prey hovering in the background of the conversation between Marion Crane (Janet Leigh) and Norman Bates (Anthony Perkins) in Hitchcock's <u>Psycho</u> (1962)? Remember little Charlie Kane playing happily in the snow outside the window in the background while inside the boarding house Ma and Pa Kane are selling him to Banker Thatcher? Polanski uses deep focus for the same effect. The subject of the verbal exchange or the physical tension of the foreground and middleground planes can be commented upon symbolically or, by means of juxtaposition, ironically by the object(s) or action(s) which are simultaneously visible in the background of the scene. Through this method of constantly connecting the three separate planes of his film frame, Polanski employs deep focus composition with a painterly sensitivity and effect.

The deep focus composition of one particularly eloquent scene late in <u>Chinatown</u> demonstrates this ability of Polanski's compositional sense to present thematic ideas by visually relating the objects, characters and actions within the separate planes of his frame. The scene begins as Jake drives up to the white safe house in the glaring sunlight. Mrs. Mulwray's big white Packard is parked out in front. Jake storms past Evelyn and Khan into the house spitting harsh words in the Chinese butler's own language as he goes. All the signs of an imminent hasty departure are in evidence in the front room-- suitcases and hatboxes sit on the floor

ready to be loaded into the Packard --as Jake confronts
Mrs. Mulwray. He shows her the twisted spectacles fished
out of Hollis's backyard tide pool and runs his own
scenario of the death of her husband past her: jealous
wife struggles with unfaithful husband by tide pool as
husband's young mistress looks on; husband stumbles,
hits head, accidentally drowns; young woman goes
hysterical and is put on ice until the Water
Commissioner's death blows over. Jake finishes his
imaginary scenario with a line which becomes
tremendously ironic in the light of the revelations which
follow: "There's no time to be shocked by the truth,"
he bullies Mrs. Mulwray. The ironies: First, Jake is still
nowhere near the "truth" of the matter and reality is
still inscrutable no matter how confidently he spins out
his version (nothing is ever what it seems); secondly, the
person who, as the scene unfolds, will be forced to take
time to be "shocked" by the "truth" is not Evelyn
Mulwray but Jake himself.

When Mrs. Mulwray doesn't react to Jake's scenario,
he phones Escobar to come and pick her up. That
elicits the violent reaction from Evelyn Mulwray which
propels the scene into its central revelation of the "real"
yet inscrutable "truth":

> JAKE: Who is she? And don't give me
>   that crap about your sister because
>   you don't have a sister.
> MRS. MULWRAY: (nervous, eyes darting, clearly
>   desperate, as if she is making up
>   some new lie) She's my daughter.
> JAKE: (slaps her hard across the face)
> MRS. MULWRAY: She's my sister.
> JAKE: (slaps her hard again)
> MRS. MULWRAY: My sister. (almost ca-
>   tatonic as if the words are
>   ricocheting out of her on their own
>   impetus with each slap)
> JAKE: (one last slap) I want the truth.
> MRS. MULWRAY: She's my daughter . . . and

my sister.

The ricochets finally die and Jake decides to take the time to be shocked. He stares at her. She taunts him quietly: "My father and I. Understand? Or is it too tough for you?" Her words slap him in the face. Her words underline the irony of how incredibly slow to see the truth Jake is. Even when he sees the reality, he doesn't want to believe it, immediately tries to change it. "He raped you?" Jake tries to impose a reality he can deal with upon what really happened, tries to give her the opportunity to deny the terrible truth that has forced him to take the time to be shocked. Unable to recast the reality, with her whole body, her whole being, shaking, she answers "no" to his question with a doomed shake of her head.

The scene is beautifully written by Robert Towne and played electrifyingly by Nicholson and Dunaway. Jake's hand smashes out of the foreground into her face as she numbly pleads with him from the middleground to understand, as she kneels below him in the middleground to make her terrible confession. The scene is written and played brilliantly, but the crowning touch of genius lies in Polanski's deep focus visual composition.

All through the scene, as Jake and Mrs. Mulwray confront each other in the foreground and middleground, a single image, a still object, which comments both symbolically and ironically upon the whole action of the scene, looks on from the background. Immediately behind and to the left of Mrs. Mulwray, never out of frame or focus, sits, on top of a hatbox, a young girl's yellow broad-brimmed summer straw hat with a white streamer. It is the most self-contained, lyrical and complex symbolic object in a film filled with exactly this kind of visual symbolic details. Sitting there, unmoving, behind Evelyn Mulwray's distraught shoulder, it comments on all that is being revealed in this tense confessional scene. As Evelyn Mulwray confesses her original sin, her loss of innocence, her ultimate violation of moral taboo, this symbol of girlish summer innocence sits in the background like the paradisal past which Jake has just realized (and Evelyn already knows) can never be regained.

The hat is Katherine's. It represents Katherine's innocence which Evelyn Mulwray is fighting a losing battle to preserve. But the hat also represents Evelyn's old lost innocence and Jake's newly lost innocence. When Evelyn shocks him with the "truth" from her past, Jake is forced to finally give up any romantic idealism, any illusion that he can actually understand or control the realities of his "Chinatown" world. The hat wryly comments that the innocent are the most alien of all the foreigners who traverse "Chinatown."

This relation of the symbolic object in the background to the action taking place in the more prominent planes of the scene is the kind of masterful compositional touch one expects to see in a painting by Cézanne or Degas. Throughout this whole scene Jake functions as a combination confessor and badgering psychiatrist to Evelyn who is tangled in the web of her own family romance. She makes Jake see, but he is too shocked to either absolve her or cure her. And, all the time, the hat sits in the background, mocking their separateness, their naivete in thinking they could ever really understand or see, its bright summer innocence directly counterpointed to Evelyn's black mourning dress. That summer hat, so clean and out of place amidst the scene's squalid revelations, represents all that is ungraspable in the world of Chinatown: Jake and Evelyn's past; reality; the ability to see clearly and understand. They live in a world where seeing and understanding no longer belong as viable possibilities just as that virginal summer hat doesn't belong in this scene of ugly sexual self-realization.

The hat only appears once in the whole film yet it triggers shock waves of thematic exposition which spread to other scenes where similar losses of innocence or attempts to protect innocence occur. For example, it justifies the opening scene of the film, a scene that

doesn't seem to have any purpose other than to
introduce Jake as a private detective who doesn't mind
doing the dirtiest types of marital showing and telling.
But after the hat defines the theme of the loss of
innocence, that opening scene makes sense as a
conscious foreshadowing of one of the film's major
concerns. That opening scene immediately shows Curly's
(Burt Young) loss of innocence as he reacts to the
picture Jake has taken of his wife copulating with
another man. The creamy summerness of the hat also
corresponds to Jake's role in that opening scene. The
first time we see Jake, he is photographed in soft light
wearing a cream-colored summer suit. Curly is grubby
and disheveled and deranged over the dirty pictures of
his wife while Jake is clean and fresh and relaxed,
seemingly the picture of a man clear of conscience and
pure in innocence. Yet, the pictures in Curly's hand
clearly signal the superficiality of that innocence.

Those thematic waves generated by the summer hat
symbol also ripple across the last scene in Chinatown.
After Jake receives his final shock of the film, looks
into the gaping empty socket of Evelyn's shot-out eye,
the camera slowly moves up off of the corpse as if
drawn by the hysterical screams, looking for their source.
The screams are Katherine's. She has just seen her
mother, sister, step-mother, protector, shot to death
before her eyes. When the camera locates Katherine,
shooting over Jake's shoulder across the barrier of the
open car, Noah Cross is moaning "Oh Lord, Oh Lord,"
and trying to cover Katherine's eyes, trying to shield her
from reality, trying to maintain her innocence. But it
can't be done. Certainly not by Noah Cross. She
shakes him off. She has already seen the terrible reality
and he can't silence her hysterical screams. The whole
theme of the loss of innocence as defined in the hat
scene culminates in this ironic bit of business between
Cross and Katherine. How absurd for the incestuous
father to try to protect the innocence of the daughter
born from the incestuous act. The whole concept is as
ridiculous as inviting the fox into the hen house.

There has never been any possibility for innocence in
the Chinatown world. Katherine can never be innocent
because she is the result of the film's original sin, the
hidden incest which has caused the major flaw in
everyone's sight and has prevented everyone from seeing
clearly the inscrutable reality of their world. The world
of Chinatown was fallen before Jake ever met Evelyn
Mulwray or Katherine or Noah Cross. No matter how
hard Jake tries, it will always be too late to cover his
eyes and block out the reality of that original loss of
innocence which sends him walking away in shock
through that empty Chinatown night.

V

Chinatown and Citizen Kane

The symbolic use of deep focus photography as in
the "summer hat" scene is the most prominent of a
number of ways in which Chinatown shows its direct
descendence from Orson Welles' Citizen Kane (1941).
Both films certainly share the central theme of the
inscrutable nature of reality. The detectives in both
films, Thompson the newsreel reporter in Citizen Kane
and Jake, are uncured victims of flawed sight
throughout. Both films gain their momentum from piece
by piece examinations of the loss of innocence; in both
films the detectives pursue an innocence doomed before
it even started to be lost.

Chinatown is not only thematically similar to Citizen
Kane, but is also the most visually imaginative film
since Citizen Kane. It signals its kinship to Welles'
masterpiece in some very specific ways. The audience is
visually instructed to start thinking Kane quite early in
Chinatown. In the barber shop, the front page of a
customer's newspaper trumpets the L.A. Water
Commissioner "Love Nest" scandal complete with
heart-bordered pictures of the illicit lovers caught in the
act by Jake Gittes, private eye. That newspaper insert
looks exactly like the front page of the newspaper
expose of Charles Foster Kane's secret "Love Nest"

planted by Boss Jim Gettys.

But the influence of Welles upon Polanski, of
Citizen Kane upon Chinatown, is much more complex
and interesting than simply direct allusion en hommage.
The central themes of Chinatown, "inscrutable reality"
and "flawed sight," are the same problems Thompson
wrestles with in Citizen Kane. Both Thompson and Jake
are detectives trying to put together the pieces of very
complex puzzles, trying to understand the reality of the
world they are constructing. Both detectives are similarly
handicapped in their attempt to complete the puzzle of
reality. Pieces are missing. Reality remains fragmented.
In Citizen Kane, the puzzle of reality is represented by
an explicit symbolic motif which appears throughout the
final third of the film and culminates when Thompson,
in Kane's warehouse, picks up a single piece of one of
Susan Alexander Kane's puzzles and then tosses it away
in defeat. The pile of puzzle fragments that Thompson
tosses his symbolic puzzle piece upon is just like the
pile of discarded objects burning in the furnace that the
sled is tossed upon in the final shot. The pieces to
the puzzle of reality are always available, but because of
flawed sight the detectives rarely succeed in putting them
together. "Rosebud," the one piece that could have
made all of the relativistic fragments which Thompson
collects come together, is always within his grasp yet he
can't see it. Thus, because that one piece eludes him,
none of the others fit together either. Kane finally
becomes just a pile of puzzle pieces, a warehouse of
crates, a string of contradictory images on newsreel film,
fragments of reality which Thompson has collected yet
never understands.

There is no overt puzzle imagery in Chinatown but
Jake's pursuit of a mystery which keeps changing shape,
a reality which he can never piece together, directly
parallels Thompson's stalking of Kane and "Rosebud" in
the maze of relativist reality which his sources create.
Jake works hard (as Thompson did) to collect and fit
the pieces, but (sharing Thompson's fate) Jake always
comes up with one piece missing. As Jake himself says,

"You don't always know what's goin' on" and as Noah
Cross warns, "You may think you know what you're
dealing with, but believe me you don't."

Polanski imitates the narrative technique of Citizen
Kane through his title metaphor. "Chinatown" is this
film's "Rosebud." "Chinatown" is that mysterious,
enigmatic world which seems always there yet is never
entered physically until the final moments of the film.
The word "Chinatown" becomes the ultimate verbal
symbol for the quicksilver inscrutability of reality.
Walsh's "it's Chinatown," the last words of the film, are
exactly like "Rosebud," the first and last word of Citizen
Kane. Both are "codas" or end symbols which capture
the essence of the world, the theme, the meaning of the
films. Both "codas" send the audience out of the theater holding the missing puzzle piece which the detectives
were never quite able to put their hands on. The irony
of both "codas" is that even though the missing piece
has been found, the reality still remains relativistic.
Each member of the audience can use that puzzle piece
in his own way, look at the completed puzzle from her
own point of view.

"Rosebud" is the symbol of the original sin that
money committed against young Charlie Kane. At one
point in Welles' film, Kane tells Thatcher, "You know,
if I hadn't had so much money, I might have been a
really great man." The last word of Citizen Kane,
"Rosebud," reiterates that original sin, represents the
love, normality and identity that Kane had to give up in
order to serve his money. Walsh's "it's Chinatown" represents acknowledgment of a similar original sin which
hovers over Polanski's movie. The original sin of incest
thrusts all of these characters into this Chinatown world
of surfaces and sub-surfaces, of deceit and illusion, of
flawed sight and the loss of innocence.

Neither "Rosebud" nor "Chinatown" are important in
their physical realities; that is, as a real object (the sled)
or a real place (Alameda Street). Like Kane's "Rosebud,"
Jake's "Chinatown" is both a real place and a symbolic
state of mind, a word symbol the purpose of which is

to trigger a kaliedoscope of meanings: memories of the past, hopes for the future, intuitions of the missing pieces in one's personal puzzle. These "coda" word symbols are the keys to meaning in both films because both films meticulously explore man's inability to see and understand the meaning of reality. Yet, neither word symbol makes reality clearer or more graspable. Both films build on the same theme and end on the same note.

The influence of Welles is, however, most evident in the totality of Polanski's deep focus conception of Chinatown. In fact, with his conscious extension of the planes of the frame, Polanski's use of deep focus actually attempts to go beyond Citizen Kane. One interesting use of deep focus which Welles exploited obsessively also plays an important visual role in Chinatown. Optic imagery, the use of mirrors, reflections, refractions and distortions, is a stream of visual imagery dear to Orson Welles' heart especially in his early films: Citizen Kane, The Magnificent Ambersons (1942) and The Lady From Shanghai (1948).

Welles was obsessed with mirrors and his optic imagery always represents the theme of the relativity and fragmentariness of reality. His use of mirrors to multiply the image of a single person or object became a variation of his deep focus conception of reality existing on several different planes of the frame simultaneously. That same use of mirrors to create multiple images underscored Welles relativist concept of narrative structure and characterization, especially in Citizen Kane.

For example, one pivotal deep focus optic image defines the whole narrative structure of Citizen Kane as well as the film's central theme. After trashing his wife's bedroom, Kane exits, walks by his servants who stand aside with mouths agape at the sounds of violence erupting from behind the closed door, turns right and walks between two wide floor-to-ceiling mirrors. As Kane walks between the mirrors, his reflection is multiplied into infinity. Kane after Kane after Kane after Kane walks by infinitely down into the receding depths of the mirror. What this single image says is what Thompson finally comes to understand after scouring the country in pursuit of "Rosebud" and Kane. There are many different Kanes. Kane consists of thousands of shards of reality, pieces in a puzzle, infinite images marching in a mirror. He cannot be grasped or understood.

Again, in The Lady From Shanghai, mirrors play a similar thematic role. The final scene of The Lady From Shanghai takes place in a hall of mirrors. Michael O'Hara's (Welles) three sharks all carrying guns move in and out of the mirrors, divide and distort and multiply. But the guns are the interesting factor in this mirror scene. Only by means of the guns which violently shatter the false mirror images can illusion be separated from reality. As the guns fire and the mirrors crash into shards of illusion, Michael realizes that only by this process of elimination can he find the true realities, the murderers whom he must trick into eliminating each other if he is to survive. Every time a gun fires, the gunman has no idea if he is firing at a real person or at a mirror image. Illusion and reality have become confused, multiplied. The only way to cope is random violence devoid of direction or understanding.

Similar streams of optic imagery appear in Chinatown. As did the photographer in Antonioni's Blow-Up, whenever Jake looks closely into something he invariably sees his own reflection superimposed upon the illusive meaning which he is trying to grasp. As the photographer in Blow-Up studies the pictures shot in the park, his eye keeps returning to that one picture in which the woman points her finger accusingly at him. In Chinatown, as Jake scans his world for pieces of the reality he is trying to understand, he keeps seeing unexpected mirror reflections of himself. In the office of Yelburton (John Hillerman), the Assistant Water Commissioner, Jake studies the pictures on the walls and sees his own reflection. Moments later, waiting for Mrs. Mulwray, Jake sees something in the tide pool, starts to fish for it, sees his own reflection just as he is interrupted by Mrs. Mulwray's arrival. Each time Jake tries to look into things to find meaning, his own reflection stares back at him. These two "himself surprised" mirror scenes signal an existential thread running through Jake's attempts to see and understand reality. One of the inscrutable realities his flawed eyes must try to see is himself.

Those two "himself surprised" mirror scenes prefigure the only scene in which Jake directly confronts himself. After his long day and night in the orange groves, at the nursing home, in Mrs. Mulwray's bed and following the white Packard to the safe house, Jake returns to his apartment for a shower and a little shuteye. He stares at himself in the mirror then walks away in defeat from the confrontation. His own reality is just as inscrutable as all the other realities he has been trying to grasp. He is no closer to understanding himself than he is to understanding his Chinatown world. Thus, though the mirror imageries take a different form-- Welles = multiple images; Polanski = superimposed reflections --they both work to the same thematic effect. Both signal that the images of reality are illusive reflections on the surface of a mirror, one-dimensional, ungraspable, inscrutable.

One other aspect of Welles' technique, his expressive use of light and shadow, is also evident as an influence upon Chinatown and, as did the Wellesian optic imagery, serves as a striking visual means of revealing the themes of "flawed sight" and "inscrutable reality." As Welles did, Polanski meticulously lights his film to express theme. In Citizen Kane and The Magnificent Ambersons, Welles repeatedly uses shadows on faces to undercut the believability of a character's words or actions and to foreshadow a threat to the speaking character's fortunes.

For example, in two scenes from Citizen Kane, Welles' lighting throws shadows over the faces of the speaker at the moment of truth. The result is the visual undercutting of that verbal truth. As Charles

Foster Kane leans down to sign his "Declaration of Principles," that highminded statement of moral responsibility which will appear on the front page of his newspaper, a shadow falls completely across his face. That shadow intimates that Kane will not live up to his "Declaration of Principles," that they are empty words which reality will ultimately obscure as that shadow obscures Kane's face. The same shadow of untruth falls across Kane's face later when his wife and Boss Jim Gettys confront him in Susan Alexander's apartment. The whole scene is played in shadow. As Kane's voice protests his innocence, describes the love the people have for him, the sinister shadows obscure his face, turn him into a hopeless voice crying in the darkness as the others stand in the light of reality. In The Magnificent Ambersons, Welles uses lighting to structure and define mood. In the first half of the film the Amberson mansion is brightly lit and teeming with people and the exterior scenes glare with the bright whiteness of the clean snow. However, in the second half of the film as the Amberson fortunes fall, the mansion empties and subsides into shadows and the pure whiteness of the snow is replaced by the soot-filtered light of the growing factory town.

VI
Polanski's Symbolic Chiaroscuro

Polanski lights Chinatown with the same clear thematic intention that Welles lavished on Citizen Kane and The Magnificent Ambersons. Whereas Welles uses shadows to comment upon the actions and intentions of his characters, often throwing shadows across their faces at precisely the crucial moment, Polanski uses shadow in a very different way. In Chinatown, the lighting serves as a means of contrast which visually delineates the oppositions of planes within the deep focus frame. Repeatedly, Polanski contrasts the foreground of his frame shrouded in deep shadow to the starkly-lit (usually by bright sunlight), even glaring, background of the image. When this opposition between shadow and sunlight, darkness and the clear light of day, occurs in Chinatown, it usually takes one of two forms, both ironic. Either the character in the scene (usually Jake Gittes) passes from shadow into light (thus signaling some progress toward revelation or clarification) or the camera composes an image in which blocks of shadow and blocks of glaring sunlight vie for possession of the action of the frame, form clear visual oppositions through which the action of the frame must pass. In the first case, the use of the lighting opposition and Jake's passage from shadow to sunlight is highly ironic because, no matter how good or how bad the light, Jake never seems quite capable of seeing the truth in his "Chinatown" world.

Jake's movement between the opposed realms of shadow and glaring sunlight begins when he first visits the Mulwray mansion. His car approaches down the deeply shaded residential street, trees overhanging create a tunnel effect, and turns left into the wide driveway. As the car moves out of the shade of the overhanging trees and into the bright sunlight, the camera pans to the white stucco hacienda on the hill, the first of a number of stark white houses (the safe house, Curly's house in Pedro) which glare in the California sunlight. The whole film follows Jake as he moves from shadow into light, night into day, trying to see and understand. But the problem isn't in the lighting of his world; the problem is in his flawed sight. When Jake enters the Mulwray mansion on that first occasion, he passes out of the sunlight into the cool, dark shade of the entranceway through which he must pass before again emerging into the rectangle of glaring white sunlight formed by the open passage onto the verandah. All of the scenes in the Mulwray mansion take place within the context of geometric blocks of light.

Every time Jake enters the Mulwray house, he plunges into that reception area of darkness while the glaring sunlight through the rectangular verandah doorway in the background persistently mocks his sightlessness.   If

anything, the framed light in the background of this
composition deepens the darkness of the foreground.
Like the windshields and windows and lenses and
fences, the shadows present an obstacle which Jake must
look through to find the truth. The ironic problem is
that even in the brightest sunlight the truth still may
not emerge from its self-imposed shadow. Later, when
Jake returns to the mansion in search of Mrs. Mulwray,
he again plunges into the shadows of the entranceway
where the Chinese maid glides like a ghost covering the
furniture in preparation for closing up the house. But
Jake doesn't linger in the cool darkness. He barges
through it into the glaring sunlight of the backyard
where he actually gains a measure of revelation. He
finds in the tide pool the broken bifocal spectacles
which prove later to be the key to solving the murder
of Hollis Mulwray.

The compositional opposition of blocks of shadow
to blocks of glaring white light is complemented by the
film's color imagery as expressed in the costuming and
the settings. Chinatown is a chessboard of a movie
where whites and blacks consistently oppose each other.
At the mansion, after Jake has traversed the blocks of
shadow and sunlight, he waits for Mrs. Mulwray in the
yard by the tide pool; she suddenly appears from her
morning ride dressed in a glaring white riding outfit
which exactly matches the glaring block of sunlight
through the doorway backing the deep shadows of the
house. Her riding outfit is too clean, whiter than any
white should be, as is the white Packard car she drives,
the white silk bathrobe she wears in her bedroom and
the white safe house where she keeps Katherine
incognito. Soon after, wearing a white suit, in Lou
Escobar's office at the police station, she is notified of
her husband's death.

But at other times, Evelyn Mulwray shrouds herself in
black, her mourning. First, in the restaurant she wears a
black dress with white pearls and, as the scene ends, she
starkly contrasts to the white of the big Packard waiting
in the background. Next, in Jake's office, she wears a

high-necked black dress topped with a black beret.
When she comes to get him after his losing
confrontation in the orange groves, she wears another
black suit, black hat, white pearls outfit. As Jake does,
she constantly moves between the blocks of black and
white, between the powers of darkness and the ironic
light which is too white to be real or true.

In other scenes the costuming or the setting itself
maintains this black/white opposition. The white suit
of the man with the knife (Roman Polanski), "the
midget" as Jake calls him, glares against the black night
as he fires at the white Packard fleeing down the
driveway of the Mar Vista Nursing Home, a scene which
in both its choreography and its lighting directly foreshadows the final scene in which another man fires a
pistol in the night at the same fleeing white car. The
exterior settings-- the Mulwray hacienda, the safe house,
Curly's house in San Pedro --are all photographed in
exactly the same way. All white, they are shot in bright
sunlight so that they appear even whiter than they are.
Polanski's picking of his locations for color, his
meticulous alternation of his blacks and whites, his
blocks of light and shadow gives Chinatown its strong
sense of composition, its painterly look, as if he were
presenting a series of still lifes through which he allows
his characters to move. The stark whiteness of Curly's
San Pedro neighborhood as viewed through the windows
of Jake's car spurs memories of the bright reds and
blues of the backgrounds in Antonioni's Blow-Up. It
has been said that Antonioni painted half of London to
create the color imagery for that film and Polanski has
clearly shown the same sort of painterly obsession with
the alternations of his blacks and whites in Chinatown.

Polanski's sectioning of his film into geometric
blocks of shadow and glaring white light, into color
patterns of black against white and white against black,
supports the hovering ironic theme of his film noir,
ironically comments on the naive approach to reality
which his central character, Jake, takes. Nothing in
Jake's "Chinatown" world is black and white. None of

the oppositions within the people or the events of
Jake's journey have that much clarity or distinct
separation. Those many scenes in Chinatown in which
the black/white oppositions are clearly defined are all
ironic. Those scenes are opposed by scenes where
shadow and light wash together to create an atmosphere
of real uncertainty as opposed to the artificial certainty
of the black/white scenes.

Each of the three major confrontation scenes of the
film is shot in this neutral light where the strongly
delineated blacks and whites, shadows and glaring blocks
of sunlight, have broken down. In the bathroom and
bedroom of the mansion as Jake and Evelyn Mulwray
fence with each other before and after making love, the
light has that filtered, muddied cast. The confrontation
between Evelyn and Jake in the safe house which goes
back and forth almost interminably before the incest
secret finally surfaces is filmed in the light of late
afternoon filtered through bamboo shades. The
nighttime confrontation between Jake and Noah Cross
takes place in the same verandah doorway in the
Mulwray mansion which was the demarcation line
between the blocks of shadow and glaring sunlight in
the earlier scenes in that house. But in this
confrontation scene, the light has changed, gone gray,
taken on the neutral cast of weak moonlight bouncing
off subdued stucco and filtering through cigarette smoke.
In the clearly defined light, nothing is clear or true or
ever resolved. In the mulatto light, where the illusion
of clear distinctions has broken down, reality surfaces.

Only when man can reject the illusion that reality
exists in any kind of black and white distinctness can
he begin to understand the dialectic complexity of the
real world. Jake has to give up his misguided desire
for the world to surrender nice black and white answers
to his questions. He has to realize that reality is just
never that simple. He has to surrender himself to the
world of dialectical synthesis where the blacks and the
whites, the shadows and the lights, flow together, mix
and release their complex, inextricably tangled secrets.

Ironically, this whole dialectical lighting schema of
the film was prefigured in the opening scene by the
barred light through the newly installed Venetian blinds
in Jake's office. In later scenes, those same blinds wrap
first Jake then Evelyn Mulwray in bars of shadow and
light. "Blinds" indeed. That wordplay on the theme of
"flawed sight" was present from the very first scene.
And, it is the same barred light which falls across the
courtroom scene in Welles' The Lady From Shanghai.

VII
Tunnel Perspective Composition

The final and most interesting aspect of Polanski's
parallel use of deep focus lighting, composition and
color imagery in Chinatown is the manner in which he
combines those visual aspects with his use of perspective
within the composition of the frame. All through the
film, Jake finds himself in the situation of trying to
look through shadows, penetrate darkness. He must
always peer through changing light down narrowing
fields of vision. Polanski uses perspective repeatedly to
create tunnels of vision down through which Jake must
either see or move. Snooping around the reservoir at
night, gunshots force Jake down into the tunnel of the
run-off channel where he is almost drowned. The same
tunnel perspective is created as he drives down the alley
next to the restaurant after meeting Mrs. Mulwray for
lunch, as he moves down the aisle of platte books in
the Hall of Records, as he guns his car between the
tight straight rows of trees in the orange groves, as he
enters the long tunnel of the courtyard of Ida Sessions'
apartment building, and as he coasts down through the
stark white walls of the alley next to Curly's house in
San Pedro. The scene in the apartment building
courtyard is the most elaborate use of this tunnel
perspective because it is shot from two different
expressive angles. The scene begins with an
over-the-shoulder shot as Jake passes through the portal
moving away from the camera and into the shadowed

tunnel of the courtyard. Immediately, however, Polanski
cuts to a reverse angle shot looking down from in front
as Jake walks up the tunnel of the courtyard toward the
camera.

Why this repeated tunnel imagery? Because it gives a
sense of enclosure and inevitability. Jake really is
trapped, narrowing his field of vision, penetrating deeper
into the heart of the underground all through the film.
The key to the symbolic meaning of Polanski's use of
deep focus perspective to create a pattern of tunnel
images comes early. Hanging along the walls of the
Department of Water and Power reception room are a
series of photographs of Hollis Mulwray and Noah Cross
in better times. Jake's eyes move from one photo to
another until they finally come to rest on two much
younger men, Cross and Mulwray, posed inside the
tunnel of a huge drainage pipe on a construction site.
There is a deterministic quality about this tunnel
imagery as if the main characters, once having entered
the enclosure of the tunnel, are destined to move
inevitably deeper into the shadowy subterranean world
that is "Chinatown." Mining the mystery, Jake's
perspective and his field of vision narrows as he
descends.

The tunnel imagery is Polanski's most expressive use
of deep focus perspective, but he also emphasizes
perspective in his major establishing shots. Twice, for
example, the railing of the Hollenbeck bridge curving
out of the foreground toward the mountains introduces
two parallel early scenes. First, that perspective shot of
the bridge railing introduces a pan along the railing to
Jake's profile as he spies through binoculars on Hollis
Mulwray's car driving through the dried-up riverbed.
The second use of that same establishing shot and pan
carries the scene to Jake poised on the edge ready to
descend into the riverbed, plunge into the mystery of
Hollis Mulwray's death. Jake Gittes follows the
archetypal mythic pattern, descends into a complex
underworld where nothing is ever what it seems to be
and where reality glides and swoops like a taunting

shade.

All of these aspects of the Polanski style in Chinatown-- the opposing blocks of light and shadow, the black/white color imagery, the use of perspective to create tunnels of vision --complement Chinatown's basic theme of seeing or attempting to see reality. These elements of the Polanski visual style all owe their existence to the deep focus concept of filmmaking developed by Orson Welles and Greg Toland in Citizen Kane. Chinatown isn't just a homage to Citizen Kane as Brian DePalma's Dressed To Kill (1981) was to Hitchcock's Psycho. Chinatown extends the expressive, symbolic possibilities of Citizen Kane's concepts of deep focus as far as they can go.

VIII
Chinatown as film noir

But Citizen Kane is not the only film upon which Chinatown draws for inspirations. Chinatown is also very much a genre film. It recognizes and plays variations upon all the major film noir conventions. It orchestrates turns of plot, characterizations, and symbolic motifs similar to those chords which sound in its classic genre predecessors. Richard T. Jameson (MTN; July 1974) shows a deep reticence toward discussing Chinatown as a part of the film noir genre. "Most reviews or remarks about Chinatown . . . have included some mention of The Big Sleep and/or The Maltese Falcon" he begins, but then he, for good reasons, denies the inevitable comparisons:

> The Big Sleep has eased past Falcon as the official private-eye film classic and has begun to be cited . . . with alarming frequency, virtually any time a halfway mysterious narrative involves murky plot convolutions or overtly seeks to trade on behavioral matter. . . . One of the heftiest compliments I can pay Chinatown is that

> while I was watching it I didn't think of any
> other movie. . . . Even in 1946 The Big Sleep
> was only one movie among many . . . it
> invented little but reinvented just about
> everything . . . Chinatown reinvents in that
> way. It provides its own highly distinctive
> map of a deliciously various genre.

Jameson is certainly right in cautioning that The Big
Sleep is not the only influential film in the genre but
if he seriously thinks that Chinatown does not show the
influence of any other films of its type, then he simply
wasn't paying very close attention.

Jameson's intentions are honorable. Chinatown is a
truly distinctive movie. It deserves better than to simply
be compared to others of its type, discussed as an artful
pastiche of Huston and Hawks. Yet, Chinatown is
highly representative of its genre's past as well as its
genre's possibilities. In other words, Chinatown clearly
shows knowledge of where the film noir genre has been
even as it demonstrates how far that genre can go.

For example, Chinatown does indeed resemble The
Big Sleep and The Maltese Falcon. The early scene in
Jake's office in which the fake Mrs. Mulwray draws Jake
into the mystery is lifted whole out of The Maltese
Falcon. The phony Mrs. Mulwray sucking coyly on her
cigarette holder has Brigid O'Shaughnessy (Mary Astor)
written all over her. Jake draws her out with Sam
Spade's (Humphrey Bogart) skeptical detachment and
businesslike smugness. Walsh and Duffy listen in the
same way that Miles Archer (Jerome Cowan) did in the
original. Chinatown then moves along the exact plot
line, even recreates the same images, of The Maltese
Falcon: surveillance of the suspect, a bridge railing, a
shot in the dark.

Similarly, the scene on Mrs. Mulwray's verandah is
conceived in terms of clear allusions to The Big Sleep.
The scene begins with Jake walking up to the front
door past the Mulwray chauffeur in the driveway washing
down the big white Packard with a hose. Remember

Owen the chauffeur hosing down one of the family cars
and glaring resentfully as Marlowe (Humphrey Bogart)
leaves his first meeting with General Sternwood?   As
Jake and the real Mrs. Mulwray meet and then sit across
from each other at the table on the verandah, their
dialog carries clear echoes of the sexual innuendos
exchanged by Marlowe and Vivien Sternwood (Lauren
Bacall) in the notorious horse racing discussion from
The Big Sleep:

> MRS. MULWRAY: I went riding.
> JAKE: You must have gone quite a dis-
> tance.
> MRS. MULWRAY: Riding bareback.

As their conversation continues, it fulfills perhaps the
most standard convention of the film noir detective
genre, the sudden attempt to get the detective off the
case before he discovers too much.   Both Brigid
O'Shaughnessy and Vivien Sternwood try the same scam
on Sam Spade and Phillip Marlowe respectively.   Jake
replies to Evelyn Mulwray exactly the same way that his
two ancestors replied to those earlier films' versions of
the film noir femme fatale:

> MRS. MULWRAY: Let's just drop the whole
> thing.
> JAKE: I'm not the one who's supposed to
> get caught with his pants down. . .
> . It's nothing personal.
> MRS. MULWRAY: It's very personal.   It
> couldn't be more personal.

As was the case with the Sternwoods, Evelyn Mulwray
doesn't want Jake to dig any deeper because she is afraid
he will unearth the personal family secret which lies
beneath the public secrets that Jake has already dug up.
    The very next scene also takes its cue from The Big
Sleep.   Jake returns to the Department of Water and
Power and confronts a very officious receptionist who

insists that Mr. Yelburton is in conference and unavailable. Jake decides to wait. Before long he has that receptionist so intimidated she is ready to jump out of her underpants. Remember Marlowe confronting Agnes, the receptionist in Alfred Gwynn Geiger's combination rare books/porno shop in The Big Sleep? Later, in the Mar Vista Rest Home when Mulvihill (Roy Jensen) shows up with mayhem on his mind, Jake directly echoes Phillip Marlowe when he says, "Can we leave the lady out of this?" Still later, Evelyn Mulwray tries Vivien Sternwood's trick: "Wait here. I need you here," she pleads just as Vivien told Marlowe to wait for her phone call which he immediately knew would never come. Spade, Marlowe, Jack Gittes-- they all harbor the same suspicions, listen to the same lies, know that they have no choice but to mistrust the women they find themselves loving. They are always the most suspicious when the woman is the most seductive.

IX
Chinatown and The Lady From Shanghai

However, despite a number of clear allusions to the two most prominent classics in the film noir genre, neither The Big Sleep nor The Maltese Falcon is the major film noir influence upon Chinatown. If Chinatown closely resembles any of its genre predecessors, it resembles Orson Welles' The Lady From Shanghai (1947). In The Big Sleep, Hawks employs the Chinese decor of Geiger's house, encourages his camera to linger on buddhas, pieces of Chinese sculpture and Chinese wallhangings to signal the exoticism, the foreignness to normality of Geiger's world of homosexuality and pornography. The Chinese exoticism of Geiger's world nicely parallels the musky exoticism of General Sternwood's orchid greenhouse, that artificial tropical jungle under glass mimicking another hemisphere even as the General himself mimics existence, lives only in the artificial heat, partakes only vicariously of other people's pleasures.

But the Chinese imagery in <u>The Big Sleep</u> is present only to define Marlowe as a normal man forced to enter these foreign worlds, adapt and finally control them, understand them. In <u>The Lady From Shanghai</u> and <u>Chinatown</u>, there can be no such understanding. In those films, the Chinese imagery functions as the key to all meaning. The Chinese theme in both <u>The Lady From Shanghai</u> and <u>Chinatown</u> signals the need for a totally new way of seeing if one is ever to understand. As Elsa Bannister (Rita Hayworth) says in Welles' film, "I was taught to think about love in Chinese. . . . The Chinese say, it is difficult for love to last long. Therefore, one who loves passionately is cured of love, in the end." Michael O'Hara answers: "Sure, that's a hard way of thinking." In both films, the death of the <u>femme fatale</u> is the only cure for the strange inscrutable Chinatown love disease which both Jake and O'Hara have managed to contract.

In both <u>The Lady From Shanghai</u> and <u>Chinatown</u>, the Chinese imagery brushes across the canvas of each film until near the end when, in both films, the story finally arrives in Chinatown. Both Elsa Bannister and Evelyn Mulwray employ a Chinese servant who serves as Butler, bodyguard and all-purpose rectifier of messy situations. Elsa's Li and Mrs. Mulwray's Khan lurk on the edges of the screen, always present but always in the background until each film enters Chinatown.

Structurally, both films take the form of a journey through a maze-like world in which reality is constantly in flux, where the rules of the game are always changing, and deceit, betrayal and revenge are the norm rather than the deviation. Michael O'Hara meets his lady from Shanghai in the darkness of Central Park, follows the lure of her siren song aboard her husband's yacht the "Circe," and journeys all the way to the other side of the continent caught in her spell. After allowing her to bewitch him into taking the rap for a murder he didn't commit, reality really starts to waiver and blur as he moves inevitably closer to Chinatown. Heavily drugged from a fake suicide attempt in the

courtroom where he has just been convicted of murder,
O'Hara escapes and staggers through the rain of the city,
his vision blurred, toward Chinatown.

Like Jake Gittes, O'Hara has been to Chinatown
before. Earlier in the film he asks Elsa where she was
born. She tells him Chi Foo. He quips that Chi Foo
is the second wickedest city in the world after Macao.
She answers that she has gambled in both of those
cities and has worked in Shanghai. They both agree
that you need more than luck in Shanghai. O'Hara
staggers through San Francisco's Chinatown looking for
some place to hide. Finally he enters a Chinese
theater, melts into the audience and groggily rests, worn
out from all the confusion, the deceit, the betrayal, just
as Jake Gittes is when he finally shows up in L.A.'s
Chinatown. Elsa follows O'Hara to Chinatown. Seeking
information, she converses in Chinese until finally led to
the theater. Backstage, she telephones Li, her Chinese
butler, to come and help her dispose of O'Hara. Like
similar climactic scenes in Hitchcock's The 39 Steps
(1935) and Saboteur (1942), chaos and gunshots come to
the theater as Li and his men spirit Michael O'Hara
away.

Chinatown closely resembles The Lady From
Shanghai in three clear ways. Structurally, it too
develops its title theme by means of a series of
intimations of Chinese imagery, brief allusions to the
influence of the Chinatown world upon the characters'
past lives and world views, until it becomes clear that
the film's characters are moving inexorably toward some
confrontation, some revelation, in Chinatown. In both
The Lady From Shanghai and Chinatown, the respective
plots turn on exactly the same idea, the central
character's realization that "nothing is ever what it seems
to be." Michael O'Hara in the theater in Chinatown
kisses his siren lover in order to avoid detection by the
police. But even as he kisses Elsa, his suspicious hand
slips into her purse and finds the gun that could have
cleared him of the murder charge. He realizes that he
has taken the fall for a murder she committed.

Secondly, both films employ an optic imagery (discussed earlier) which underlines the distortion, multiplication and ultimately the illusion of trying to see and understand reality. Early in The Lady From Shanghai Grisby (Glenn Anders) repeatedly spies on Elsa and O'Hara through a monocular which gets him close to the action while keeping him at a distance. Jake employs exactly the same optic spying technique in the use of his binoculars and camera lenses in Chinatown. The problem that both Grisby and Jake encounter, however, is that though they can see and even magnify reality from a distance, they still cannot understand it. Despite the tools of optic magnification, their sight remains flawed and reality remains elusive and inscrutable.

Thirdly, both Michael O'Hara and Jake Gittes are drawn into closely similar relationships to their film noir fatal women, to the mysteries they find themselves entangled in, to the Chinatown worlds they are trying to understand. Both become entangled in the deadly web spun by the fatal woman. In Chinatown, as the white/black color imagery of her costuming so aptly demonstrates, Evelyn Mulwray becomes a true black widow who places Jake in a position where he has an excellent chance of getting his head taken off. He actually does get a piece of his nose cut off. Both Michael O'Hara and Jake Gittes spend their whole respective relationships with the fatal women as outsiders, as employees. In fact, in Chinatown Jake being on the outside looking in is a recurring visual motif. Remember his position outside the window in the initial safe house scene? In The Lady From Shanghai, O'Hara's role as outsider is even kinkier than Jake's. While Jake rather quickly takes the dead husband's place in the black widow's bed, Michael, it seems, has been hired by an impotent husband to keep his young wife happy. Both Jake Gittes and Michael O'Hara are used as tools to divert attention from the real mystery which lies beneath the initial mysteries.

The Lady From Shanghai and Chinatown both end

with exactly the same image, a deconstructive image. It
is a high overhead shot of the <u>film</u> <u>noir</u> protagonist,
victimized by inscrutable reality, doing the only thing
left to do, walking away. Michael O'Hara turns his back
on the dying Elsa, makes his way out through the
turnstile of the "Crazy House" and walks slowly away in
the early morning light of the empty parking lot. In
<u>Chinatown</u>, after Walsh offers the final benediction--
"Forget it, Jake. It's Chinatown." --the only remaining
alternative for Jake is to turn and walk away. The
camera pulls back to that high overhead angle as Jake is
led away down that shadowy, neon-lit street and the
audience knows that everything has been lost, nothing
gained, and what has happened on the screen cannot
even be fully understood, certainly not by Jake.

The Chinatown world demands that one leave that
American hunger for answers, for resolution, behind and
embrace the Chinese way of dealing with reality, taking
it as it comes, never believing it, knowing that nothing
is ever what it seems. Or, as the narrator Michael
O'Hara says in the final scene of <u>The</u> <u>Lady</u> <u>From</u>
<u>Shanghai</u>:

> He said the world's bad, we can't run
> away from the badness and you're right there.
> But she said we can't fight it. We must deal
> with the badness, make terms. But then the
> badness deals with you, makes its own terms
> in the end surely.

In the end, surely, all that Jake knows is that when you
enter the Chinatown world you give up your control of
reality, give up the power to evaluate and determine
outcomes which your senses normally exert in western
society, give up your ability to see the enemy and deal
with him on your own terms. Following Jake into
Chinatown is a metaphorical equivalent for America's
descent into Vietnam.

One last thematic similarity which both <u>The</u> <u>Lady</u>
<u>From</u> <u>Shanghai</u> and <u>Chinatown</u> share involves the illusion

which those films' respective protagonists, Michael O'Hara
and Jake Gittes, both nurture, the illusion that they can
actually swim and survive in the destructive element, the
illusion that they can continue to breathe beneath the
murky surface of the dangerous waters in which they are
submerged.   In The Lady From Shanghai, Michael
O'Hara, in a parable-like speech about a school of
sharks in a feeding frenzy, introduces that film's theme
of man's potential for self-destruction, for testing the
destructive element, for descending into the heart of
darkness never to be seen again:

> You know, once off the hump of Bra-
> zil, I saw the ocean so darkened with blood
> it was black. . . . A few of us had lines out
> for a bit of idle fishing. It was me had the
> first strike.   A shark it was, and then there
> was another, and another shark again, till all
> about the sea was made of sharks, and more
> sharks still, and the water tall. My shark had
> torn himself away from the hook, and the
> scent, or maybe the stain it was, and him
> bleeding his life away, drove the rest of them
> mad.   Then the beasts took to eating each
> other in their frenzy, they ate at themselves.
> You could feel the lust of murder like a
> wind stinging your eyes, and you could smell
> the death, reeking up out of the sea.

In The Lady From Shanghai, O'Hara finds himself
swimming in a school of self-destructive sharks. It takes
all the agility he can muster to keep them from feeding
on him as they feed on each other. In the end they
tear each other to pieces as first Broome then Grisby are
shot, and then Bannister and Elsa kill each other in the
Hall of Mirrors.   Only Michael swims away from the
widening, darkening pool of blood. Jake Gittes finds
himself drawn into the same sort of bloody maelstrom
where he must struggle to keep from drowning as Hollis
Mulwray, Noah Cross and Evelyn Mulwray thrash out

their incestuous frenzy all around him and, in the end,
kill each other off as Jake fights to stay afloat.

X
The Destructive Element

One elaborate, multi-faceted, multi-level pattern of
visual/verbal imagery in Chinatown represents the
Conradian theme of Jake's struggle to survive in the
destructive element of the film's throbbing heart of
darkness. As does The Lady From Shanghai, Chinatown
employs a consistent imagery of water and fish, of
breathing, finally of drowning, all intricately and meticulously connected into a thematic motif which defines
the nature of Jake's existence in this Chinatown world,
the nature of the city of L.A.'s existence in Noah Cross's
corporate world, and the nature of the audience's
existence in the seventies world of Vietnam, Watergate
and OPEC. The water/fish/breathing/drowning imagery
defines theme on each of these three levels of meaning:
the EXISTENTIAL (Jake's struggle to survive in the
Chinatown world); the SOCIAL (L.A.'s water as a target
for corporate greed); and the POLITICAL (the events of
the film as a metaphor for America's seventies struggle to
survive Vietnam, Watergate and all the other pressures
upon her society).

This symbolic motif begins in Jake's office as he
ushers one client out, Curly the fisherman, and is
immediately introduced to another client, supposedly the
wife of the Head of L.A.'s Department of Water and
Power. Once on the Mulwray case, Jake follows the
trail to a city council meeting where a new dam is
being discussed, to the dry L.A. riverbed, to a runoff
channel that empties into the ocean. The pattern of
the investigation is taking such clear shape that Walsh
exclaims, "The guy's got water on the brain."
Immediately after Walsh presents this succinct evaluation,
Duffy telephones to report that Mulwray and a young
girl are meeting in a rowboat in the lagoon in Echo
Park. "Water again," Jake cocks a wink at Walsh while

dashing out of the office. Floating amidst this opening
deluge of water images are two introductory fish
references which only take on significance when they
resurface later in the film. While being ushered out of
the office by Jake, Curly apologetically mutters about
how the albacore and skipjack aren't running and as
soon as they are he will be able to pay Jake's fee.
Then Walsh reports that the only word he picked up of
the "terrific" argument between Hollis Mulwray and Noah
Cross in front of The Pig and Whistle was "applecore."

Jake thinks he has caught Mulwray in a simple little
sexual affair. He has no sense of the depth of the
watery surface which he has barely broken. First, his
simple little sex case ends up splashed all over the front
pages of the L.A. papers, then the real Mrs. Mulwray
shows up and Jake realizes that he has been played
neatly for a sucker. Jake goes to the Department of
Water and Power where he meets Russ Yelburton, the
Assistant Commissioner, whose office walls are hung with
mounted fish. From there he pays a visit to the real
Mrs. Mulwray. They chat on the patio next to the tide
pool in her back yard. Next Jake drives to the reservoir
and arrives just in time to see the drowned corpse of
Mulwray fished out of the water.

A trail of water, a series of verbal then visual
references to fish, all leading to a drowning-- some kind
of pattern seems to be forming. But what does it
mean? At this point in the film, perhaps Morty the
chain-smoking, hard-coughing coroner has the best
answer of all, which is no answer at all. "Middle of a
drought," Morty laughs between coughs, "and the Water
Commissioner drowns. Only in L.A." Morty's ironic
resignation to his city's tradition of weirdness, "Only in
L.A.," carries the same intonation of helpless
bewilderment that Walsh's "it's Chinatown" carries at the
end of the film. Morty goes on to tell Jake that,
strangely enough, the Water Commissioner is the second
drowning victim of the day. The other is a bum who
passed out in the L.A. riverbed under the Hollenbeck
bridge, the same bridge Jake followed Mulwray to earlier

in the investigation. "That river's dry," Jake blurts out. Morty just shrugs it off and puffs and coughs some more. "Forget it Jake," Morty seems to be saying, "It's L.A., city of weirdness." But Jake can't leave it alone. He goes back at night to the reservoir where Mulwray died to see if he can find some of the answers to all of these questions about water and drowning that have been raised.

It is in this night scene at the reservoir that the first significant definition of this whole verbal/visual motif of water/fish/breathing/drowning images is offered. At the reservoir when shots are fired at Jake, he takes refuge in a run-off channel where he is immediately blindsided and swept away by a wall of rushing water. He manages to save himself from drowning but two thugs, Mulvihill (whom he met in the Water and Power building earlier) and a midget in a white suit carrying a very sharp knife, are waiting for him after he drags himself out of the water. While Mulvihill holds Jake, the midget (Roman Polanski) sticks the stilletto up Jake's nose:

> MIDGET: Hold it right there, kitty kat.
> JAKE: Hello Claude, where'd you get the midget?
> MIDGET: Know what happens to nosey people, kitty kat? I cut it off and feed it to my gold fish.

With the verbal connection between noses and fish made, the midget slits Jake's nostril with a quick flick. They leave him on his knees with blood spurting between the fingers of his hands. The scene does have a dark irony to it. What more appropriate thing to cut off if you want to stop a detective from nosing around? After this night scene, Jake's nose and images of fish pepper the middle third of the film. Jake gets off a series of breathing jokes at his poor mutilated nose's expense. In the restaurant with Evelyn Mulwray he says, "I goddam near lost my nose and I like it. I like breathing through it." Then soon after when Yelburton asks about his nose and if it hurts, Jake answers, "Only when I breathe." These wry verbal jokes establish the connection between drowning and breathing which was established visually in the night scene at the reservoir. Water is clearly the dominant element in Chinatown. It can be a destructive element as it was for Hollis Mulwray, or, if one is quick and can adapt, one can keep one's head above water, keep breathing, survive in the destructive element.

The scene at the Albacore Club where Jake meets Noah Cross for the first time gives a full clear definition to the meaning of all of Chinatown's water/fish/ drowning/breathing visual/verbal references. The scene begins with the Albacore Club pennant, a fish's head in profile dominated by one wide eye. Jake joins Cross for lunch and, at Cross's insistence, they are served fish with the head left on. In a threatening close-up, the dead fish's eye stares from Cross's plate as their conversation begins. "This Escobar. Honest?" Noah cross-examines Jake. "As far as it goes," Jake answers. "Of course, he has to swim in the same water we all do."

That single line in the middle of this crucial scene clarifies the meaning of the whole pattern of interlocked symbolic references to water, fish, drowning and breathing which have floated throughout the whole first half of the film. Jake is adrift in the Chinatown world. He can either sink or swim, drown or learn to breathe underwater the way the fish do. Jake's struggle in the destructive element is existential and Sisyphusian. He must learn to tread water, to survive, without ever being able to understand or control the inscrutable world in which he has been cast adrift.

While the water and drowning and breathing images are symbolic allusions to the existential aspirations and the individual crimes of the swimmers in the sinister sea of Chinatown, those images also carry meaning on a more universal level, point to the social and political themes of the film. In one of the final scenes, Jake confronts Noah Cross at the Mulwray mansion and accuses Cross of drowning Mulwray in the backyard tide pool. In the face of that accusation, Cross admits nothing but rather delivers a small philosophical speech on tide pools: "Hollis was always fascinated by tide pools. You know what he used to say, that's where life begins, slews, tide pools." Cross might have added "and ends" to his little speech and come much closer to the reality.

As Jake exposes the whole Cross conspiracy that led to the drowning death of Hollis Mulwray, Cross just shrugs, amazed that Jake is getting so upset over little things like the theft of some water and a murder. "Either you bring the water to L.A. or you bring L.A. to the water," Cross instructs Jake as if lecturing a schoolboy. The water is the life source for the city of L.A. and Noah Cross has a strangle hold on that city's future just as he had on Hollis Mulwray's neck the night of the murder. The water is the central social issue of the film; it can float the city, give it life, or, it can kill the city, cut off its ability to breathe. The most frightening aspect of this whole Conradian pattern of interlocked images is that Cross knows exactly what he is doing. "I don't blame myself," Noah Cross tells Jake. "Most people don't ever have to face the fact that at the right time in the right place they are capable of almost anything." This is Jake's second eye-to-eye confrontation with inexplicable human evil. Earlier he had faced the grim taunting of Evelyn Mulwray: "My father and I. Understand? Or is it too tough for you?" Jake, stunned, asks, "He raped you?" begging for a "yes" answer. Evelyn sadly shakes her head "no," her eyes never flinching until Jake looks away. In both of those scenes, Jake confronts the human heart of darkness, the potential for pure evil within all men. Noah Cross becomes his Kurtz who exudes like a deadly essence "the horror, the horror." In the final scene of the film, Jake descends all the way into the fatal heart of darkness, drowns in the inscrutable reality of Chinatown. Only Walsh's "Forget it, Jake, it's Chinatown" saves him, brings him back to the surface and keeps him afloat.

<h1 style="text-align:center">XI</h1>

Chinatown as American Metaphor

Appearing in 1974, Chinatown presents a metaphorical vision of an America where "nothing is ever what it seems," where sight is so flawed that no one can see the light at the end of the tunnel, where the American dream is drowning in corporate greed and political deceit and personal betrayal. What Chinatown is saying is that America will survive, but that is all that is left for her to do. Vietnam destroyed any global credibility which had once given her identity. Watergate, spreading like a cancer across the whole decade, destroyed her from within, forced Americans once and for all to amputate any vestiges of political trust left over from the Kennedy optimism of the sixties. Chinatown's social historical message is captured with succinct eloquence in that last line "Forget it, Jake, it's Chinatown."   The seventies world truly is a Chinatown world and there isn't really very much any of us can do about it.   The Noah Crosses, the corporate villains, are in control and there is really nothing anyone can do to keep them from controlling our lives and getting away with murder every day. Forget it, America.

Chinatown, in all its social historical meta-phoricality, is, above all else, a film, much like Blow-Up, in which little things mean a lot-- a summer hat in the background, a single black lens in a pair of broken sunglasses, the involuntary blowing of an automobile's horn. It is a brilliantly composed film in which every inch of the frame, every plane of the deep focus image is used to present visual meaning. It is an eloquently written film, the words combining with the images to define complex themes which offer meaning on multiple ideational levels. Chinatown's themes define ourselves, our society, our national consciousness.

And finally, Chinatown is an exquisitely acted movie.   Jack Nicholson is totally convincing as the

cynical, one-step-behind private eye.   It is his movie.
The audience looks over his shoulder.   His Jake Gittes
is always the outsider looking in, the middle-class man
in the middle, a step above the servant or employee
class but never equal to the rich and powerful moneyed
class which employs him to clean up their messes.   Self-
employed yet employed, welcome nowhere (the banker
tries to harrass him from the barber shop, Khan closes
the door in his face, Escobar asks him how he got into
the reservoir, the clerk at the Hall of Records whines
"This is not a lending library," the valley farmers try to
drive him off with shotguns), Nicholson plays Jake as a
slick twentieth-century Odysseus, man of cunning, liar,
wanderer, soldier.   His only problem is that in the
twentieth century everybody knows about his Trojan
horse trick.   Noah Cross, in fact, has a bigger Trojan
horse.   Trying his small deceits in Cross's complex
world, Jake is swallowed up by the constantly
shape-shifting mystery.   Then both he and Cross in the
end are swallowed up by the biggest Trojan horse of
all, the Chinatown world where nothing is ever what it
seems.
  Nicholson is perfectly cast, but Faye Dunaway steals
the show with the best work she has done in any of
her films, better than her hormonal adolescent in Bonnie
and Clyde (1967), her cool user in The Thomas Crown
Affair (1968), her frightened doe in Three Days of the
Condor, her hard bitch in Network and her menacing
monster in Mommie Dearest (1982).   In Chinatown, her
Evelyn Mulwray is so high-strung that one pluck could
break the eardrums of every dog in the L.A. basin.   From
scene to scene she plays Evelyn as a woman balanced on
a razor's edge, jittery verging on hysterical, constantly
fighting for control of her own emotions, so tight that
her hands and voice twitch from the tension.   It is one
of the most subtly jumpy performances in recent film
history.   The slightest word or intimation sets Evelyn
off, triggers her twitchy struggle for control.   All Jake
need do is mention Noah Cross and Evelyn folds into
her protective coloration, circles her wagons.   If Jake is

an overmatched Odysseus shipwrecked in this Chinatown
world, Evelyn is a hunted Aphrodite carrying the
unpardonable sin. In the restaurant, when Jake mentions
that he has talked to her father, she lunges for a
cigarette as if it is all that can keep her from going
over the edge. Jake, seeing but not understanding (as
usual), wryly advises her that she's already got one going
in the ashtray. "Does my talking about your father
upset you?" Jake goes on. She tenses further, coiling
into herself like a spring, and tries to answer: "No.
Yes. Hollis and my, my," her voice snaps but she
winds it back under control, "my father had a falling
out." Jake, having no idea what he is saying, asks:
"Over you or over the Water Department?" His blind
words wind her even tighter. "Why should it be over
me?" she manages without breaking every straining wire.
Later, in her bed, she is naked before Jake when her
father's name once again witlessly surfaces in his
conversation. Like a plant closing protectively, she folds
her arms across her breasts at the mere mention of her
father's name. Terribly uncomfortable with her sexuality,
Dunaway's Evelyn is the highest strung, jumpiest
performance since Ingrid Bergman's in Notorious (1946).

Chinatown is a film directed by a Polish refugee
using the best of America's actors to catch in complex
images not only the essence of its genre but the essence
of American life in the seventies. Chinatown is Jack
Nicholson's, Faye Dunaway's, Robert Towne's, Roman
Polanski's and Hollywood's best work. It gives the lie
to any voice which argues that Hollywood is incapable
of producing great art. Greatness only surfaces
infrequently. It did in Citizen Kane and it did again
in Chinatown.

6. THE VIETNAM WAR FILMS

One, Two, Three, what are we fightin' for?
Don't ask me; I don't give a damn,
Next stop is Vietnam.
>   --Country Joe and the Fish,
>   "I-feel-like-I'm-fixin'-to-die
>   Rag"

Country Joe, the head cheerleader at Woodstock, posed a question which is still, more than a decade later, being asked. What were we fighting for? What really happened "over there" (to use the title of a very different war song)? Early in The Deer Hunter (1978), Stevie's babushka'd mother pleaded with her parish priest:

> I do not understand father. I un-
> derstand nothing anymore. Can you ex-
> plain? Can anyone explain?

Her words link the world of The Deer Hunter to the worlds of inscrutable reality presented in Blow-Up and Chinatown. Her words best capture the dilemma of all of America, then and now, concerning Vietnam.

The 1980s now. Teenagers and college kids going to movies, movies about the Vietnam War; a war they hardly remember, a war they may never understand.

1970s then. The older brothers of these college kids and the older brothers of kids who rarely go to the movies and may never go to college were sweating, fighting and dying in Vietnam.

Where does the 1980's generation go if it wants to understand its older brothers?

Unfortunately, few will encounter the meticulous sociological, psychological and historical data on the Vietnam War compiled by academic studies in the last ten years. More perhaps will read the literature: Michael Herr's Dispatches or Tim O'Brien's Going After Cacciato. But most will go to the movies and, in all but a few exceptions, won't learn a thing, won't ever understand.

Is it possible to understand life by watching motion pictures? Is realism attainable only documentarily or can it be found symbolically? These are the kinds of questions that a subject like "The Vietnam War Films" automatically posits. These Vietnam War films are all about a real event which meant and has come to mean a lot of different things. Each movie tries to approach some part of that meaning.

Do they succeed? In most cases they don't. Yet some succeed much better than others mainly because they are more in tune with the social history of the decade.

1978. A man in San Francisco starts selling tee shirts bearing the map of Vietnam over the caption "SOUTHEAST ASIAN WAR GAMES, 2nd Place." Has it all become a bad joke?

If it has, Hollywood is at least partially to blame. With few exceptions, the films supposedly about the Vietnam War have been jokes. With few exceptions, Hollywood has made little attempt to understand. As Rex Reed wrote in Big Screen, Little Screen (New York: The MacMillan Co., 1971): "When Hollywood goes to war, it usually drops nothing but bombs." Take for example a film like More American Graffiti (1979). It turns a theme, walking away from the war, which Tim O'Brien treated seriously in Going After Cacciato, into a production number from a Crosby/Hope "Road" movie played to a soundtrack of "The Happy Wanderer." Perhaps M*A*S*H (1970), which is really a Vietnam War film though set in Korea and which is a real breakthrough movie which paved the way for the realistic treatment of the Vietnam War in the films of the late seventies, had the right idea when it turned the reality of war into a bloody black comedy.

Since 1976, the movies have been picking persistently at the scab of memory. The majority of the Hollywood portrayals of the Vietnam War or the effects of the war on Americans involved have been misguided, insensitive, exploitative, cliched, inauthentic and just plain stupid. Writing in the Chicago Tribune (3 June 1979), Gene Siskel poses an important question: "Does any one film tell the whole story?" He answers:

> No. . . . Of course not. How could any one film possibly attempt to capsulize a war that lasted 10 years, cost 56,000 American lives, 1.3 million Vietnamese lives, staggered the American economy, and divided our nation.

Certainly, no film could ever tell the whole truth. However, it seems reasonable to expect that purportedly serious films (again, with a few notable exceptions) should not consciously twist and obscure the fractional truths which they attempt to approach. Jack Fuller, also writing in the Chicago Tribune (1 October 1978), directly examines the phoniness of the Vietnam War movie medicine show:

> They are breaking the silence that fell on Hollywood almost at the very beginning of the fighting. They now present a vision of history and its effect on the people caught up in it. And they want the nation to believe it is real.

In fact, the majority of the so-called Vietnam War movies have nothing whatsoever to do with the war in Vietnam. They are set in the States. They attempt to metaphorically superimpose Vietnamese culture on American culture. However, in order to make this superimposition, they ignore the fact of the absolutely cut-off situation of the men fighting in Vietnam, a world different in every way from life in the United States, then, now, ever. If ever there was a "Chinatown" world where "nothing is ever what it seems to be," Vietnam was it.

Thus, point #1, many films don't qualify for consideration simply because the Vietnam War just doesn't work as a metaphor for life in America. Two different worlds. Two different cultures. Two utterly different perspectives on life and death and conducting war. These differences were never resolved during 10 years of American occupation incountry and they are never going to come together now no matter how close Hollywood tries to draw its metaphorical parallels. Jake Gittes couldn't go into Chinatown and understand its inscrutable reality and Americans had no better luck in Vietnam.

Four particularly clear examples of this type of pseudo-Vietnam War film are Taxi Driver (1976), Rolling Thunder (1977), Who'll Stop The Rain (1978) and Heroes (1977). Each has a climactic firefight scene meant to conjure images of Vietnam. Travis (Robert DeNiro), a Vietnam vet heavily firepowered, makes a night sweep on a mean streets brothel, flushes Charlie and wastes him in Taxi Driver. In Rolling Thunder, Col. Rane (William Devane) and Johnny Vohden (Tommy Lee Jones), returned POW's, search out and destroy a group of torturer-killers in a Mexican whorehouse. In Who'll Stop The Rain, Ray Hicks (Nick Nolte), another super-vet psychologically trip-wired, stages a firefight on a New Mexico desert mesa that lights up the night like a full-scale NVA rocket attack.

The firefight at the end of Heroes is more complicated than the others. By means of psychological flashbacking, the streets of Eureka, California are turned into the Vietnam battlefield where a best buddy was killed. Seared in his mind, Jack Dunne

(Henry Winkler) carries his own image of the war with him wherever he goes.

Besides firefights, each of these films offers a scene in which the returned veteran worships his combat weapon. In Taxi Driver, Travis prances with his guns before the mirror. Johnny Vohden in Rolling Thunder assembles his assault rifle as a prostitute discovers his sexual impotence. In Who'll Stop The Rain, Ray Hicks digs up his buried M16 with rocket launcher and lovingly reassembles it. And in Heroes, Kenny (Harrison Ford), Jack Dunne's vet friend, shoots at the stars with his M16, and misses.

Each of these films (except Rolling Thunder) has redeeming qualities. Taxi Driver is one of the most visually exciting films of the decade. Travis is like America in Vietnam. He tries to impose a highly conventional way of life on a perverse and chaotic world. When it doesn't work, only one solution remains, bomb it flat. For all its good points, Taxi Driver was one of the first films to exploit "PVS" (Post-Vietnam Syndrome), a label most veterans particularly resent. "PVS," a generalization fostered by the mass media, offers the negative image of the disturbed Vietnam veteran often strung-out on drugs and prone to sudden acts of ungovernable violence and criminality.[1] Each of these four films sustain that generalization as do scores of TV shows and stories in the print media.

Heroes, however, is an honest, if simpleminded and slapstick, version of a more important psychological syndrome of the returned Vietnam veteran: the nightmare of guilt at having survived yourself yet having left dead buddies behind.

Who'll Stop The Rain, adapted faithfully from Robert

---

[1]Cf. Charles R. Figley and Seymour Levantmen, Strangers At Home: Vietnam Veterans Since The War (New York: Holt, Rinehart & Winston, 1980); and Tim O'Brien, "The Violent Vet," Esquire, December, 1979.

Stone's brilliant novel of Vietnam's burnt-out cases, Dog
Soldiers, is the best film of this group.   While it too
supports the oversimplification of "PVS," it also deals
with the overpowering reality of existential emptiness.
Ray Hicks knows that his own self and its survival in
the fields of fire is the only thing that is important.
He is an old-style samurai confused by the most
ill-conceived of wars.

     But none of these films is about Vietnam. They are
about America, and the Vietnam War is simply closest at
hand to provide a metaphor for violence and mindless
inhumanity.   Who'll Stop The Rain is the only one
which spends any extended time incountry in Vietnam.
Its first ten minutes give graphic representation to the
horror of the war: napalm, rocket-ripped bodies,
soldiers turned into "vicious freaks," corrupt politicians
dealing heroin in Saigon.   Converse the journalist
(Michael Moriarty) takes pictures of it all until he can
stand it no longer. The terror of the war touching him
so closely breaks him down, turns him aimless.
Somehow, vaguely, the war serves as his motive for
becoming a heroin smuggler.   Though the brief scenes
of the war are vivid, their connection as motivation for
the ensuing action in the States is irretrievably muddled.
The film becomes, with its final image of the heroin
blowing in the New Mexico wind, a rock and roll
version of Treasure of the Sierra Madre (1948).   Ray
Hicks, early in Who'll Stop The Rain, makes the most
lucid comment on the Vietnam war:

          CONVERSE: Don't they say that this is the
                       place where everybody finds out who
                       they are?
          HICKS: What a bummer for the gooks!

     One other returned veteran film set in the United
States is less easy to dismiss.   Coming Home (1978)
combines a perceptive and compassionate documenting of
the unique situation of the disabled Vietnam veteran
with an all-too-familiar soap opera love affair set in the

naval base suburbia of San Diego with an unexplainably clumsy handling of "PVS." Vietnam veterans have mixed emotions about Coming Home. They agree that it gives much-needed visibility to the special situation of the disabled Vietnam veteran, but they react negatively to the ending. As one said: "I didn't like it. It makes the Marine out to be just an asshole."

Coming Home deserves mixed reviews. The good is its hard-hitting revelation of the situation of the disabled Vietnam veteran, a new species of American "invisible man." In a central scene, as Luke Martin (Jon Voight) is chaining himself and his wheelchair to a military base gate, he is caught in the act, lit up by the headlights of an entering staff car. But they never see him. He really is invisible as he has told Sally Hyde earlier: "When I dream, I have legs. . . . I'm still the same person. When people look they don't see me." When Sally (Jane Fonda) tries to convince the Marine Wives Club to give the disabled veterans some attention, insert some pictures, in the base newspaper, her idea is rejected out of hand. Finally, when a young, mentally confused vet commits suicide in the ward of a VA Hospital, the orderly calms the restless group of milling, wheelchaired men with the words, "It's alright." It's not alright! The kid is dead! "It's alright" was what America kept saying as the bodies, the paraplegics, the invisible men came home. "It's alright," America said, and then turned away.

What Coming Home does best is show how during that time of war in America everyone was disabled in one way or another. The contrast between the innocence of a past forever lost and the experience of a present reality too grim to accept is strikingly defined in the wheelchair football game. Luke, the high school star, once again sweeps around end carrying the ball. Sally is a cheerleader again. But it just isn't the same. As Vi says about America: "They tore down my past and built a shopping center."

The bad about Coming Home is the soap-opera quality of the triangular love affair and the clumsy,

insensitive handling of the character of Bob Hyde (Bruce
Dern). Early in the film Bob makes love to Sally to
the slow-spoken words of the Marine Corps Hymn.
Under him, she wears a look of orgasmless pain. Later,
above Luke Martin, she finds ecstacy for the first time.
Her whole husband can't bring her to orgasm but her
paralyzed lover can. Ironies like this one may represent
the upside-downness of Vietnam era America where the
healthy are crippled and impotent and the crippled are
healthy and potent, but it is still a soap-opera cliche.

Some subtle images of loneliness and separation fail
to rescue this shop-worn love story. Fences symbolize
separation. Through the chainlink fence on the
basketball court, Sally tells Luke that she is going to
Hong Kong to meet her husband as the ironic strains of
"My Girl" play on the soundtrack. When Bob
disembarks, limping, from Vietnam, Sally and he face
each other through another chainlink fence. The men
in the VA Hospital watch helplessly through the wire-
glass of a door as Billy (Robert Carradine) commits
suicide. Everyone is separate. Unfortunately, Coming
Home offers no possibility for reunion. Everyone is
simply "LUCKY out" as the final image of the film, a
sign on a supermarket door, directs.

What clinches the cliche quality of the love triangle
in Coming Home is Bob Hyde's muddled characterization
and sentimental demise. It is the writer's fault, a clear
case of writing oneself into a familiar yet complex
human situation then failing to write oneself out. Bob
Hyde running naked into the surf in Coming Home is
every bit as maudlin and unbelievable as James Mason
trudging wearily into the sea in the 1954 version of A
Star Is Born.

The one aspect which disqualifies Coming Home as
a real Vietnam War film is its detachment from the war
itself. The closest Coming Home gets to Vietnam is the
obligatory atrocity description of off-stage action. Bob
Hyde tells of his men chopping off heads. In answer,
Sally massages his temples and flees back to her lover in
the States. In later films (Go Tell The Spartans, The

Deer Hunter, Apocalypse Now) similar atrocities happen,
are presented realistically on-screen, and carry a much
greater moral impact, actually bring the audience into
close relation to the horror of dehumanized war.

The climactic scene of Coming Home, in which
Luke, Sally and Bob all confront each other, is, like
major scenes in other returned veteran films, dominated
by an M16.   Bob grimly assembles it and snaps its
bayonet into ready position.   The rifle with the bayonet
fixed erect is Bob's only remaining potency.   Ironically,
when the impotent Luke backs Bob down, the rifle
becomes simply the same old phallic cliche, as
meaningless and empty as the war was for both Luke
and Bob. As Blow-Up examined the phenomenon of a
whole variety of forms of contemporary impotence and
as Chinatown probed the impotence of seventies man in
the attempt to understand reality, Coming Home
graphically demonstrates the impotence of a whole
generation of young Americans toward the act of
understanding the war in which they fought.

In the opening scene of Coming Home, a rap
session, one disabled vet tells another: "You got to
justify it to yourself, so you say it's OK.   If you don't
do that the whole thing was a waste."   In a bar in
Hong Kong, Bob tells Sally: "I know what it's like.   I
wanna know what it is."   As Sally pushes Luke along
the beachwalk after receiving a letter from Bob, Luke
says: "Whatever he says, it's a hundred times worse."
And in Luke's closing scene he tells a group of high
school boys that "It ain't like it is in the movies."
Each line of dialogue signals how difficult it is to
understand what the Vietnam War was, tries to express
the "inscrutable reality" of it.   Unfortunately, Coming
Home never takes its attempt far enough.

Julian Smith in his book Looking Away: Hollywood and Vietnam (New York: Charles Scribner's Sons,
1975) writes:

> Vietnam was like a movie that had gotten
> out of hand: gigantic cost overruns, a

shooting schedule run amuck, squabbles on
the set, and back in the studio, the first
<u>auteur</u> dying with most of the script in his
head, the second quitting in disgust, and the
last swearing it was finally in the can, but
sneaking back to shoot some extra scenes.

When the war in Vietnam began, everyone thought all it
would be was an extension of an established metaphor,
just another familiar image-in-frame moving from World
War II to Korea to Vietnam, just another John Wayne
movie.

Point #2, many of those films which actually take
the viewer into the Vietnam War don't succeed because
they follow the same formula of movies made about
earlier wars, couched in the same Cowboys and Indians
terms.   What Hollywood initially failed to recognize was
the uniqueness of the Vietnam War.   Because of
Vietnam's ambiguous circumstances, its strategy, its
identity, the old images just didn't fit.   Hundreds of
thousands of young Americans rode off to Vietnam as if
it were a John Wayne movie and found themselves in
the middle of a surreal Fellini-esque enigma, the Little
Big Horn set in a tropical jungle with ghosts for
Indians.   Two films especially must be dismissed because
of their formula approach: John Wayne's incredibly
cliched remake of <u>Fort</u> <u>Apache</u> (1948), <u>The</u> <u>Green</u> <u>Berets</u>
(1968), and <u>The</u> <u>Boys</u> <u>In</u> <u>Company</u> <u>C</u> (1978).

<u>The</u> <u>Green</u> <u>Berets</u> is nostalgic <u>deja</u> <u>vu</u> rendered so
meticulously in John Wayne's anachronistic image and
likeness that no viewer can help but immediately realize
that the Monument Valley in Utah must have been
rented that weekend and Big John forced to find a new
landscape in which to play Cowboys and Indians.

Like <u>The</u> <u>Green</u> <u>Berets</u>, <u>The</u> <u>Boys</u> <u>In</u> <u>Company</u> <u>C</u>
reminds of about forty other movies.   In this eternally
recycled script, the camera follows a cross-section of
recruits through the rigors of training to the terrors of
the front lines.   <u>The</u> <u>Boys</u> <u>In</u> <u>Company</u> <u>C</u> even pulls
out the most overworked cliche of the whole war film

genre, the old jumping-on-the-grenade-to-save-your-buddies chestnut.

As did The Green Berets, The Boys In Company C uses children to prod the viewer's transmission of war guilt. In The Green Berets, one child was evacuated by helicopter in the nick of time while another was gang-raped and killed thus giving a previously non-combatant journalist (David Janssen) reason to pick up a gun on the side of truth, justice and John Wayne. In The Boys In Company C, the children are killed outright and their deaths serve as a motive for a previously pacifistic Marine to grab his machine gun and start blazing away. In a much more interesting film, Go Tell The Spartans (1978) a realistic twist is given to the children-caughtin-the-war-zone cliche-- the children turn out to be Viet Cong and gun down the sentimental Americans.

The most puzzling weakness of The Boys In Company C is its confusion of its own identity. It can't decide whether it wants to be a realistic documentary or a political metaphor. The Marine boot camp, the military convoys, the firefights, are realistically presented as they have been so many times before in so many other movies about so many other wars. Near the end, however, as in M*A*S*H (1970), the script calls for an athletic contest to serve as a metaphor for the nature and conduct of the real war.

As an isolated metaphor, the soccer game works. The American Marines, rigorously trained to be winners, are soundly beating their Vietnamese opponents at halftime when their commanding officer orders them to throw the game. Clearly, the metaphor's message is that the war was thrown; we put the fix in ourselves from Washington. As in so many recent films-- The Parallax View, Network, The China Syndrome, Apocalypse Now --the brass, the administrators, the people running the corporation, are portrayed as the villains. The second half of the soccer game turns into a joke like those "2nd Place" tee shirts. As a metaphor for what happened politically in Vietnam, this soccer game might have some cogency. However, set down in the midst of this otherwise starkly documentary portrayal of the war, it is so extravagant a symbol that it trivializes all that has gone before.

A third film, Go Tell The Spartans, succeeds where the others fail because it consciously focuses on the contrasts between World War II and Vietnam. Whereas WWII films like the most recent extravaganza A Bridge Too Far (1977) are filled with bon vivants (Anthony Hopkins packing his tuxedo for the battle of Arnheim bridge) and merry pranksters (Elliot Gould darting around like a happy munchkin), Go Tell The Spartans, set at the same time as The Green Berets in 1964-65, is a maverick war film about a maverick war.

In Go Tell The Spartans the war is not plotted on maps by brilliant strategists like Eisenhower or Rommel, but on computer screens by corporate clerks. Only the computers seem capable of comprehending the deceptive flux, the illusive ghostliness, the inscrutable reality of the enemy.

Go Tell The Spartans portrays the war as a constant opposition between appearance and reality. It is a theme right out of Blow-Up and Chinatown, a theme of never knowing what is going on, of nothing ever being what it seems.

Another type of formula war film resurrected for the Vietnam era is the "coming of age in war" film. In films of this type such as Big Wednesday (1978) or Our Winning Season (1978) or More American Graffiti (1979), the Vietnam War is trivialized or alluded to only as a tangential backdrop against which more important American initiation rites like surfing and drag racing are foregrounded. In Big Wednesday and Our Winning Season, characters leave the film to grow up in the war. The Vietnam War, handled sentimentally in both cases, is the cliched crucible in which all the high school carefreedom and innocence is burned away. Conversely, a film like Go Tell The Spartans deals with the theme of growing up in the war but deals much more thoughtfully and widely with the reality of both growing up and grownups returning to war for another tour.

Thus far, this chapter reads like just another scoff-at-Hollywood exercise. However, two films, The Deer Hunter (1978) and Apocalypse Now (1979) come to grips with the Vietnam experience in both realistic and symbolic terms. Often it is a major intention and accomplishment of a film is turn real experience into art, not just by reporting it which is what the journalist does or catching it which is what the photographer does or analyzing it which is what the critic does, but actually finding and transforming that experience using all these different approaches to reality in order to give that experience meaning. This is the act of approaching life by means of style. It is an act which tells everyone not only how it was or what it meant but also what everyone's life can be and mean in relation to the event being presented. This sort of approach by means of style is accomplished in Michael Herr the journalist's Dispatches, in Tim O'Brien's Going After Cacciato and in Michael Cimino's The Deer Hunter.

One of the most convincing arguments for the power and significance of The Deer Hunter is the palpable fear of the film which so many people exhibit. They are literally afraid to see it because they don't want to get that involved. Much has been written about the emotional power of the film, but few have plotted its metaphorical structure, attempted definition of its full thematic meaning.

The Deer Hunter's simple, linear plot is structured in three movements like an abbreviated symphony. Many of the events which occur in the film are either factually non-existent (Saigon Russian Roulette parlors) or unbelievable (a Sergeant, or anyone, getting back into Saigon during the final days). But it simply doesn't matter because The Deer Hunter is a film which lives and means through its metaphors. It opens in fire, men walking through a Dante-esque inferno (Something Director Cimino, actor DeNiro and the other Italian members of the company surely envisioned) of the steel mill. The fire image is but one of many metaphors which appear and recur throughout the film. The middle section, set in Vietnam, begins with a napalm drop and Michael (Robert DeNiro) again walking in the fire, killing with a flame-thrower. Before, Hell was simply one's place of employment. In section two, the flames are beginning to burn out of control. In the final section, in Saigon, Michael returns to float through a world going up in flames. Come finally to the Seventh Circle, he learns from Nick (Christopher Walken) the hopelessness of Hell, the lostness of a whole new generation.

The opening section of The Deer Hunter stresses "community" whereas section two stresses psychological aloneness and section three attempts to synthesize the dialectic, resolve the distance between the two poles. Unfortunately, the opening section of the film seems plagiarized while the rest is starkly original and imaginative. The two central scenes of the opening section, the ethnic wedding and the deer hunt, are lifted respectively from The Godfather and Deliverance (1972). But it doesn't matter, they work.

The scenes, the characters, the ironic action of section one all focus on a single central theme, American naivete. The characters see life as a comprehensible and predictable game. They jauntily bet on its outcome. The words of the song, "You're just too good to be true," which echo ironically all through section one define that naivete. During the wedding reception, all the central characters line up for a group picture. Smiling, in white dresses and sharp tuxes, the band playing "You're just too good to be true" in the background, the camera catches their last moment of innocence. The wedding itself, occasioned by the bride's pregnancy, is ironic and directly connected to the departure of the boys for Vietnam. Both the forced wedding and the departure are cases of young men doing things they don't really want to do, yet going ahead and doing them anyway without considering the consequences, without really knowing what they are getting into. They are like Jake Gittes being inexorably drawn toward Chinatown even though he knows it is a place where "You can't always tell what's goin' on."

Section one seeds the film with images of naivete which in the later sections grow and flower with irony. On strong, lithe legs, Stevie (John Savage) leads the Russian folkdance. He will return legless from Vietnam. "If you don't spill a drop, it's good luck for the rest of your life," the announcer predicts as the wedding ritual unfolds, but three tiny drops of red wine stain the breast of the bride's white dress predicting the red splashes of blood on Nick's white shirt in the film's other, later ritual. Michael asks a zonked-out Green Beret who wanders into the wedding reception "what's it like over there?" The man's grim, obscene answer is the one full and real statement of futility in the opening section. Naturally, the boys, in their naivete, laugh at him. Like America in Vietnam, they have no idea what they are getting into.

On the way to the mountains for the deer hunt, Welsh the bartender (George Dzunzdas) gets caught outside the car in a classic "sucker" practical joke. But they are all "suckers," walking into an illusion. Michael's words, as they sit on the car in the mountains, dominate the most important scene in this opening section. He holds up a bullet and says, "This is this!" They laugh. In their fun-loving naivete, the others reject Michael's sudden seriousness and even he can't explain what he means. As he has told Stan (John Cazale), they all have to learn.

In the last scene of section one, Welsh the bartender plays pensive piano the night before Stevie, Nick and Michael leave for Vietnam. The camera pans slowly over their faces as they try to envision what is in store for them. Nick spends most of his time in section one of the film betting . . . and losing. He bets Michael can't pass a semi on the inside and loses . . . his truck. Michael gives him back the registration with the advice, "There's no such thing as a sure thing." In the bar, Nick bets on every shot in the pool game, tossing dollar bills away without a thought. This motif of betting

which appears in section one prepares for the central
metaphor of the film which dominates section two, the
ultimate gamble, Russian Roulette.

"This is this!" Michael had said, holding up a
bullet.   In a Viet Cong prisonhouse, the ultimate
visceral reality of Michael's words, one man/one bullet,
the self in clear and direct confrontation with the threat
of immediate death, rises and is frozen in the Russian
Roulette game. The Cong officer holds up the bullet.
Later, the master of ceremonies of the Russian Roulette
parlor also holds up the bullet as Michael did earlier.
The Russian Roulette is a superb metaphor because it
has meaning on so many different levels.

Literally, the Russian Roulette recreates the AP
Wirephoto of the Saigon chief-of-police putting a gun
to the head of a Viet Cong and pulling the trigger.
Structurally, it underscores section one's theme of
naivete: forced to gamble with their own lives, they bet
blindly on survival; later, they choose to face death even
when unforced.   Politically, it depicts the gamble of
American intervention in Southeast Asia, a gamble which
must ultimately be lost (as Nick does) or withdrawn from
(as Michael urges).   Psychologically, the Russian Roulette
metaphor captures the frozen moment of sudden death
which haunts the flashbacking daymares of a whole generation of American veterans.   After his escape, Nick is
drawn back into the Russian Roulette experience as he
wanders through the chaotic night streets of Saigon.
But most important, when Nick enters the Russian
Roulette parlor, Michael is already sitting in the gallery.
Each man has been drawn back to the one experience
of his life which he has been doomed to repeat forever.
The Russian Roulette metaphor captures the essence of
the flashbacking experience with which so many Vietnam
veterans must live.

The Russian Roulette metaphor also underscores the
central thematic purpose of section two of the film.
Where in section one all were together in a human
community, in this second section each is alone:
Michael in battle, Stevie in the pit, Nick in the

hospital. In the opening battle scene of section two, Michael doesn't even recognize Nick and Stevie when they walk up and greet him. He stumbles in the grip of the sudden catatonia which afflicts a whole range of characters-- Stevie, Nick, Stevie's wife --throughout the rest of the film. This catatonia is the limbo where people whose naivete has been suddenly shattered temporarily walk.

In the Russian Roulette game, each character finds himself isolated with the gun in his hand; each must look at the gun and repeat Michael's earlier words: "This is this!" By shooting most of the Russian Roulette games in brutal agonizing close-ups, the Director visually underscores the tormented aloneness of the characters.

After rescuing the others, Michael walks alone down the burning refugee road. After escaping, Nick quietly and alone goes to pieces on the windowsill of the hospital. Michael experiences the same aloneness at home in Clairton but his reaction is different. He fights his isolation, his catatonia.

Section three is the most analytic and introspective section of the film. The focus is on Michael as he tries to understand all that has happened and put it all back together. This third section takes place in two separate sequences: first, an interlude in Clairton which includes the last deer hunt; second, the return to Vietnam and the final resolution of what is left of the community. Two major themes dominate. In the Clairton interlude, the theme of change is explored through Michael's eyes. In the Saigon scenes and in the ending, the theme of homecoming and reintegration to community is resolved humanly, and, unlike in Coming Home, realistically.

When Michael returns from Vietnam, his friends want to welcome him home, but instead he squats alone against the wall in a motel room in a scene reminiscent of Nick on the hospital windowsill. The next morning, from a distance, he watches his friends leave the house. They pull the same "sucker" play with the car on Welsh. Michael realizes that nothing has changed with them, but he has completely changed. The fire of the steel mill is reprised. "Nothin's changed," says Stan. In the bowling alley, on the deer hunt, the others are still able to laugh and have fun, but for Michael all is different. He stands and hunts alone. The metaphor of the deer hunt comes to its best symbolic resolution when Michael wastes his one shot and screams "I'm OK!" to the cataract. The scene echoes a line which DeNiro playing Bruce Pierson spoke in Bang The Drum Slowly (1973), "I didn't feel like killin' anymore." In the VA Hospital, Stevie tells Michael: "I don't wanna go home. . . . I don't fit." With Stevie's words, Michael is offered the challenge of bringing everyone home, of putting the community back together.

When Michael reenters the fire of Vietnam in search of Nick, he is playing out a fantasy which flashes in the minds of many Vietnam veterans, the same fantasy upon which the film Heroes was based, the survivor guilt fantasy, the desire to go back and bring through combat buddies who didn't make it. In the final reprise of the Russian Roulette game, the capturers, the torturers, are Michael and Nick's own minds. Nick dies in the trap of eternal return. His bright blood spattering over his white shirt fulfills the ominous prophecy of the wine soiling the wedding dress earlier.

The final scene in which the survivors gather together for a communal meal, even sing "God Bless America," has cliche written all over it, but it works. It is the way things are. They are Americans, survivors, friends. They sing to affirm their wounded, no longer naive, community. The major contribution of The Deer Hunter is its tenderness toward its characters. They are real. They are us. What The Deer Hunter does better than any of the other films, including Apocalypse Now, is show how everyone was touched by the war, how we all were victims, all were wounded.

If The Deer Hunter is a symphony, then Apocalypse Now is a rock and roll light show. It captures the audience visually with action, spectacle and dramatic shock. Where The Deer Hunter is an intensely literary film whose images can be read like a work of literature, Apocalypse Now suffers from being based on Heart of Darkness. The Conrad connection distracts rather than serves as an illumination round. It makes little sense to write about the structure of Apocalypse Now because of its faithfulness to Heart of Darkness's myth of the allegorical journey. It does, however, capture the theme of Conrad's novella, man's capability for giving up all civilized restraint, for being attracted to all the possibilities of evil.

Coppola seduces the audience into a suspension of all civilized restraint, all moral judgement, all abhorrence of that which is innately evil. He makes war so beautiful, so fascinating, presents atrocity and obscenity with such routine frequency and visual virtuosity, that the audience becomes used to it, morally immune, forgets the lethal reality. When napalm suddenly explodes across the screen, the audience is mesmerized by its beauty and forgets its reality. That napalm is liquid fire sticking to the bodies of men, women and children, burning them to death. The audience is attracted by the same beautiful, hypnotic, unrestrained horror which captured Kurtz.

The central meaning of Apocalypse Now lies in its ironic meditation upon the human obsession for moral judgement. In a war, this film is saying, no one has the right to accuse or judge because everyone partici-pates in the evil. Those who do judge are so ludicrously shortsighted about their own action that they miss the built-in irony. An Army general and a CIA spook give Capt. Willard (Martin Sheen) his mission. On tape, Kurtz (Marlon Brando) comments ironically: "And they call me an assassin!" Because Kurtz has assassinated four enemy agents, they are sending an assassin to assassinate him. "He's out there operating without any human restraint," the General (G.D. Spradlin) judges, yet Willard's mission is "top secret" and "doesn't even exist nor will it ever exist," because it too is beyond all human restraint. As Willard comments: "charging a man with murder was like handing out speeding tickets at the Indy 500."

The most important speech defining the lunacy of judgement in war falls to Kurtz. He tells of an atrocity committed by the enemy and of the ensuing realization which changed his whole perspective on the war:

> You have to have men who are moral and at the same time are able to utilize their primordial instincts to kill without feeling, without passion, without judgement . . . because it is judgement which defeats us.

Both Kurtz and Willard know that the war has made the world inhospitable for men. As Willard says early, "when I was here I wanted to be there. When I was there all I wanted to be was back in the jungle." What men aren't willing to admit is that with all judgement suspended, they can exist within that war. That is what Apocalypse Now sees as the reason for the Vietnam War causing so many psychological casualties. That war was the apocalypse, the end of restraint, of civilized judgement, for the men who fought there. When they returned from the heart of darkness, they were asked to resume business as usual as if they had never changed, as if they had never entered the jungle.

The political statement of Apocalypse Now doesn't work nearly as well as the ending of The Deer Hunter. Apocalypse Now chooses to celebrate rudimentary hindsight. It criticizes the way the war was run; all those beautiful machines, that elaborate organization, those Playboy bunnies, and yet they can't win or leave or survive. The major political metaphor of the film is Chef's (Frederick Forrest) panicked self-exhortation: "Never get outa the boat!" In Willard's mind, Chef's terrified mumbling becomes political metaphor: "Never get outa the boat unless you were goin' all the way." Scene after scene in Apocalypse Now stresses America's need to learn to leave things alone, to not "get outa the boat."

Willard tells the Chief (Albert Hall) to leave the

sampan alone, but it is searched and a whole Vietnamese family dies for no reason. Coppola follows this scene with a long blank screen pause to let the uselessness sink in. At the spooky bridge, the Chief (who has learned his lesson) argues for turning back: "Why don't we just leave it alone." But Willard can't, and the Chief dies a few clicks upriver because (not having learned his lesson well enough) he needlessly steps out of the wheelhouse to fire wildly into the jungle.

Is it possible to understand life by watching motion pictures? A survey of a subject like Vietnam War films must pose that question. These films are about a real event which took on many different meanings. Each film tries to approach some part of that meaning. But what do you do when you are confronted with a reality so dramatic, so shocking, frightening, confusing, that it makes Alfred Hitchcock look like Walt Disney? You distance it. In most cases-- with Go Tell The Spartans, The Deer Hunter, and Apocalypse Now the exceptions --that is what Hollywood has done for the Vietnam War. That distancing was what Jake Gittes tried to do with his past in Chinatown but inevitably he kept being drawn back into it until all that was left for him to do was walk away. Those three successful Vietnam War films also realized that ultimately the basic social realities of the seventies couldn't be distanced. Those three films have presented visual and verbal metaphors which strike right to the heart of one of the darkest periods in the American experience.

7. THE FORGOTTEN VIETNAM FILM

1979 was the 100th Anniversary of the birth of Albert Einstein. Perhaps his theory of relativity-- the proposition that the properties of a thing, an event, a person, remain constant but seem to vary depending upon the point from which that object is observed --offers the best method of all for examining the subject of the Vietnam War and the films which that war has generated. Year by year, that war takes different shape in the hands of new writers and filmmakers. Whether from a grunt's eye view or from a firefight-hopping helicopter, whether from Saigon or Khe Sanh, whether from Chicago or Kent State or through the eye of a documentary movie camera in the act or in fictional metaphoric commercial film hindsight, the war has accrued a great deal of relativity. As we move further away in time and space, the war itself becomes more and more remote while images of the war assert themselves more and more prominently. Images can never be the war, but they should at least try to reflect the war accurately. As the previous chapter pointed out, only a small percentage of the films about the Vietnam War to appear in the seventies succeed with any sort of realistic or metaphorical accuracy.

Three successful films are always mentioned, but only two are ever discussed. The two are, of course, The Deer Hunter and Apocalypse Now while the other is Go Tell The Spartans, a 1978 film directed by Ted Post and starring Burt Lancaster.

Why is Go Tell The Spartans the forgotten Vietnam

film? First, the film's title gives no signal that it is a
Vietnam film (for all the average filmgoer can tell, Go
Tell The Spartans could be a Victor Mature gladiator
remake). Its publicity budget was about a dollar-fifty. It
received few major reviews. It played for a grand total
of about 15 minutes in American theaters. Few people
have seen the film and fewer people have written about
it. Yet, Go Tell The Spartans is a fine, perceptive,
well-acted, high production value film whose meanings
work on a number of representative levels to attempt
definition of the situation of American involvement in
Vietnam during the earliest stages of the war.

Go Tell The Spartans is based on Daniel Ford's
short novel Incident At Muc Wa, written and published
while the war was still going on (Doubleday and Co.,
1967); in fact, while the war was still in its infancy. In
this light, Incident At Muc Wa is a startlingly prophetic
book. Not nearly as prophetic as Graham Greene's The
Quiet American, but prophetic nonetheless. The plot of
the novel embodies the thoughtless futility of the
American presence in Vietnam. It involves an old French
outpost that the Americans don't want to garrison and
the Viet Cong have no desire to attack yet which
becomes the site of a major firefight. The book was
written a year before Khe Sanh existed and eighteen
months before the famous siege of Khe Sanh was "won"
and the encampment abandoned.

But the prophetic qualities of Ford's Incident At
Muc Wa do not outweigh the fact that it is a bad
novel filled with characterizational cliches and
embarrassing writing. It is such a haphazard and
frivolous book in so many ways. One of the outposts is
named "BOO JUM". One of the central characters, a
ticket-punching Captain, is named after Ford's typewriter.
"She went over to rescue her typewriter from Captain
Olivetti," the narrator at one point draws attention to
the novelist's little exercise in cuteness. Corporal Ackley
has acne and the General is named Harnetz (guess what
the men call him behind his back?). In a different kind
of novel, all of this might be acceptable playfulness. But

in a novel this purportedly serious, it is all in trite bad taste. Perhaps the most embarrassing part of the novel is a subplot involving a young Jewish newspaper reporter for a stateside tabloid called, what else, The Liberal. The scriptwriters have had the good sense to completely excise this Lois Lane character and this silly subplot from the film.

In its time, 1967, Incident At Muc Wa was an interesting novel about a confusing war. It has all kinds of factual and historical value-- Ford closely observed the bric-a-brac, motives and mannerisms, if not the language, of the war --but very little literary value. It has been superceded by other, much better, combat memoirs and fictions. Its major value for a filmmaker is its wealth of unrealized characters and incidents. In Go Tell The Spartans, these characters are not only realized, they are given symbolic, even mythic, significance. Perhaps the relationship of Incident At Muc Wa to Go Tell The Spartans proves once again an old Hollywood maxim: "Bad books make good movies."

Go Tell The Spartans is brazenly unfaithful to Ford's Incident At Muc Wa. Though the film does get rid of the stupid girl reporter, it keeps most of the book's characters. However, the film changes many of those characterizations drastically. Only three characters from Ford's novel stay essentially the same in Post's film: Corporal Courcey (Craig Wasson), the romantic innocent; Captain Olivetti (Marc Singer), the ticket-puncher; and Corporal Old Man, a Man Friday Vietnamese. All of the other major characters change either in terms of the substance of their characterization or their plot action.

In terms of plot action, for example, Sergeant Oleonowski (Ron Liebman), in the book, marries a Vietnamese refugee girl named Butterfly and manages to take her back to Penang to have their child. In the film, Sergeant Oleo commits suicide and Butterfly leads a Viet Cong ambush of the American advisors. In the book, confused Lieutenant Hamilton, who spends his brief tour in Vietnam skirmishing with a #1 case of the

runs, is med-evaced out due to malnutrition; in the
film, Hamilton (Jonathan Goldsmith) is killed leading a
foolhardy mission across a river which the Viet Cong
have zeroed in with deadly crossfire.

The film also takes characters from the book and
either realizes full characterizations where only flat
cardboard effigies stood before or changes characterization
drastically to emphasize theme. In the film, Major Barker
(Burt Lancaster) becomes the central character. In Ford's
book, Barker was only a confused, drunken, publicity-seeking buffoon of a minor character. Major Barker
carries much of the thematic statement of the film and
chooses to die a soldier at Muc Wa with the Vietnamese
Raiders when all of the other Americans except Courcey
abandon them. Two other characterizations which are
mere shadows in Ford's novel-- Cowboy, the Kit Carson
scout and an old, ghostly Viet Cong --become extremely
important thematically in Go Tell The Spartans.
Cowboy, in his unsentimental brutality and his
instinctual, pragmatic knowledge of the treachery of the
territory, serves as an important counterpoint to the
sentimental romanticism of the American presence in
Vietnam. He knows how to deal with the Indians,
something the Americans never learn. The ghostly,
one-eyed Cong who haunts the French graveyard in Go
Tell The Spartans becomes a mythic image of the
"secret sharer" that so many Americans who fought in
Vietnam sensed.

Go Tell The Spartans, therefore, is something
different altogether from Daniel Ford's Incident At Muc
Wa. The film creates whole new themes which Ford's
novel never realized even if it did sense them. The
film's characters also speak those themes in completely
new dialog none of which is carried over from the
novel.

Go Tell The Spartans is set in 1964 when Americans were supposedly still advisors in Vietnam, before
that first cocky battalion of Marines landed in DaNang
for their "splendid little war" as Phillip Caputo called
it in his Pulitzer Prize-winning memoir A Rumor of War

(New York: Ballantine, 1978). Set at the same time as The Green Berets (1966), Go Tell The Spartans tells it like it really was, not as John Wayne, caught up in some Fort Apache wet-dream, imagined it to be. In The Green Berets, John Wayne's troops win a huge set-piece battle. In Go Tell The Spartans, Major Barker's troops get wiped out from ambush by a group of ragtag refugees. The film begins conventionally enough with the static introduction of a group of transparently type-cast soldiers: the college boy, the stupid green Lieutenant, the battle-hardened sergeant, the rich-boy doper, the ticket-punching officer who wants to go back to the States and be a politician, and the nails-for-breakfast General Harnetz (nicknamed "Hard Nuts"). You expect some war hero type like John Wayne or Charlton Heston or Glenn Ford or Henry Fonda to play the lead role in a formula war movie like this, but all you get is a limping Burt Lancaster: subdued, tired, cynical. Major Barker and Cowboy, a Kit Carson scout who is first seen giving a VC the water torture in order to extort information, are the only break in the war movie stereotypes of the first one-third of the film. But despite the flat opening and just when the film seems to be settling down to become just like every other Army movie since Sergeant York (1941), Darby's Rangers (1958) and The Dirty Dozen (1967), Go Tell The Spartans comes alive. The characters start vibrating into roundness. The writing (particularly the dialog) gets interesting. The Vietnam War starts to take graphic shape. The film starts making highly ironic verbal and visually symbolic comments about the Vietnam War on HISTORICAL, PHILOSOPHICAL and MYTHIC levels of representation.

The historical meaning of the film focuses upon the differences between the Vietnam War and World War II, differences which the American military command never recognized before it was too late. The film examines how the world and the way war is conducted have changed since World War II and how America hasn't kept up. One aspect of this theme is represented by Barker's reactions to Sergeant Wattsburg, a computer intelligence specialist. Wattsburg sets up an elaborate computer system, his "Incident Flow Indicator," to track the whereabouts of the Viet Cong. "You mean you're gonna tell us where the VC are gonna attack before they do it," a skeptical Barker taunts Wattsburg. For all his experience, Barker isn't prepared to fight this kind of war. Wattsburg's computer is better prepared. In World War II, the command decisions were made by men; personalities like Patton (or Barker) could emerge and control the action. Not so in Vietnam. Only the machines seem capable of comprehending the baffling invisibility of the enemy. However, the real irony of this new computer war becomes evident when considered in the light of an earlier incident as commented upon by the battle-wise Sergeant Oleo. When a booby-trapped roadblock suddenly appears in the path of a secret truck convoy, Oleo says: "VC know everything we're going to do. That roadblock wasn't there yesterday. They knew that convoy was coming." The VC don't even have a computer, yet they are more than holding their own against all that sophisticated American technology.

But the historical theme is most heavily concentrated in the characterization of Major Barker. To Wattsburg, Barker is a dinosaur who doesn't trust technology and ought to be extinct. To Cowboy, Barker is, like Courcey, a kind of sentimentalist. Experienced as Barker is, the primitive savagery of Cowboy (who kills anything that moves) still makes him nervous. Barker longs for a more understandable, yes, a more "civilized" war, a war like World War II. But what Barker gets is Vietnam.

He realizes that he and the other Americans are just not equipped to fight this new kind of war. When Courcey says, "Maybe I just wanted to see what a war is like," Barker chomps down on his cigar and in his tired soldier's voice answers:

> You know what you are? You're a tourist.
> Too bad we couldn't have shown you a
> better war. Like hitting the beach at Anzio

or smashing through to Bastogne with Patton. That was a real tour. This one's a sucker's tour. Going nowhere. Just around and around in circles.

By the end, Courcey accepts the truth of a phrase which has echoed throughout the film as he finally agrees, "It's their war." Barker ends up naked and dead at Muc Wa. Confused, lacking terms to explain this new kind of war, trying to make the old terms fit and failing, not only failing but completely missing the point, Barker is like so many Americans during that time in that place.

On a philosophical plane of meaning, Go Tell The Spartans defines the Vietnam War as a surreal and unresolved dialectic in which nothing is ever what it seems, where contradiction rules and where established human truths are constantly ambushed and blown away. Einsteinian relativity and inscrutable reality rules the world of the film. Courcey sees the war as an educational experience. Olivetti sees the war as a political opportunity. Barker sees the war as "a sucker's tour."

Early in Go Tell The Spartans, Barker asks, "Where are we?"

His Adjutant answers, "Penang, Vietnam."

"You sure it's not a loony bin?" Barker shoots back. "Sometimes I think we're in a goddam loony bin."

This "appearance versus reality" dialectic is understood by only one character in the film. Cowboy trusts no appearances. He instinctively senses all the masked realities of the war.

Early in the film, when a group of refugees are spotted in a jungle clearing, the following exchange occurs:

COWBOY: Cong. We attack?
COURCEY: Let's be damn sure before we start
          shooting.
COWBOY: They Cong. Shoot first then look.

All through the film Cowboy keeps saying "They Cong" but nobody listens to him. Courcey takes in and befriends the refugees. In the end, the refugees ambush Courcey, Barker and the Raiders and an innocent young girl pops out of a hole in the ground and machine-guns Cowboy.

The ruling tone and controlling vision of the film is irony. A pretty little girl is a killer. A corpsman named Abraham Lincoln is a junkie. Lieutenant Hamilton catches the quickstep and dies of his own stupidity because he doesn't know enough whereas Sergeant Oleo commits suicide because he knows too much. Barker who says that Vietnam is "a sucker's tour" dies because he is a sucker for his concept of duty. Cowboy, the most unsentimental character in the film, dies because of others' sentimentality.

In terms of this theme of the illusoriness of reality, Go Tell The Spartans can be compared to Chinatown. In both films, "nothing is ever what it seems to be." The last line of that film, "It's Chinatown," with only slight revision, could be the last line of Go Tell The Spartans. The Americans in Vietnam didn't understand the people, the culture, the language, the jungle or the war itself. All through the film the Americans try to understand the Vietnamese, try to communicate with the Vietnamese, try to predict the intentions of the Vietnamese, but they never succeed. When the Americans look for answers to why they never succeed, they can't find any. About the best they can do is shrug their shoulders and say "It's Vietnam" or some equally hapless equivalent like "It's their war."

Perhaps Go Tell The Spartans' best symbolic representation of the futility of America's tussle with appearance and reality in Vietnam comes in one scene where a camera angle and an editing choice offer a wealth of symbolic meaning. The scene involves the simple landing of a huge transport helicopter. Like a pregnant pelican, it roosts in the paddy, thumping out streams of air. But the grass simply bends with the cur-

rents, never gives or breaks. When the chopper lifts off,
the camera lingers on the ground and no sign is left of
the American machine ever having been there.

But Go Tell The Spartans also goes on to examine
the Vietnam War from a mythic perspective. This level
of meaning focuses upon a theme of the "secret
sharer(s)" in the world of the war. The title of the film
comes from an inscription over the gate of an old
graveyard in which a full company of French soldiers are
buried in unmarked graves. The inscription, written by
the French commander, refers to the battle of Ther-
mopylae and the three hundred Spartans who died there.
It reads: "Stranger, when you find us lying here, go tell
the Spartans we obeyed their orders." This inscription
which links the ancient Spartan soldiers to the French
soldiers to the Americans captures the layered nature of
the war, how every soldier shares the same reality with
every other soldier not only in this war but across the
ages. "Go tell the Spartans" is a mythic epitaph for the
"universal soldier" (of the Vietnam-era folk song) and
"The Unknown Soldier" (of Jim Morrison's Vietnam rock
lyric title).

Directly associated with this mythic graveyard in Go
Tell The Spartans is an image which embodies the
mythic intentions of the film. When Courcey first enters
the graveyard, he gets a brief glimpse of a man with a
gun. Immediately, the man disappears. From the very
beginning, the relationship between Courcey and the old
Cong fluctuates between the real and the surreal, between
appearance and reality. The next two appearances of the
old Cong occur in the form of portentous cutaways. At
crucial points in the American presence in the film, the
camera cuts away to close-ups of this old,
battle-wizened, hollow-cheeked, one-eyed, Viet Cong
soldier with his head wrapped in a dirty bandage and
his blackened, burnt-out eye socket sighting blindly
down the barrel of a rifle so old that it even pre-dates
the French in Vietnam. After Courcey in the pouring
rain has counted the graves of the 302 Frenchmen who
died in the earlier battle of Muc Wa, idiotic Lieutenant

Hamilton says: "All brave men. They fought the battle and lost. But we won't lose. We're Americans." As Hamilton finishes his speech and runs off through the rain to shit in the jungle, the camera cuts away to that old one-eyed Viet Cong, waiting, staring enigmatically, perhaps inwardly laughing at the insane <u>hubris</u> of the Americans.

That mythic image of the one-eyed Viet Cong soldier captures that vague sense of a "secret sharer" which many American combat soldiers in Vietnam experienced. One combat veteran described it in these terms: "I always sensed he was out there, used to think about him all the time, like he was my twin or something. Some VC, like me, wondering what the hell was going on, doing the war, but not understanding the war."[2] That old Viet Cong images what the Vietnam War was. He is just there, trapped in a war that makes no sense. He is just there, waiting for something to happen. "This is this," Michael says enigmatically in <u>The Deer Hunter</u>. "I'm here, always here," the old, one-eyed Viet Cong might well be thinking in <u>Go</u> <u>Tell</u> <u>The</u> <u>Spartans</u>.

In the last scene of the film, Courcey, wounded, the only survivor of the ambush, makes his way back to the graveyard where he confronts his "secret sharer." The two face each other across the graves of all the soldiers of antiquity. The old Viet Cong soldier raises his antique rifle, but doesn't fire as Courcey staggers across the graveyard crying "I'm goin' home, Charlie."

Perhaps a lyric by David Crosby from a song called "For What It's Worth" (1966) best captures the meaning of <u>Go</u> <u>Tell</u> <u>The</u> <u>Spartans</u>. It is a lyric that vibrates with ambush and firefight and surreality and old, evil-eyed Viet Cong:

>   There's something happening here,

----

[2]Private interview with Vietnam veterans conducted as part of English 232, "The Literature of the Vietnam War," Purdue University, Spring 1979.

What it is ain't exactly clear.
There's a man with a gun over there,
Tellin' me I've got to beware.
I think it's time we stopped, children,
What's that sound?
Everybody look what's goin' down . . .

From Go Tell The Spartans, innocence meets insight in
the "Chinatown" of the seventies, Vietnam. Courtesy of
MOMA/Film Stills Archives.

8. SUPERIMPOSED REALITIES: THE VISUAL/VERBAL THEMES IN APOCALYPSE NOW

When Apocalypse Now opened in late 1979, the critics fell upon it like scavengers on a C-rat dump. By consensus, they found five major flaws. One, the journey upriver is visually exciting and humanly compelling,but the final section in Kurtz's compound fails. Two, though Conrad's Heart of Darkness provides structure for the film, it ultimately gets in the way of dramatic resolution. Three, Martin Sheen's Captain Willard remains undeserving of sympathy and detached throughout while the central character, Brando's Kurtz, is an incoherent and obese embarrassment. Four, the voice-over narration is intrusive and melodramatic. And finally, the film is an ambitious war epic which fails due to its inability to involve the audience on the human level.[3]

Although the critics formed up in almost unanimous agreement about Apocalypse Now, they failed to look closely enough at either Coppola's techniques or his

---

[3]Stephen Farber (New West 9/10/79) writes of Apocalypse Now: ". . . this fiasco is as shocking and painful to behold as the first staggering defeat suffered by a brilliant general." Veronica Geng (New Yorker 9/3/79) maintains that "the movie collapses, as '2001' does, in a final attempt to show the unshowable." Gene Siskel's headline (Chicago Tribune 10/5/79) clearly agrees

(Footnote continued)

symbolic images which serve as the major vehicles for
the conveyance of meaning in the film. Not only does
Coppola's film offer a wealth of visual and verbal
symbols but it also undertakes to examine the reality of
what it was like, on the outside and the inside, to be a
grunt in Vietnam. Unlike its major competitors among
the Vietnam War films, Apocalypse Now doesn't worry
about the difficulties of coming home, nor does it base
its meaning upon metaphors which have no foundation
in fact. It presents the reality of the surreality, the tormented psychology which never came through on the
five-o'clock follies, the six-o'clock news or in any of
the previous Vietnam War movies with the limited
exception of Go Tell The Spartans. Of all the Vietnam
War films, Apocalypse Now is the most characteristically
a seventies movie. It graphically presents the theme of
corporate conspiracy as well as consistently reiterating the
dominant truth which man in the seventies must learn to
accept, that "nothing is ever what it seems to be." Most
critics overlooked Apocalypse Now's seventiesness and
wrote it off either because the film wasn't quite what
they expected or because Vietnam and the war as
portrayed in Coppola's film wasn't quite what they had
expected.

In fact, point by point,the five major critical
objections to Apocalypse Now display an astounding
tactical misapprehension. For example one: while
nibbling away at Brando and the final one-third of the
film, the critics failed to see the appropriateness of
Brando's casting and appearance, and, they ignored the
most important speech of the film which he delivers.

------

[3](continued)
with the others: "VIET NAM FILM ENDS UP FIGHTING
ITSELF." Vincent Canby excoriates the film (especially
the ending) in terms very similar to those of Siskel. Of
the major reviewers, only Charles Champlin (Los Angeles
Times 8/12/79) and Roger Ebert (Chicago Sun Times
9/26/79) wrote enthusiastic reviews.

For example two: only Veronica Geng defined the dominant textual influence upon Apocalypse Now, Michael Herr and Dispatches. For example three: Willard, not Kurtz, is the central character in Apocalypse Now (as Marlow also is in Heart of Darkness). For example four: while scoffing at the voice-over narration, the critics failed to search for any thematic meaning in Coppola's visual/verbal technique, particularly the recurring use of superimposition. And finally, Apocalypse Now is a psychological study, not a war epic in the genre tradition of The Longest Day (1962), A Bridge Too Far (1977), and Tora, Tora, Tora (1970). Ironically, the very things in Apocalypse Now which have been misinterpreted most often are the things which most expressively serve Coppola's intention.

I
"Mistah Kurtz, he dead."

Coppola's handling of the final Kurtz section of Apocalypse Now drew the most concentrated fire. Yet, the casting of Brando was as inspired as was the casting of John Wayne as a dying gunfighter in The Shootist (1976) or Paul Newman as an aging star in Buffalo Bill And The Indians (1976). If one is going to kill a sacred cow, who better to play that cow than Brando. Jack Kroll noted (Newsweek 8/20/79) that in this final section

> the parallel with Conrad becomes closest and most dangerous. Coppola handles it shrewdly . . . . Faced with a grotesquely obese Brando, Coppola swathes him in a mythic mantle of light and shadow, his shaven head looming from the darkness like a moon of evil.

Few other critics appreciated either Brando's shaven head or Coppola's photographing of it. However, that shadowy, looming, enigmatic head links Coppola's Brando to a classical symbology representative of American megalomania:

> . . . a vast form shot lengthwise, but
> obliquely from the sea. Shrouded in a thin
> drooping veil of mist, it hovered . . .
> strangely vibrating his predestinating head,
> sent a broad band of over-spreading
> semicircular foam before him as he rushed.
> Retribution, swift vengeance, eternal malice
> were in his whole aspect, and spite of all
> that mortal man could do, the solid white
> buttress of his forehead smote . . .

Thus Melville described Moby Dick. "Forehead to
forehead I meet thee," Ahab voiced the challenge. In the
shadowy shaven skull of Kurtz, not Conrad's Kurtz but
Coppola's American Kurtz, Willard encounters a modern
version of the white whale, an image of primordial evil,
chaos and, perhaps, revelation. Coppola might have been
analyzing the relationship between Ahab and Moby Dick
when he said:

> Willard going up the river to meet Kurtz
> was perhaps also a man looking at another
> aspect or projection of himself. I always had
> the idea of Willard and Kurtz being the same
> man-- in terms of how I made my decisions
> to do whatever we did. And I feel that
> Willard arriving at the compound to meet
> Kurtz is like coming to the place that you
> don't want to go --because it's all your
> ghosts and all your demons.[4]

As Coppola sees it and photographs it, Willard's
meeting with Kurtz is a moment of classical American
discovery comparable to that which Melville embodies in

---

[4]Greil Marcus, "Journey Up The River: An Interview
With Francis Coppola," Rolling Stone (11/1/79).

the forehead of Moby Dick. Or, more recently, it is the sort of confrontation with "the horror" rising up from the depths that was given a contemporary embodiment in Steven Spielberg's Jaws.

Kurtz's forehead becomes for Willard a mirror in which he sees himself. In one of the most visually effective and symbolic shots in Apocalypse Now, Willard, on his way to murder Kurtz, rises from beneath the surface of the river, his head smooth, glazed with the mud of the unconscious. He has brought the darkness of his deepest self to the surface and, as a result, has taken on his closest resemblance to Kurtz.

The casting of Brando as Kurtz is also important because of the demands of the single speech which defines one of Coppola's major themes. In that speech, Kurtz describes an atrocity committed by the enemy and his ensuing realization which changed his entire conception of the war:

> My God the genius . . . trained cadres . . . men who fought with their hearts, had families, had children, and had the strength to do that. If I had ten divisions of such men, our troubles would be over. You have to have men who are moral and at the same time are able to utilize their primordial instincts to kill without feeling, without passion, without judgement . . . because it is judgement which defeats us.

That speech, shot completely in close-up, captures the one reality of the Vietnam War which no one in America wanted to face. Judgement is a psychological act which does not effect reality because judgement can only deal with past action. Judgement becomes especially useless in war where criminal action and duty blur into each other. Therefore, Kurtz defines judgement as a weakness which the enemy has overcome but which is too deeply engrained in the American consciousness to ever be subdued. Speaking out of the shadows of human depravity, Brando's voice delivers the message with a leprous resignation, a tortured anguish, an alienated clarity and a compelling vulnerability. He whispers the shadowy truth. Few other American actors could deliver that speech convincingly.

II

The Influence of Dispatches

A second major offensive against Apocalypse Now concerns the film's literary genesis out of Conrad's Heart of Darkness. As Veronica Geng in her New Yorker review put it, "as a conventional updating of Joseph Conrad's Heart of Darkness . . . Apocalypse Now looks like not much more than a cannibalization." Geng and Charles Champlin were the only critics who veered away from discussing Apocalypse Now as a slavish literary modernization of Conrad's novella. Champlin wrote in his Los Angeles Times review:

> Whatever the literal borrowings of dialogue and incident from Conrad, "Apocalypse" must work or fail on its own. After one viewing, it seemed to me that the film was weakened by its debt to Conrad and had grown too consciously literary.

Geng and a later critic, Terry Peavler writing in PMLA (March 1980), both questioning, as Champlin did, the usefulness of comparing Apocalypse Now to Heart of Darkness, posited that perhaps the major literary influence upon the film is not Conrad, but rather Michael Herr.

At different stages of the Apocalypse Now production adventure, Coppola entertained the vague sense that he wasn't just making a war epic or remaking Conrad's Heart of Darkness. All along during the seemingly endless script revising, production rethinking and ending juggling, Coppola was moving toward the realization that his film could indeed capture, as no other films had, the reality of the incountry Vietnam experience. Perhaps this realization occurred just prior to Coppola's decision to bring Michael Herr, Vietnam news corps veteran and author of the most highly acclaimed non-fiction prose work on the war, Dispatches, aboard to write Captain Willard's first-person voice-over narration. As Coppola notes in the Marcus interview in Rolling Stone, Herr's Esquire pieces on Vietnam had already influenced the earliest scripting of Apocalypse Now, so bringing Herr on at the end to write the narration was most appropriate. Almost all of the episodes which emphasize the surreality of the war experience are directly adapted from Dispatches as is most of the voice-over narration. As Veronica Geng writes in her New Yorker review, "Apocalypse Now seems indebted to the special intensity of Herr's vision of the heart of the Vietnam War's darkness."

Knowledge of the influence of Dispatches and of the Coppola/Herr collaboration upon Apocalypse Now explains Coppola's and Sheen's handling of the characterization of Captain Willard. Most of the critics, unaccountably misreading both Apocalypse Now and Heart of Darkness, base their arguments on a mistaken conception that Kurtz is the central character in both works.[5] In fact, Willard (Marlow/Herr) is always the central character and his importance is dictated by the specific type of war film which Coppola chose to make.

Apocalypse Now simply is not a traditional war epic. It is a psychological study. "The first thing that happened after my involvement was a psychologization

---

[5]Stephen Farber in New West writes: "While Kurtz is the central figure, he does not make his first appearance until the last half-hour of the film. A novelist can conjure up an impression of an unseen character simply by describing the narrator's thoughts and feelings. But Coppola's cinematic substitute for the interior monologue -- a portentous voice-over narration (written by Michael
(Footnote continued)

of Willard," Coppola insists in his <u>Rolling Stone</u>
interview with Greil Marcus. "Marty approached an
impossible character: he had to be an observer, a
watcher. A lot of reading of dossiers, a totally
introspective character. In no way could he get in the
way of the audience's view of what was happening, of
Vietnam." Sheen's view of his character and of the film
as presented in a <u>Rolling Stone</u> (11/1/79) interview
conducted by Jean Vallely backs up Coppola: "As
Willard makes his journey up the river in search of
Kurtz, he makes another journey inside himself . . . .
This is the first war movie made that is a trip inside a
man's mind."

The making of a psychological film always involves
the confronting of one major problem which has plagued
filmmakers since the days of Griffith and Porter-- How
do you photograph psychology? Close-ups, expressive
looks and facial tics, superimpositions, flashbacks and
flashforwards, dream sequences, offstage and voice-over
narrations, sound effects, soliloquys, all of these
techniques exist for but one purpose, to externalize the
inner psychological workings of a character's mind. In
<u>Apocalypse Now</u>, Kurtz is a totally externalized character.
The evidences of his madness-- severed heads sprouting
from the ground like cabbages, trees bearing crucified
human fruit --are outwardly displayed everywhere in his
compound. Beyond these evidences, Kurtz talks
incessantly and when he talks, his only subject is his
own mind. His major speeches, including the early
tape-recorded "snail on the edge of a straight razor"

---

[5](continued)
Herr) --seems totally inadequate to the task of defining
the invisible Kurtz." Mr. Farber has missed the point
twice here. First, Willard is the central character. Second,
the monologue defines Willard rather than attempting to
define Kurtz. Charles Champlin in his <u>Los Angeles
Times</u> review makes the same mistake: "Kurtz, and not
(Footnote continued)

Apocalypse Now

219

speech, are all Shakespearean soliloquys devised for the express purpose of revealing the inner psychology of the character. He conducts a guided tour of his own psyche and Willard is the developing consciousness who finds himself trapped, like all the Vietnam grunts, into that tour.

Thus, not only is Willard the central character in Apocalypse Now, but portraying Willard's psychology is also the central problem. As a means of solving that problem, Coppola chooses two techniques, one visual, one verbal, to portray the inner workings of Willard's mind. The visual use of superimpositions combines with the voice-over narration to not only externalize Willard's psychological dilemma, but also to make a major thematic point about the Vietnam war itself, a point quite similar to the central themes of both Blow-Up and Chinatown concerning the multiple dimensions of reality.

III
Superimposition As Theme

The very nature of the Vietnam War and the psychological uniqueness of the men who fought there dictated the parallel visual/verbal structure of Apocalypse Now. Vietnam was a war fueled by two distinct types of violence:

> 1) the terrible physical violence and stress from terrain, climate and fatigue as well as battle;
> 2) the numbing psychological violence of uncertainty, fear, loss, confusion, cultural dislocation, abandonment and boredom.

---

[5](continued)
he, is the crucial figure in the story, and it is frustrating not to know anything like as much about the assassinating Captain as we know about Kurtz."

The first type of violence, the physical, is endemic to any war situation; the second, the psychological, was perhaps more acute in Vietnam than in any previous American war. Conventionally, the visual images in a war film represent only externalized violence. In <u>Apocalypse Now</u>, the visual effects symbolically support the verbal interiorization of the voice-over narrative to present the psychological stress, confusion and violence of this particular war.

In <u>Apocalypse Now</u>'s opening scene, Coppola chose the technique of superimposition as his means of initially defining the psychology of his grunt Everyman, Captain Willard. That technique introduces the symbolic conception of life in the Vietnam War as a layered phenomenon, a situation in which widely separate realities are constantly being overlaid, superimposed, upon one another. It is a theme similar to those which the other major films of the decade, specifically <u>Chinatown</u> have already encountered. Life in the war as the continuous superimposition of the psychological upon the physical, of the inner world upon the outer world, becomes another central theme of the film. Over the image of a simultaneous napalm strike/helicopter assault is superimposed the looming, inverted head of Willard. The helicopter blades thumping out death and destruction in the physical image of the war dissolve into the revolving blades of a ceiling fan superimposed on Willard's enlarged forehead, a forehead which prefigures the photographing of Kurtz's forehead later. But we have been misled. What seemed to be the physical reality of the war is really the psychological reality of Willard's possessed mind. The ceiling fan symbolizes Willard's wounded psyche pulsing out the waves of nightmare. And, over these superimposed visual images is superimposed yet another layer, the verbal images in the words of Jim Morrison's apocalyptic song "The End": "Lost in a Roman wilderness of pain/And all the children are insane." As Mikal Gilmore wrote of this opening scene in <u>Rolling Stone</u> (6/28/79) " we see

that it is simply the fire of Martin Sheen's reverie--
deathly dreams." As the scene goes on, the verbal
interior monologue, the voice-over, is superimposed thus
adding another layer. The words of the monologue speak
of other psychological superimpositions: "When I was
here, I wanted to be there. When I was there, all I
could think of was getting back into the jungle." Images
upon images, layers upon layers, separate realities
overlaying each other like mismatched transparencies in
some mad animated cartoon; the opening scene of
Apocalypse Now signals Coppola's whole strategy in the
film, his intention to constantly emphasize the way in
which the Vietnam War was a mad nightmare of many
separate realities all simultaneously piling up in layers
upon each other to create a bedlam so confused that
only an apocalypse could ever restore order. This theme
of the layered complexity of reality in the Vietnam War
closely approximates the "nothing is ever what it seems
to be" theme of Chinatown and the theme of man's
impotence toward understanding the distortions of
contemporary reality in Blow-Up.

Superimposition was the rule of life and of
psychological survival in the Vietnam War. Grunts tried
to superimpose past American life upon a world and
situation so cut off from America it seemed as if, as
Conrad wrote in Heart Of Darkness, they had been
"kicked . . . loose of the earth."[6] Apocalypse Now, after
its opening scene, proceeds from one scene of
superimposition to another. Each scene portrays the
constant effort of the grunts to control and muffle the
terrible reality of the war by overlaying that reality with
separate, more palatable, realities. But the irony of this
existence is also emphasized. Invariably, this
superimposition strategy fails. No matter how many layers

---

[6]Joseph Conrad, Heart of Darkness (New York:
Norton Critical Edition, 1963), p. 67. All subsequent
quotations from Heart of Darkness will be from this
edition.

of other past reality are superimposed upon the present reality, the reality of the war always reasserts itself. The true and present horror always defeats the superimposition strategy.

After the opening scene, Apocalypse Now proceeds from one symbolic superimposition to the next. All of the narrative devices employed to reveal factual material about Kurtz-- the briefing, the dossiers --are tri-level superimpositions of Kurtz's past reality upon Kurtz's present reality upon Willard's own developing psychological reality. Even the tape recording of Kurtz's voice, superimposed upon the present voices at the briefing, ironically perceives its subject, assassination, in terms of a layered superimposition. "And they call me an assassin," Kurtz's voice intones out of the tape machine. "What do you call it when the assassins accuse the assassins." Or, when the assassins send an assassin to assassinate the assassin? The General (G.D. Spradlin) tells Willard how Kurtz is "out there operating without any human restraint" and then directs Willard to "terminate" Kurtz "with extreme prejudice," in other words without any human restraint. "You realize Captain that this mission doesn't exist, nor will it ever exist," the General finishes, disavowing all restraint and all responsibility, and launching Willard into a world even more inscrutable than Jake Gittes' Chinatown, a world where reality isn't just puzzling, but, at least according to this General, doesn't even exist.

The next major sequence, Willard's time with Colonel Kilgore (Robert Duvall) and the Air Cav, offers a number of historical and psychological superimpositions. All the old romantic Cavalry traditions-- the hats, the bugle --of a lost past out of movies like She Wore A Yellow Ribbon (1949) have been artificially superimposed upon the mindless mechanized menace of the new Air Cav. Dreams of galloping horses can't dispel the ugly hovering reality of the skeletal choppers. Kilgore's Air Cav unit further attempts to superimpose California dreams of surfing and beach parties upon the reality of the war, but that doesn't work either. "They choppered in the T-bones and the beer and turned the LZ into a beach party. The more they tried to make it just like home, the more they made everybody miss it," Willard says.

Willard's time on the PBR going upriver invokes a number of similar symbolic superimpositions of the past at home in another world upon the frightening and deadly present incountry Vietnam. In an attempt to become again what he once was, Chef (Frederick Forrest) searches in the jungle for mangoes, but a tiger rips open his reverie. Listening to a tape recording from his mother at home, Cleen (Larry Fishburne) is ripped open by machine gun fire. Of all the superimpositions of an American world of past reality upon the present frustrating and lonely reality of the war, the Bunny scene at the upriver supply depot is the most elaborate. The PX displays rows of motorcycles as if it were a K-Mart back in Toledo. The Bunnies, in Cowboy and Indian outfits, erect past images of sexual arousal and release in the crowd of men who watch them dance, but the phallic gunhumping of the dancers under the phallic pillars rising behind the bleachers is but a sinister representation of the only release available to these men, the release of war.

In the same manner in which Willard's journey upriver had been introduced by that opening scene of superimpositions, the final section of Apocalypse Now which takes place in Kurtz's compound, an Angkor-Wat-like Cambodian ruin, is also introduced by a superimposition scene. Visually, this superimposition sequence is strikingly similar to the opening sequence of the film. It contains all of the same components: the jungle, the machine of war, a face. The PBR weaves its way up the river toward Kurtz with the jungle overhanging and closing in all around. Like an enigmatic God, the stone face of the Cambodian idol is superimposed over the boat wending through the jungle maze. As in the earlier superimposition scene where the burning jungle was but a deadly dream in the mind of Willard, in this scene, Willard, the PBR, the whole

mission, has become some deadly dream in the unfeeling
mind of a stone God. Willard's gods, the prime movers
of his mission, are present in that stone face. The stony
expressionlessness of the General is implied. But the CIA
spook (Jerry Zeismer), who in his one line in the film
assigns the power of life and death to Willard, actually
physically (forehead, eyes, cheekbones, lips) resembles the
idol.

Faces mirror each other throughout Apocalypse Now.
Willard at the end of the film comes to closely resemble
Kurtz. Chief's (Albert Hall) head floats disembodied on
the surface of the river as Chef's severed head later
floats in the mud at Willard's feet. Lance's (Sam
Bottoms) playful camouflaged face becomes the deadly
painted face of Kurtz. Colby, the earlier assassin sent to
terminate Kurtz, greets Willard with a drugged catatonic
face and bloody knuckles perhaps from punching his
own mirror image as Willard did in the opening scene.
Faces are superimpositions which mask all of the evil
and darkness within each human being. As Coppola
defines the psychological intention of Apocalypse Now:
"The big moment, the big scene, is not another
helicopter battle, but it's a guy, a face, alone in a dark
room, telling the truth."[7] In the Marcus/Rolling Stone
interview, Coppola talks about Brando's characterization
of Kurtz: "Finally, he shaved his head-- and that did it
. . . . That terrible face. . . . in this movie the most
terrifying moment is that image: just his face." Those
two faces, Willard's and Kurtz's, in the end superimpose
themselves upon each other and are turned to
emotionless stone by the horrors of the war. As Kurtz
says at the beginning of his central speech: "Horror has
a face."

The final visual image (before the extraneous credits
sequence begins) culminates both the theme of

---

[7]Tony Chiu, "Francis Coppola's Cinematic 'Apocalypse' Is Finally At Hand," The New York Times
(8/12/79).

superimposition and the motif of faces while also completing the circular journey of the film. The final shot juxtaposes three components in superimposition. Over the shot of the burning jungle, the opening shot of the film, is superimposed the now-muddied face of Willard next to which is superimposed the face of the stone idol. The fire burns in the lower left background of the frame. Willard's numb and stricken face hangs in the center middleground. The huge still face of the stone idol looms in the right foreground. Slowly, as the fire burns behind, the face of Willard and the face of the idol converge and Willard's face is consumed by, disappears into, the face of the stone idol. This superimposition image is the coda, the last statement, of the film. What does it mean? That war turns men into emotionless stone gods, enigmatic and beyond any human judgement.

IV
Willard As Narrator

The most omnipresent layer of superimposition of Apocalypse Now is Willard's voice-over narration written by Michael Herr. Most critics agreed with Vincent Canby's evaluation in his New York Times review that it is a "soundtrack narration that makes one's flesh wet with embarrassment." Even Charles Champlin in the single most enthusiastic review of Apocalypse Now in the Los Angeles Times wrote: "Sheen's voice-over narration grows too portentous and threatens to turn grandeur into grandiosity." However, some conduit into that confused darkness behind Willard's tortured face in the final frame of the film is needed. Coppola followed Conrad's example by deciding upon a supposed third-person limited narrator looking back. The chosen tense of the monologue opening-- "It was a real choice mission and when it was over I'd never want another." --signals that Willard has survived the experience and is evaluating what went on inside himself as well as what went on

amidst the action of the world.[8] It is a third-person
limited narration as in Coleridge's The Rime of the
Ancient Mariner, Conrad's Heart of Darkness and
Fitzgerald's The Great Gatsby.

However, if Willard is the central character, not just
a detached observer or a minor participant (like Lance,
for example, the only other survivor of the journey
upriver), how can it be a third-person limited narration?
A major problem arises with all supposed third-person
limited narrations. If the narrator is an intelligent and
interesting character who is too closely involved in the
story's action, the danger arises of that narrator allowing
himself to become the major vehicle for development
and change in the story. This invariably happens in the
finest third-person limited narratives. and it is exactly
what happens in Apocalypse Now just as it similarly
happened in Michael Herr's Dispatches. Like Marlow and
Willard who started out to tell about Kurtz, like Nick
Carroway who started out to tell about Gatsby, Herr in
Dispatches started out to tell about the Vietnam War: "I
went to cover the war and the war covered me."[9] Herr
became the central character in Dispatches: "I stood as
close to them as I could without actually being one of
them, and then I stood as far back as I could without
leaving the planet. . . . until one night when I slid
over to the wrong end of the story. . . . and I wasn't a
reporter, I was a shooter (65-66)." Marlow, Carroway,
Herr, Willard: In the end, these narrators realize, just as
the photographer in Antonioni's Blow-Up does, that all
along their real subject has been themselves; not Kurtz
or Gatsby or the Vietnam War or the lovers in the park,

---

[8]Both Veronica Geng and Jack Kroll argue that
Herr's narration reads like a Raymond Chandler narrator,
however Willard's voice displays none of the first-person
immediacy of the Chandler narrator.

[9]Michael Herr, Dispatches (New York: Alfred A.
Knopf, 1977), p. 27. All subsequent quotations will be
noted by page number within the text.

but their own inner hearts of darkness.

Because Apocalypse Now is about the psychological effects of the Vietnam War upon the men who fought it as captured in Coppola's complex vision of the war as layers of superimposed reality, an interpreter and guide is needed. Some voice must escort us into the heart of the dark many-layered experience; some voice must guide us down through all the circles of this Vietnam river hell and into all the spirals of pain inside the minds of those condemned to Vietnam. Just as Apocalypse Now has been superimposed upon Heart of Darkness, Dispatches has been superimposed upon Apocalypse Now. Therefore, Herr's voice-over narrative is strikingly appropriate. It protects Apocalypse Now from becoming either a slavish imitation of Heart of Darkness or an obscure mythic conundrum. Whereas Coppola's visual images offer the "look" and "feel" of the Vietnam War and Coppola's superimposition style symbolizes the layered reality of the Vietnam experience, Herr's narrative matches up with those images and gives them a subjective voice, the voice of a man trying to understand his own past.

V

The Fascination of the Abomination

But despite the heavy verbal influence of Dispatches, Apocalypse Now is always a Director's film and the final, most important theme, the most universal statement about war and man which Apocalypse Now makes, is presented in purely visual terms and emanates from the very earliest influence upon the film, Conrad's Heart of Darkness.

The Heart of Darkness influence is important not so much for the structure of the journey upriver, the plot and the characters, but rather for a single central idea which inspired Coppola's visual intention in Apocalypse Now. That intention is to make the theater audience actually participate in Conrad's idea of "the fascination of the abomination"(6). That intention is to seduce the audience into momentarily living, as Kurtz and Willard do, with "no restraint"(52), to make the audience itself actually experience the beauty and attraction of "the horror"(71).

Two critics, Vincent Canby and Gene Siskel, tiptoe in the vicinity of Coppola's major visual intention. Canby describes Apocalypse Now as "Coppola's perfectly sound, sometimes incredibly beautiful, meditation upon war." "Coppola, a fine showman as well as a fine filmmaker," Siskel writes, "found the condemnatory scenes so physically attractive that he couldn't bear to part with any of them." Both critics (note the "incredibly beautiful" and "so physically attractive") have a vague sense of what Coppola is really doing. He is intentionally making war so beautiful, so fascinating, presenting it with such visual virtuosity, that the audience is seduced into a suspension of all civilized restraint, all moral judgement, all abhorrence of that which is innately evil. The audience is captured by the awesome beauty to the point that it forgets the lethal reality.

Apocalypse Now opens with a still-life of a jungle treeline. Suddenly, napalm blossoms the whole width of the screen. Captured by the hypnotic beauty, the audience forgets the reality, the horror of human beings burning to death inside that treeline. Later, a formation of Phantom jets called in by Colonel Kilgore of the Air Cav for another napalm strike on another treeline, this one filled with children, hangs in the air breathtaking and clean like a cluster of modern sculpture. Further upriver, as the boat approaches the Do Long Bridge, the camera's point of view switches to that of a soldier who has just dropped a tab of LSD. "It's beautiful," Lance exclaims. In the eerie and bizarre blur of his acid eyes floats a lacey string of Japanese lanterns with fireworks flashing above and flowers of pulsing fire burning below. Lance is right. It is indeed beautiful. But for all its spooky beauty, what Lance is seeing in his blurred dope dream is a mindless battle raging out of control with no one in charge, ignorant armies clashing by

night. The beauty which initially attracts, up close turns
into insane chaotic reality. Fleur du mal. The Medusa
smile. That is the central visual, thematic intention of
Coppola's camera.

In its three major themes-- of judgement, of
superimposed realities, of "the fascination of
abomination" --Apocalypse Now presents a vision of the
American experience in Vietnam which is both physically
and psychologically accurate. His film is built upon the
guiding perception that film meaning can only be made
available through technique.

9. THE AUSTRALIAN WAR FILMS

Far removed in space from the "Hollywood" visions of the Vietnam War of Michael Cimino, Ted Post and Francis Coppola but coexistent in time and theme and Vietnam era social consciousness are the late seventies films of the thriving Australian film industry. Filmmaking in Australia is truly a national industry both stimulated and encouraged by government support. In fact, the turning point in Australian filmmaking came in 1971 with the establishment of the Australian Film Commission. Not only has the Australian film industry in the short span of about nine years (1975-present) filmed its way out of total obscurity to a high position in film production circles, but it has built this reputation on quality rather than quantity, on a small number of thoughtful, socially conscious, well-acted and brilliantly photographed films. What made Australian films so popular and successful worldwide in the late seventies was those films' judicious choices of subject matter. Every recent major Australian film has been identifiably "Australian" in its characters, its landscapes, its reliance upon real events from Australian social and military history, but each of these films has also dealt with more universal social themes, such as racial prejudice and war, with which film audiences worldwide can identify.

The Australian film industry made its breakthrough in the late seventies with a group of haunting, imagistic films which exploit both the Australian landscape and the mythical possibilities of aborigine culture. Following in the footsteps of Nicholas Roeg's Walkabout (1971),

Picnic At Hanging Rock (1975) and The Last Wave (1977)
as well as parts of The Chant of Jimmie Blacksmith
(1978) and Gallipoli (1981) present symbolic visions of
the Australian mountains and deserts and ocean beaches
reminiscent of the manner in which John Ford creates an
archetypal landscape of the American West out of the
persistent use of the Monument Valley of Utah in each
of his Westerns.

The major films which account for the rapid rise in
reputation of the Australian film industry generally fall
into two thematic categories. The first category could be
dubbed ANTHROPOLOGICAL films. This particular type
of Australian film takes its example from Walkabout
which in its stark, allegorical juxtaposition of the natural man, an aborigine, to two city children abandoned
in the outback who represent civilization and its
corruptions struck initially what has become a dominant
thematic chord in Australian film. In Picnic At Hanging
Rock and The Last Wave, the camera lingers on the
symbolic rock formations, wall paintings and panoramic
landscape views and then counterpoints those images of
nature to the expressive, tragic aborigine faces and the
dying aborigine rituals. Few American films, for example,
ever exhibit the strong mythic sense of landscape found
in a Thomas Hardy novel or a recent Australian motion
picture. In recent American film history perhaps only a
film like Jeremiah Johnson (1972) comes anywhere near
approximating this mythical, anthropological vision of
reality.

What films like Picnic At Hanging Rock and
especially The Last Wave are concerned with is the
manner in which the mythic land itself resists the
attempts of society to corrupt it, to obliterate it. In The
Last Wave, the images of the landscape become symbols
for the endurance of the aborigine culture even in the
biggest cities like Sydney where that culture has been
forced underground, where the mythic aborigine culture
can only continue to exist in sacred caves which tunnel
even deeper than the city's sewer system can penetrate
and corrupt. This ANTHROPOLOGICAL category bases

its imagery upon a strong sense of natural myth, a sense that essential human truths are to be found in the messages of nature, the look on the face of nature, man's relation to nature. Mythic tragedy, in a film like Picnic At Hanging Rock, occurs when man has lost touch with nature, has defaced nature, can no longer understand the truths which nature is trying to convey.

But though the Australian film industry made its breakthrough in this lyrical style with this mythical focus, it quickly followed its American counterparts in turning to more socially conscious films. But even in those films, such as The Chant of Jimmie Blacksmith and Gallipoli, the Australian landscape-- its hugeness, its openness, its violent beauty, its shimmering mythicality and mystery --still plays a strong visual part. Australian films made the switch from the examination of the meaning of place to the examination of the meaning of people, but the anthropological pull of the Australian landscape still broods in the background of all of the more recent Australian social consciousness films. In this switch from myth to social consciousness, the one major seventies issue which Australian films focus upon most intently is the subject of war. WAR films (expressing either direct or symbolic interest in the Vietnam War in which Australia was one of America's major allies) comprise the second major category of interest of the Australian film industry of the seventies.

Both the ANTHROPOLOGICAL films and the WAR films involve a strong sense of Australia's social history. What distinguishes them from each other is the ability of one theme to overpower the other. In The Last Wave, for example, the whole central theme of ancient aborigine religion is presented by means of a plot device-- an aborigine civil rights trial --which raises very modern questions of social consciousness, yet the whole interest of the film clearly lies with the anthropological discovery of aboriginal culture rather than social justification as in a film like To Kill A Mockingbird (1962). Conversely, striking images of the great Australian desert carry strong natural meaning in Gallipoli, brood with mythic power, yet Gallipoli makes it very clear that it is a film about WAR. And finally, it is the Australian war films which thrust Australia into the mainstream of worldwide filmmaking. Those films aligned themselves with the American Vietnam War films which were appearing at approximately the same time to show that Vietnam was not just an American obsession, an American wound, an American guilt, an exclusively American experience.

Three films in particular either directly or by means of historical analogy and symbolic scene or situation, align Australian experience with the context of the Vietnam War. The Odd Angry Shot (1979) directly portrays the experiences of Australian soldiers in Vietnam. Breaker Morant (1980) and Gallipoli employ past events of Australian military history to make clear symbolic statements about the nature of the Vietnam War and the universal evil nature of war. As in Blow-Up and Chinatown and Apocalypse Now, a major theme which each of these Australian war movies share is the manner in which reality consistently betrays the soldier. For young Bill (John Jarrett) in The Odd Angry Shot, for Breaker the soldier-poet (Edward Woodward), and for young Archie (Mark Lee) in Gallipoli, the idealized conception of the possibilities present in the war experience, the cloudy perception of what war's reality ought to mean, is totally betrayed by the surrealistic events they encounter in the war. It is as if they had actually been transported to another planet. In all three of these films, the soldier-protagonists find themselves caught in a Chinatown world where nothing is ever what it seems to be.

Each of these three Australian war films examines a political theme in which Australians (and by implication Australia itself) become willing allies and ultimately victim/scapegoats in wars always waged on foreign soil far from Australia by larger global powers whose only interest in Australia or the Australians is to exploit them for cannon fodder. Thus, each of these three films is about the futility of war as filtered through the particular Australian sense of national self. Australia's identity is that of the eager, bumptious, upstart innocent being cruelly awakened to the corruption of the more mature, experienced world powers who use the Australians as expendable pawns in their deadly games of global chess.

In these films, Australia awakens to its role in world society. By means of the individual awakening to inscrutable reality of Bill and Breaker and Archie, these films define Australia's sense of its own national destiny, its political identity: always a valuable ally yet never a major decisionmaker. These films forthrightly face up to Australia's role as a second-level world power, as a continent still trying to shake off the stigma of its convict colony origins. What these films affirm, however, is the strength, the old-fashioned idealism, the resistance to cynicism even in the face of inscrutable Chinatown reality. What these films affirm is the purity of the Australians in comparison to the debilitated cynicism of the Old World powers. In the end, what all of these Australian war films realize is that though it is good to still be innocent, one must always be responsible for that innocence, must pay the price for that innocence, must eventually lose that innocence. Both Breaker Morant and Gallipoli end with exactly the same image-- bullets needlessly piercing the bodies of men. These final images, of men dying for bad reasons as political tools, capture the essence of the Vietnam situation.

The Odd Angry Shot is an initiation movie just as Vietnam was a renewal of the basic initiation experience of the Australian soldier in world politics. The Australians fought in Vietnam as minor partners to the Americans just as they had fought in the Boer War in South Africa (as portrayed in Breaker Morant) and in the Gallipoli Campaign in Turkey in World War I (as portrayed in Gallipoli) as auxiliaries to the British. In all three of these films, the Australian soldier is cast in the same role, that of a second-class citizen either being exploited by the larger powers who are in charge or trying to prove himself by toughness and courage in comparison to those larger powers.

In The Odd Angry Shot, Bill (John Jarrett), the young Australian enlistee, is the initiate. He is an innocent virgin who in the opening sequence of the film fantasizes about taking his girl's clothes off and then has his dream come true. When he gets to Vietnam, he is forced to face reality for the first time and the whole film involves the process of his growing up, his losing of his macho, idealized view of life and war which, in all three of these Australian war films, seems built-in, directly connected to an endemic Australian inferiority complex toward their relationship to the larger global powers with whom they are allies. In other words, the consistent characterization of the Australian soldier is a political one which directly mirrors the Australian nation's role in world politics. The bumptious Australians always feel that they have to be better, stronger, smarter soldiers in order to prove themselves to their more powerful allies.

Yet, from the very opening sound of The Odd Angry Shot, the film consciously draws attention to the similarity of the Vietnam experience for both the Australian soldier and the American. The film displays an ironic consciousness that, despite the political inequalities of the two allies, in human terms their experience is very much the same. The first scene opens with the strains of one of the Top Ten incountry hits of the Vietnam War, "Leavin' On A Jet Plane" by the American folk group Peter, Paul and Mary. This song was played daily as a sort of ritual on Armed Forces Radio in Vietnam because its lyrics embodied both the past and the fantasized future for the Vietnam grunt. The past: when he had to leave his loved ones, his lover, to go far away to fight in this surreal land. The future: in that the reigning fantasy in every grunt's mind was that day when his incountry tour would finally end and he would board the "Freedom Bird" and escape the 13-month hell of Vietnam.

This clear comparison of the Australian war experience and the American continues throughout the

film. The reactions of the young men at the going-away
party in <u>The</u> <u>Odd</u> <u>Angry</u> <u>Shot</u>-- one shouts "Get one
for me" as the party breaks up --are exactly the same
reactions that the young men in the steel mill locker
room in Clairton have for Michael, Stevie and Nick on
the last day of work before leaving for Vietnam in <u>The</u>
<u>Deer</u> <u>Hunter</u>. The Australians in <u>The</u> <u>Odd</u> <u>Angry</u> <u>Shot</u>
encounter all of the same problems that the Americans
encounter in movies like <u>The</u> <u>Boys</u> <u>In</u> <u>Company</u> <u>C</u> or <u>Go</u>
<u>Tell</u> <u>The</u> <u>Spartans</u>-- foot rot, "Dear John" letters, REMFs
(Rear Echelon _ _) resentment, morale problems. At one
point in <u>The</u> <u>Odd</u> <u>Angry</u> <u>Shot</u>, Harry (Graham Kennedy)
expresses the universal grunt realization of his place, his
status, in the Vietnam War:

> HARRY: Don't get any ideas that you're
> anything special just because a few
> nogs have been takin' shots at you.
> You've got to get it through your
> head that the majority of the
> people at home don't give a stuff
> whether you live or die.

American, Australian, it made no difference, the grunt in
Vietnam knew very quickly that he was cut off from
"the World," knew that he was alone in a hostile place
that nobody at home could ever understand, a
<u>Chinatown</u>-type world where nothing was ever what it
seemed to be. "Leavin' On A Jet Plane" plays as a
recurring audio motif in the background signaling the
lingering reality in the back of everybody's mind once
they get to Vietnam-- that the only reason they are
there is so they can get out. In a sense, the strains of
"Leavin' On A Jet Plane" which permeate <u>The</u> <u>Odd</u>
<u>Angry</u> <u>Shot</u> are the equivalent of Walsh's "Forget it,
Jake, it's Chinatown." Once the reality of Vietnam is
faced, even if it isn't understood, all that is left to do
is walk away.

    In so many ways, <u>The</u> <u>Odd</u> <u>Angry</u> <u>Shot</u> is such a
typical Vietnam War movie. It is a platoon movie like

The Boys In Company C, Go Tell The Spartans and M*A*S*H in which the camera follows a group of stereotypical soldiers-- the young innocent, the old wise veteran --through their experience in the war. It is a better movie than The Boys In Company C because its lyrical and symbolic qualities generate political and existential themes. The Boys In Company C is never much more than a documentary of what it is like to be in Vietnam, never much more than a series of events strung together at random. But The Odd Angry Shot is not as good a movie as Go Tell The Spartans because it doesn't have the hard, ironic edge to either its characters or its story that Ted Post's film has. In fact, there is really no story as such at all in The Odd Angry Shot. It is a typical checklist film: that is, a film concocted out of a collected list of typical and unusual combat experiences. The characters serve as the main unifying aspect of the structure. The checklist experiences are tied together because they all happen to the same group of people in the same time in the same place. Certainly all of The Boys In Company C, the first half of Go Tell The Spartans and the middle section on the PBR on the river in Apocalypse Now display this same checklist quality which is so prominent in The Odd Angry Shot.

The technique of The Odd Angry Shot supports the checklist structure of the film. It is a "jump cut" movie. What gives unity to these jump cuts is the establishment of a number of visual and verbal motifs in the background of the action which form bridges between scenes. For example, the "Leavin' On A Jet Plane" motif ironically comments from the background all through the film. More important however is the visual motif of rain which triggers all of the more introspective scenes of the film. The rain comes down in sheets so hard and so fast that it forms a moving transparent wall between the camera and the scene. The rain explodes down upon the soldiers in the very way that the ambush violence of the war explodes. Even nature mirrors the random violence of the war in this film. The phrase "This fuckin' rain!" becomes a litany, a reflex response to the relentlessness of the grunt's relationship to his world. In Vietnam, like the forces of nature, death and violence are elemental parts of the atmosphere, the landscape, capable of exploding, drowning you in the destructive element at any time. The rain motif also serves as a tool of the jump cut technique. The whole film is built upon a progression of counterpointed scenes, counterpointed landscapes. Scenes of comedy and tragedy, scenes in the firebase and in the jungle repeatedly alternate. The rain often serves as a transitional device to bridge the jumps between scenes. The explosion of the rain can douse the threat of violence in the jungle or trigger the wry complaints of the soldiers being soaked in the base camp. In a sense, this alternation between black comedy in the basecamp and death in the jungle is what makes this film so reminiscent of M*A*S*H.

In an overall view, however, The Odd Angry Shot is a very conventional war movie about a very unconventional war. It is basically a simple character study: Young man goes to war; learns to survive under tutelage of older and wiser Sergeant Major; changes and matures. Bill, the callow youth, represents innocence. Harry, the Sergeant Major, represents experience. Harry becomes the moral norm and philosophical voice of the film while Bill serves as his sounding board. The major scenes of the film which define the social and political themes of the Australian soldiers' relationship to the war and to his homeland all take the same shape: Harry sits Bill and the others down and gives them a little lecture on what life and war is all about.

In the first-class luxury of a Quantas jet flying to Vietnam, the platoon is cocky, laughing, drinking Foster's lager, the Australian national beverage. "This is the way to go to war, eh Harry?" Bill the innocent laughs as Harry nods wryly. But the bravado of Bill and the others doesn't last long after they land incountry. After Bill experiences his first brush with death, gets the blood of one of his mortared comrades all over him,

Harry is right there to teach him his first lesson in detachment: "Come on Bill. We'll get those clothes off of you and I'll buy you a beer." This scene directly prefigures the final expressive scene of the film. Harry becomes the soldier-poet figure in this film just as Breaker Morant is in that later film which bears his name. Harry sketches all of the members of the platoon as Breaker immortalized his comrades in Kiplingesque poetry.

> BILL: Why'd you join the Army?
> HARRY: My wife left me. . . . Said I wasn't her type of people. She just didn't want to be with me.

Harry sets out the problems of life and war very clearly for Bill's perusal and, as time passes, Bill learns more and more to accept Harry's realistic, dark comic, resigned and detached view of the soldier's relationship to his world.

Yet there is irony in the relationship between these two also. Just in from the bush at the rear firebase when a "REMF" sergeant calls them "bloody tin heroes," it is Harry who looks him right in the eye and explodes, tells him to "get fucked" and then calls him "a great sodden bag of shit." Harry never romanticizes the identity of the combat grunt but he also won't let anyone who hasn't earned the right run that identity down. When Bill finally comes out and asks him: "Think we're doing any good here?" Harry gives him a purely socio-historical answer:

> HARRY: When we get home we'll be an embarrassment.
> BILL: What are we doing here then?
> HARRY: Because you're a soldier like everyone else in this tossed-up, never-come-down land. And you're here.

In the climactic scene of the film, a firefight at an
enemy occupied two-lane bridge that looks like it could
be across a trout stream in either New Hampshire or New
South Wales, Harry and Bill lose one of their close
buddies to a Viet Cong ambush that literally rises out
of the ground as in Go Tell The Spartans. "Looks safe
enough" Bill had said only moments before to his mate
who moved out onto the bridge and into the ambush.
It is just another Vietnam scene in which "nothing is
ever what it seems to be." As the corpse of their friend
is pulled out of the water, Harry gives Bill a smoke and
they turn their backs on the dead body:

> HARRY: Makes you wonder, doesn't it? A
> whole morning's work for noth-
> ing.

The final scene of the film is an expressive ironic
commentary on the theme of the futility of these men's
participation in this Vietnam War. The scene is a "coda"
to all of the maturation and disappointment which has
come before. The scene jump cuts from Vietnam to a
bar overlooking a scenic harbor in Australia. Bill and
Harry in uniform enter and the barman asks: "Just back
from Vietnam?" Harry answers "No" and refuses the
barman's offer to buy them a beer, outwardly rejecting
the barman's gesture of pity. In fact, Harry has been
playing at barman all through this film, selling beer for
20 cents a bottle to his closest friends, making sure that
everybody pays their own way. The drinking of beer
together has been an image of camaraderie for the
Australian soldiers. They drink beer as a way of
proclaiming themselves working class, of asserting a basic
Australian identity. In this last scene the two close
friends sit down to have one last beer before putting
the Vietnam War behind them. They sit down, put their
feet up and gaze out the window at the serene blue
harbor:

> HARRY: Hasn't changed a bit, has it? Seems

>   like only yesterday.
> BILL: What? This joint?
> HARRY: So here we are.   Terrific (sar-
>   castic).
> BILL: Terrific (subdued).

But they aren't happy. They don't smile when they say
"Terrific." It is much like the last scene of The
Graduate in the back seat of that bus. Bill and Harry
just sit back and drink their beers and think about how
much they have learned, how little they understand and
how little anybody cares.

Harry and Bill's inability to get any satisfaction out
of their confrontations with the inscrutable realities of
Vietnam takes other form in The Odd Angry Shot. The
most symbolic sequence in the movie is very reminiscent
of the symbolic technique of superimposition used in
Coppola's Apocalypse Now. Midway through the film the
Australian platoon assaults an ancient Vietnamese temple.
Inside they find a ferocious stone idol which stands
guard over this sacred place. Water drips like blood from
the bared fangs of the stone idol as the camera lingers
on a close-up of its terrible face. Later in the film,
after a bloody raid on a ville, Bill has a nightmare in
which the face of his girl, whom he dreams his sexual
dream about in the opening sequence of the film and
who sent him a "Dear John" letter in the middle of the
film, appears. Suddenly her face disintegrates into the
face of the stone idol with its teeth bared, and then,
over that image is superimposed the flashback image of
Bill and his girl making love. This symbolist sequence
encompasses the past at home and the savage present in
Vietnam and shows how the one has replaced the other,
how innocent love can no longer exist in the horrible
world of the war. It is an image of how Vietnam
becomes an overlay on the life of everyone who serves
there, changes them, destroys their innocence forever. The
symbolic sequence ends with a sound bridge and a jump
cut to the platoon venting their murderous emotions in
a "mad minute" on the weapons range. Innocent love

has been transformed by Vietnam into the ultimate in violent chaos.

The Odd Angry Shot is a thoughtful and intelligent movie, but it is very predictable very much like so many of the other Vietnam War movies, so clearly following a stereotyped formula for war movies from Pork Chop Hill (1959) to The Guns of Navarone (1961) to The Dirty Dozen (1967) and The Devil's Brigade (1968). In the tradition of this particular type of war movie, the films of the seventies simply aren't that much different from the formula war movies of the fifties and sixties.

The other two important Australian war movies of the late seventies make their socio-historical comments upon the Vietnam War in a very different way than does the conventional The Odd Angry Shot. Both Breaker Morant (the Boer War) and Gallipoli (WWI) are Vietnam War movies in the way that M*A*S*H (the Korean War) is a Vietnam War movie. Both are distanced in time and factual reality from the Vietnam War, yet both focus upon events and themes which directly mirror (or symbolically recall) events and issues central to the Vietnam War. When Robert Altman's M*A*S*H appeared in 1971, even though it was set in Korea in the early fifties, the people who flocked to see it knew what war it was really about, knew that its satire was aimed directly at the war that was in session not the long gone war in which it was set. M*A*S*H was an anti-war movie that captured a whole anti-war generation by taking the historical past and showing its symbolic relevance to the socio-historical present. That is exactly the thematic and symbolic intention of both Breaker Morant and Gallipoli. They take the distant past of Australian military history and show its relevance to the more recent past of Australia's (and America's) blooding in Vietnam.

Breaker Morant, like Apocalypse Now, is a Heart of Darkness movie. Breaker (Edward Woodward), like Marlow and Captain Willard, comes to learn what depths of evil can exist in the heart of man. The story of Breaker Morant turns on a single event of the Boer War and its

legal, political, existential aftermath. A company of
specially trained Australian counter-insurgency troops
walk into a Boer (guerilla fighters against English rule in
South Africa; an earlier version of the Viet Cong)
ambush. The company is totally annihilated and the
mutilated body of their Captain is brought back to the
base camp where it serves as a catalyst to anger and hate
against the Boers for the remaining members of the
company and their new commander, Breaker Morant. First
the Boers are tracked down and some are killed, some
captured and caged in the Australians' base camp. Then,
the Boers' suspected informant, an itinerant Dutch
pacifist cleric, is assassinated. Finally, all of the captured
Boers are executed. In Australian military history, this
event is the equivalent of the My Lai massacre in
American military history. In her book <u>Long Time
Passing: Vietnam and the Haunted Generation</u> (New
York: New American Library, 1985), Myra McPherson
makes a very similar comparison in her short discussion
of <u>Breaker Morant</u>.

  After the factual events take place, <u>Breaker Morant</u>
becomes a film very much like <u>Blow-Up</u> or <u>The
Conversation</u>, a film which takes an event and disects it,
analyzes it from every possible angle, constantly flashes
back to it in the attempt to understand it. The final
two/thirds of <u>Breaker Morant</u> is the trial of Breaker and
the two other officers (John Waters, Bryan Brown) who
allegedly carried out his orders to assassinate the
Dutchman and massacre the Boer POWs. What makes this
such an interesting film thematically is that as the trial
unfolds it becomes clear that the personal guilt of
Breaker and the others is not what is at stake here at
all. In fact, from the beginning of the trial, nobody,
except the defense lawyer (Jack Thompson) and the
defendents themselves, even seems interested in the
individual guilt of the men on trial. Whether they did
it or not, whether they were right or wrong, just isn't
the issue. The trial is completely a theatrical exercise in
political expediency which underlines the inferiority
complex of the Australians in their relationship with

their British allies.

For a seventies audience, with the atrocity trials of Calley, Medina and the whole American military chain of command still fresh in mind, the characterization of Breaker Morant is a fascinating one. He is not a William Calley. He is much more intelligent, experienced and introspective than the expert testimony of the My Lai investigation showed Calley capable of ever being. Breaker is the archetypal soldier-poet of myth and romance, and yet the evidence is quite strong that he ordered both the assassination and the massacre under a loose interpretation of orders passed down the British chain of command, orders which the British commander in South Africa persists in disavowing. In a sense, Breaker is much like Colonel Walter Kurtz in Apocalypse Now who also takes the war into his own hands. The film is about two very different things. First, it examines the potential in even the best and the brightest, the most respected of men, for evil; the Heart of Darkness theme. Second, it examines just another incident in a tradition of Australians being used as scapegoats by their more powerful political allies.

What makes this a particularly Australian film is its lyricism of the sort passed on from films like The Last Wave and The Chant of Jimmie Blacksmith. The poetry of Breaker, the introspection of the man, glides through the film in counterpoint to the brutal violence of the war and of the acts he and the others are accused of committing. What Breaker himself does in his poetry is what this film does in its examination of the nature of war. He takes the evil in man and turns it into metaphor.

Of the three major Australian war films, Peter Weir's Gallipoli is the most expressive in its visual/verbal images, the most universal in its themes. Gallipoli is Chariots of Fire (1981) for the real world. Like Chariots of Fire, it has two runner heroes whose personalities are quite different, a similar double narrative which shifts from the motives and actions of one to the similar development in the other, and even similar individual

scenes such as the foot race at the West Australian
provincial fair. But in Gallipoli, the young men are not
running for the sport of it, they are running for life and
death. Early in Chariots of Fire, Eric Lyddel (Ian
Charleson) runs a race at a provincial fair for the glory
of God, but in Gallipoli Frank Dunne (Mel Gibson)
runs a similar race for money. Late in Chariots of Fire,
Abrahams (Ben Cross) and Lyddel run for personal glory,
racial pride, national glory and the glory of God in the
Olympic Games, but late in Gallipoli Frank Dunne runs
his lungs out in a desperate effort to save lives at the
Nek in the Gallipoli Campaign. In Chariots of Fire,
Abrahams and Lyddel succeed and win medals for Great
Britain. In Gallipoli, Frank fails to get the message to
the trenches in time and Archie (Mark Lee) and 472 of
the 600 Australians in the battle of the Nek are killed.[10]
That, dear reader, is the difference between romance and
reality.

All the political themes of Breaker Morant are also
present in Gallipoli: the exploitation of the Australians
by the British; the Australians' resentment of that
exploitation yet their stubborn determination to prove
themselves a first-class nation to their haughty British
allies. Like The Odd Angry Shot, Gallipoli is also an
initiation movie with this theme focused in the
characterization of the younger of the film's two heroes,
Archie Hamilton. In the first half of the film, before
the two heroes embark for the Gallipoli Campaign, these
political and initiation themes are given their strongest
visual/verbal representation. Early in Gallipoli the
initiation theme is given clear verbal definition as
Archie's Uncle Jack reads aloud the story of Mowgli from
Kipling's The Jungle Book:

---

[10]My thanks to Professor S.F.D. Hughes of Purdue
University for his research into the factual events
portrayed in Gallipoli as presented in his review of the
film for the Cinema Now film series notes.

> BAGEARA: No, Little Brother. . . . Now I
> know thou art a man, and a man's
> cub no longer.
> MOWGLI: Now I will go to men.

Later, immediately after Archie wins a thrilling race at a
provincial fair just besting Frank Dunne at the tape, the
recruiters for the Light Horse arrive. "Come and find
out how to get into the greatest game of all," the head
recruiter announces to the assemblage of strong young
backcountry men.

With this line drawn between running and war, with
the ironic "game" metaphor established, the political
theme of Gallipoli involving Australia's need for
self-definition as a nation begins to surface. After a
series of misadventures on their way to enlistment in the
fabled Light Horse, Frank and Archie find themselves
faced with crossing fifty miles of outback desert on foot
in order to get where they need to be:

> ARCHIE: You can always find water if you
> know how.
> FRANK: How?
> ARCHIE: Cockatoos.
> FRANK: (Amazed) We put our lives in the
> hands of a mob of parrots?

In the light of what happens in the Gallipoli Campaign
later, Frank's incredulous choice of words becomes highly
ironic. In specific terms, the disorganized and insensitive
British become the "mob of parrots" into whose hands
the Australians put their lives. In more universal terms,
Frank's comment underscores the universal illogic of
young men on their way to war. Frank and Archie cross
the desert and enlist in the Army; in other words, they
freely opt to take their chances with the "parrots."

The comic irony of Australia's minor involvement in
world politics is again clearly presented in an exchange
between Archie and an old prospector who rescues them
from the desert:

> ARCHIE: I'm off to the war.
> PROSPECTOR: What war?
> ARCHIE: With Germany.
> PROSPECTOR: I knew a German once. How'd
> it start?
> ARCHIE: I don't know but the Germans
> started it.
> PROSPECTOR: Australia's fighting already?
> ARCHIE: In Turkey.
> PROSPECTOR: Turkey? Why?
> ARCHIE: They're a German ally. If we don't
> stop them there, they could end up
> here.
> PROSPECTOR: And they're bloody well
> welcome to it.

This comic exchange crystallizes a whole series of themes which will be fleshed out as this film goes on: the ignorance of the Australians toward their role in the Gallipoli Campaign; the fallacious "Domino" theory which was used in World War I and was still being used in the Vietnam War of the 1970s; the naivete of the young eager political innocent counterpointed to the total detachment of the old Australian man of the land.

In Perth, the night before the boys are to sign up to join the Army, Frank's father takes him aside and asks:

> MR. DUNNE: What the hell do you wanta
> sign up for? The British killed your
> grandfather, hung him at a
> crossroads outside Dublin.
> FRANK: I'm not going to fight any British
> war. I'm going to keep my head
> down, maybe come back an officer.

Frank is not as naive as Archie but his sense of the political relationship of Australia to the British is extremely naive. As Australia always has, he's allowing himself to go to war as an inferior ally of the British despite the fact that Britain's relationship, especially in military terms, to the Australians has never been anything but exploitative.

The ironies multiply when the soldiers of the Light Horse leave Australia to train in Egypt for the Gallipoli Campaign. Just as Archie and Frank did earlier in the film, the Infantry and the Light Horse march out into the desert to rehearse for the war. They are practicing for the fatal charge at the Nek at Gallipoli even though they don't know it yet. The young soldiers charge each other and fall down laughing like children playing at war. This foreshadowing scene is both symbolic and ironic: Ironic in that their playacting deaths will be very real later; symbolic in that they are once again young men marching willingly out into the twentieth-century wasteland of war.

The political theme of Australia's inferiority complex in the presence of her British allies is also comically represented in these Egyptian scenes. Frank, Archie and the others ride burros through the streets mimicking the British officers on their saddle horses and singing "If England needs a hand well here it is." Then they raise their canes like the Four Musketeers and charge into a curio shop to get restitution for a fake Tutankamen statue. "You're dealing with Australians here, you know," they shout at the Egyptian merchant as they demolish his shop. But when they get outside, the offended party realizes: "Hey fellas, it was the wrong shop." Just as they will later at the Nek, the Australians have illogically gone to great lengths to defend their honor in the wrong place for the wrong cause.

Like the infamous Ball before the Battle of Waterloo as recounted in Lord Byron's Childe Harold's Pilgrimage and Thackeray's Vanity Fair, the young men of the Light Horse dance with the girls of the Nurse Corps on the night before their departure by ship for Gallipoli. To the soundtrack accompaniment of choral music, their troop ships glide out of the night fog toward the Gallipoli Peninsula. The camera reverses its angle and the nighttime view of the Peninsula encampment spreads

out like a panorama across the screen. It looks like a
huge carnival with brightly colored lights strung its
length and the artillery shells exploding like fireworks in
the night sky. In fact, it looks very much like the
reverse angle scene in <u>Apocalypse</u> <u>Now</u> when the PBR is
approaching the multi-colored lights and the exploding
fireworks of the Do Long Bridge.

What is left in the film is the fateful battle itself.
The scenes leading up to the charge from the trenches
at the Nek are peppered with visual images of time and
running. As that recruitment officer said earlier, the
clocks have started and "the greatest game of all" is on.
The watches of the officers in the Headquarters station,
the watches of the field officers in the trenches, Archie's
own antique watch given to him by his Uncle Jack, fill
up the screen, ironically comment on the Army's attempt
to time its attack, to control time, and tragically symbolize how quickly time is running out for the
Australian soldiers in the trenches. Frank Dunne has
become a runner for the Headquarters station and, when
there is a communications breakdown between the
Headquarters and the trenches, he is given the message to
stop the fruitless charge and told to "go like the wind."
In effect, he is running for everybody's life.

In the trenches, the camera pans not the faces of the
men waiting to make their last sprint but their valuables
hung from bayonets along the walls of the trench. The
camera pans across watch after watch, last letter after last
letter, until it comes to rest on Archie's watch from his
Uncle Jack and his racing medal from the provincial
fair. Time has stopped. Frank is racing his heart out to
try to halt reality and Archie is poised for his last
sprint across the sixty yards of the Nek to the Turkish
trenches. But Frank doesn't make it with the message and
the order to go over the top is given. The film ends
with a freeze frame of machine gun bullets tearing into
Archie's running body.

Where <u>Chariots</u> <u>of</u> <u>Fire</u> opts for sentiment and belief
in God, sportsmanship and order in the world, <u>Gallipoli</u>
opts, as <u>Chinatown</u> did, for the inscrutability of reality.

Both Gallipoli and Chinatown are films set in the past
which metaphorically comment upon the state of society
and the world in the seventies. Both portray worlds so
complex, so out of control, that the indivi- dual can no
longer have any kind of ordering impact upon them, in
fact, can't even understand them much less control them.

The one unifying theme which all three of the
Australian war films affirm is the futility of young men
going to war to fight for causes which are not even
their own, for reasons which they don't understand, in
foreign countries far from their homelands in which they
are ill-equipped to survive much less triumph. In other
words, because all are seventies movies, all three comment upon the waste of sending young men to fight in
Vietnam.

But the social consciousness of the Australian film
industry doesn't end with that war of the seventies. If
two of their most successful recent films, Mad Max
(1980) and The Road Warrior (1982) both starring Mel
Gibson, are any indication, the Australians are already
looking ahead to the next war. The Australia of these
two films is a very different one from the 1950s
Australia of Stanley Kramer's On The Beach (1959) but
the social situation of the aftermath of a nuclear war is
still the same. The Australian war films of the late
seventies captured the futility and disappointment of
that decade with highly perceptive accuracy. Let's hope
that Mad Max and The Road Warrior are mere holocaust
fantasies and don't participate in this Australian
socio-historical accuracy trend.

10. THE FILMS OF THE EIGHTIES

Robert Sklar, at the end of <u>Movie</u> <u>Made</u> <u>America</u>, includes a short chapter entitled "The Future of Movies" which attempts to predict what will be the trends in the films of the seventies. From the vantage of the eighties, that chapter has proven far from prophetically accurate. Yet, despite the perils of prophesying, the temptation is strong to go out on a limb, to make the informed prediction. Indeed, in the early years of the decade of the eighties, clusters of films have already begun to form around topics of social concern worldwide: nuclear war films, films about terrorism, farm films, the return of the existential film, feminist films. Yet these trends are still in their infancy and the real direction of the films of the eighties still is dependent upon what happens in the history of the decade. One single event, like a Watergate or a Vietnam, could change Hollywood's whole emphasis. The temptation is strong but any observant film historian or social historian must be constantly aware of how quickly the trends can change or die out, how quickly predictions can become shortsighted mistakes, how quickly the world may be blown up.

My only hope is that the seventies and the issues which the social consciousness of the films of the seventies reacted to will be over forever. The movies examined in this book, the social issues and themes and events which those movies built on, are not positive themes or issues. The films themselves are not optimistic. The seventies was not a decade of optimism or progress or prosperity or hope. It was a decade of

insecurity and the films of that decade showed it. It was
the decade of Vietnam and Watergate and international
corporate conspiracy and Three Mile Island. The films
took those events and turned them into metaphors for
the helplessness and confusion of the individual caught
in the regressiveness of a dark age. The films of the
seventies are proving, however, to be a rather hard lot to
get rid of, the trends don't seem to want to die out. In
the early years of the eighties, for example, films with
Vietnam themes are proving even more popular than they
were in the late seventies. The corporate villain remains
entrenched as the faceless purveyor of menace and evil
in society in the films of the early eighties.

Ian Jarvie, in 1970, writing about the films of the
previous decade clearly defined the relationship of
American film to its society. His perception has become
a continuing fact and is worth reiterating more than
fourteen years later in regard to the films of the
seventies and early eighties. Taking his cue from the
French critics, Jarvie realized

> there was something else that was vigorous
> and exciting about the American cinema,
> something deeply entwined in the relation it
> bore to its society: its ability to portray every
> aspect of American society with almost
> clinical accuracy: from the urban, rural, and
> negro slums, through suburbia, to its highest
> social and political realms: American film men
> knew their society and put it on their screens
> . . . . there has always been in the American
> cinema a vigorously critical attitude to
> society. It has criticized, condemned, satirized,
> and lampooned its home society quite
> mercilessly. This is a general truth about
> America: its best critics are Americans.
> Gangsterism, political corruption, lynching,
> prejudice (against Jews and Negroes), fascism,
> witch hunting (ancient and modern), war,
> and, recently, the Bomb, have been the object

of critical films made within the mainstream
of American cinema.

As a prophet (though prophecy was not his purpose in
the above quote), Jarvie has proven amazingly accurate.
The films of the seventies bear out his perception of
"Hollywood's" involvement in the portrayal and critical
analysis of the major events and social trends in
American society.

In the late sixties and seventies, that impulse toward
social criticism, always so strong in American films since
the thirties, heightened internationally. Film art dissected
and exposed the state of the global society in which it
was produced. In the late sixties and seventies, film
became a barometer and a conveyor of the truth of how
far society has fallen, of the confusion and hopelessness
of the individual's relation to society.

It is hard to predict the future state of the movies
relationship to society, however, if the evidence of the
seventies decade means anything, one basic truth should
hold into the future: no other popular entertainment
medium, not music nor television, has the ability to
dramatize, analyze and comment upon social history
better than the movies. In the seventies, reality may have
been inscrutable, but the films of that decade tried their
best to examine that reality in terms of metaphorical
truth.

If nothing else, this study of the "state of the art"
of film at the end of the seventies can end on one very
positive note. "Hollywood" and its product, though not
always mimetically accurate or totally objective, is not as
distorted or shallow or escapist or exploitative or
insensitive as the majority of its critics and
commentators charge it to be. In sometimes overt,
sometimes submerged, often direct but more often
complexly symbolic ways, "Hollywood" takes the reality
of social history and turns it into metaphor thus
illuminating it through the function of art.

INDEX